D1426714

A Wealth of Wild Species

Norman Myers

A
Wealth
of
Wild Species

Storehouse for
Human Welfare

Westview Press / Boulder, Colorado

Copyright © 1983 by Synergisms, Ltd.

Published in 1983 in the United States of America by
  Westview Press, Inc.
  5500 Central Avenue
  Boulder, Colorado 80301
  Frederick A. Praeger, President and Publisher

Library of Congress Cataloging in Publication Data
Myers, Norman.
  A wealth of wild species.
  Bibliography: p.
  Includes index.
  1. Nature conservation–Economic aspects. 2. Biology, Economic. I. Title.
QH75.M93 1983   333.7'2   82-20121
  ISBN 0-86531-132-3
  ISBN 0-86531-133-1 (pbk.)

Printed and bound in the United States of America

10   9   8   7   6   5   4   3

While Dorothy and I have roamed around Africa, and during the course of our travels to America and China and lots of lands in between, we have wondered how much wildlife will be left for our children to enjoy when they are old enough to start out on safaris of their own. So I dedicate this book to our daughters

Malindi and Mara

in the hope that they will find that their present elders and betters have done a good job of conserving all people's wildlife for all time.

Contents

PART FOUR   GENETIC ENGINEERING

EPILOGUE

Preface

When I wrote *The Sinking Ark* in 1979, a book describing the mounting problems of disappearing species, I devoted an early chapter to the topic of "What Are Species Good For?" I looked at the ethical and aesthetic arguments, then I went on to the ecological arguments, and I wound up with the economic arguments.

I started the chapter with spirited commitment: I knew just what I wanted to say, I knew how I wanted to say it, and the words flowed as if of their own accord. The middle part of the chapter was reasonably straightforward, no problem. But when I came to the last section, the words dragged. A chapter that I had started to write with a spirit of conviction ended up with a tone of calculation. By the time I finished it, my heart was no longer in it. Surely, I felt, we should feel a sense of "gut identification" with our fellow species. Anyone who thinks there is need to argue a case for the worth of elephants and butterflies and sea anemones does not know the true value of wildlife. Nor will he ever know as long as he looks in that direction. Wildlife is its own justification.

So I was surprised when magazines that wanted to run excerpts from the book often chose those parts that cover the utilitarian benefits of wildlife for humanity. While roaming around the lecture circuits, I frequently found that listeners' questions would focus on the contributions of plants and frogs and insects to our daily welfare. I began to wonder, and I started to delve deeper. I soon found that there was a mountain of research to show how much we depend on our fellow species for our material life-styles—and, sometimes, for our survival.

Further support for the economic view of wildlife emerged as I traveled around the Third World. Developing nations' leaders are more likely to be turned on to conservation through an economic argument than through talk about the "intrinsic beauty" or the "moral imperative" of wildlife. After all, developing-world people like to hear how wildlife can earn money, especially when they realize that seven out of every ten of Earth's species reside in the tropics, meaning in developing nations.

The more intrigued I have become with the economic argument, the more I have become involved with it. I now recognize how my own life is enriched in a dozen ways before breakfast each day, thanks to the foods and drinks, the medicines and pharmaceuticals, and the welter of industrial products that we derive from wild creatures. As I get through with brushing my teeth each morning, using a toothbrush with "improved" bristles and best-quality toothpaste (from an extra-efficient toothpaste tube) applied to teeth kept in shape through the dentist's latest plumbing materials—all products that have been enhanced through contributions from plants and animals—I feel like raising my glass with its mouthwash and offering a toast through the window to the great wild world out there: "Here's to you, fellow species."

This book tells how our welfare is ever more intimately tied up with the welfare—indeed the continued survival—of the millions of species that share the One Earth home with us.

To prepare a book like this, I have consulted with colleagues in dozens of countries. A list of all the persons who have helped me with my inquiries would fill several pages with names. To all these people with their diverse professional backgrounds, I can offer no more than a "blanket thanks." This is not to say that I do not appreciate the support of each of you. Without your ready assistance, there would be no book.

I confine my individual thanks to those professional associates and friends who have gone out of their way, time after time, to be of help. They have clarified obscure points for me, they have drawn my attention to new advances in their fields of science, they have offered me fresh insights of endless types. They are all busy persons, but they have been unstinting with their time, whether in protracted discussions with me or in checking through chapters of the manuscript. So I wish to record my special gratitude to Professor Herbert G. Baker, Department of Botany, University of California at Berkeley; Dr. W. Hugh Bollinger, Director of Native Plants Inc., Salt Lake City, Utah; Dr. Paul A. Brooke, Wertheim and Co. Inc., New York City; Dr. Dana G. Dalrymple, Bureau of Science and Technology, U.S. Agency for International Development, Washington, D.C.; Dr. James A. Duke, Economic Botany Laboratory, U.S. Department of Agriculture, Beltsville, Maryland; Professor David O. Hall, Department of Biology, University of London; Professor J. W. Hastings, Biological Laboratories, Harvard University, Cambridge, Massachusetts; Professor Carl B. Huffaker, Division of Biological Control, University of California at Berkeley; Professor Barbara Kingsolver, Office of Arid Lands Studies, University of Arizona; Dr. Lloyd Knutson, Chairman of Insect Identification and Beneficial Insect Introduction Institute, U.S. Department of Agriculture, Beltsville, Maryland; Professor Walter H. Lewis, School of Medicine, Washington University, St. Louis; Dr. Annalee Ngeny-Mengech, Department of Chemistry, University of Nairobi; Dr. Lowell R. Nault, Ohio Agricultural Research and Development Center, Wooster, Ohio; Dr. Lambert H. Princen, Northern Regional Research Center, U.S. Department of Agriculture, Peoria, Illinois; Dr. Peter H. Raven, Director of Missouri Botanical Garden, St. Louis, Missouri; Dr. George D. Ruggieri, Director of New York Aquarium, Brooklyn, New York; Dr. Matthew Suffness, Natural Products Branch, National Cancer Institute, Bethesda, Maryland; Dr. Wayne Teel, Menonite Central Council, Nairobi, Kenya; Professor H. Garrison Wilkes, School of Botany, University of Massachusetts, Boston, Massachusetts; and Professor Sylvan H. Wittwer, Director of the College of Agriculture, Michigan State University, East Lansing, Michigan. To all these persons I offer the thought that my manuscript has been improved in one place and another, and another and still another, by their suggestions and criticisms and corrections. Any deficiencies remaining are the responsibility of the one who perpetrated them in the first place.

Although this is the shortest of the four books I have written to date, it has required the greatest amount of drafting—i.e., redrafting and re-redrafting. Each time I thought I had gotten on top of some aspect of the book's theme, I would come across some ultrarecent research report, meaning that a chunk of some chapter would have to go back for a new draft. I asked my secretary so many times to have a go at a "final draft" of some section that, on being handed a pile of dictaphone tapes from me, she would listen to my assurances that this was to be the last go-around on that particular stuff, and she would smile to herself, put her head down, and reach for the typewriter keys. On the day when I told her that several entire chapters had been consigned to the file marked "Finally final manuscript," she could hardly believe that we were approaching the end of the tunnel. A long, indeed endless, tunnel it must have seemed to her at times, but she never gave the impression that she was finding it a long dark tunnel. I could not have wished for a more assiduous secretary and a more congenial colleague to work with than Mrs. Sharmi Bhalla of Nairobi. I rarely feared for the typing energy or the good temper of Sharmi, though I sometimes suspected I would find the typewriter reduced to a heap of molten metal.

As I mentioned at the start of this preface, I have long mulled over the topic of wildlife's economic values. But it was not until I met the vice president and associate publisher at Westview Press that my thoughts began to be shaped into a form that could appear between the covers of a book. For a splendidly catalytic impulse I must thank

Lynne Rienner of Westview. Lynne has been not only encouraging throughout the entire exercise of producing this book, but she has been exceptionally patient as her author failed to meet one deadline after another. Also within the walls of Westview Press, I have found constant support from, and genial (as well as superswift) rapport with, Associate Editor Jeanne Remington. Thirdly, Jeanne handed my manuscript over to one of the most incisive, constructive, and agreeable copy editors that it has ever been my pleasure to work with, Don Meyer. To this troika of publishing colleagues across the Atlantic, my many thanks. When a writer – or at any rate, this writer – tries to write a book, he is not simply producing a lengthy series of words. He is laying something of his self "on the line," something quite deep and personal. On the basis of my 14 years in the writing field, I believe I could scarcely have looked for a more sensitive bunch of people, now friends, with whom to work.

I write these words at my desk in Nairobi, shortly before I take a last long safari to the airport. After 24 years of splendid sojourn in dear old Kenya, I must take my leave. Family concerns require that I seek "pastures new": however hospitable Kenya has been to me, the country will certainly not provide a resting place for my children's bones, so the sooner they start their new life in another land, the better. Yet the spirit of the place lingers with me. Beyond my desk and out of the window stretches a half-hectare where a visiting friend has just recorded 43 different birds during a weekend stopover. Within this single landscape outside my window, there are more kinds of flowers and trees than I shall find in the whole of London's Hyde Park or New York's Central Park. Above the scene are gathering some rain clouds – clouds that bring smiles to local people's faces, rather than the frowns that people wear in Europe and America when showers threaten. I shall miss Kenya, which has not only been a home to me, but a wellspring of inspiration for many of my writings, and especially for this book. What will my daughters find if, in another 24 years' time, they choose to come back to Kenya? How many wild creatures will they see in the skies and savannas and streams? And if they lever their daddy out of his rocking chair to accompany them, will he still enjoy that sense of knowing he is in a land where many other manifestations of life's variety go their wild way without let or hindrance?

Actually my delight in wildlife is something that I did not possess when I first set foot in Kenya. I have learned a good deal of it from African friends, especially from the Masai tribe with whom I have spent hundreds of days and nights on safari. But most of all, I think, I have learned to enjoy African wildlife – as opposed to lions and antelopes and crocodiles and other individual entities – from my wife,

Dorothy. I remember the pleasure that lit up her face when we first drove together across the Serengeti Plains, and she was content just to *be* with the wildlife throngs. She did not need to photograph them, or "do" anything much with them, she just wanted to sit and watch them. When I live in Britain, I shall feel that the blandness of that country's landscapes could be redeemed if I could ever suppose that I might one day turn a corner and come face to face with a giraffe. We could stand and look at each other, and all would be well.

For that sense of wildlife's ultimate value, I must thank Dorothy. I also need to thank her for the support she has shown while I have been writing this book—even though she may be less committed to its theme than I am. As with two of my other books, Dorothy has accomplished the most difficult part of the entire writing—she has watched with equanimity the toils and tribulations of a writer trying to meet his deadlines.

And while living in Britain, I shall know that I can retain my dream of giraffes in Kenya only if wildlife there can be enabled to pay its way. Hence my wish to demonstrate the economic value of species in terms of their contributions to our daily rounds. I realize that this approach will not sit well with every reader. Indeed some observers view an economic rationale for conservation as a perversion, even as something "evil." But in developing nations especially, there is little space for the luxury of wildlife that exists for its own sake. In face of an incoming tide of humanity, with its growing numbers and growing expectations, an ethical stance or an aesthetic argument will achieve little more than a Canute-like gesture. However much I may agree that every species has its own right to continued existence on our shared planet, I do not believe that the world yet works that way. So in a practical workaday world of politicians and economists and planners, we must make the best case we can in favor of wildlife. While waiting for the millennium, we must set about some pragmatic conservation strategies that will stand up in our marketplace-motivated societies. To the extent, then, that I can demonstrate that wildlife means something in terms of dollars and cents, and pounds and francs and yen, I believe there will be a better chance of wildlife aplenty left at the end of the century, and at the end of all centuries to come. If species are enabled to survive through crass economics, should that detract from the pleasure of the purist who gazes at zebras and polar bears and flamingos with a spirit that is not jaundiced with considerations of mere money?

Norman Myers
Nairobi, Kenya

Prologue

Wild Species:
A Key Factor
in Our Daily Lives

From morning coffee to evening nightcap we benefit in our daily life-styles from the fellow species that share our One Earth home. Without knowing it, we utilize hundreds of products each day that owe their origin to wild animals and plants. Indeed our welfare is intimately tied up with the welfare of wildlife. Well may conservationists proclaim that by saving the lives of wild species, we may be saving our own.

It is fitting, then, that we remind ourselves of these connections. This book aims to document the myriad contributions that wildlife makes to our material well-being. Of course wildlife offers many other benefits: it can cater for the human spirit as well as for the body. But this book focuses on material contributions.

Our daily bread, for instance. The wheat and corn crops of North America, like those of Europe and other major grain-growing regions, have been made bountiful principally through the efforts of crop breeders rather than through huge amounts of fertilizers and pesticides – and crop breeders are increasingly dependent on genetic materials from wild relatives of wheat and corn. In common with all agricultural crops, the productivity of modern wheat and corn is sustained through constant infusions of fresh germ plasm with its hereditary characteristics. Thanks to this regular "topping up" of the genetic or hereditary constitution of the United States' main crops, the U.S. Department of Agriculture estimates that germ plasm contributions lead to increases in productivity that average around one percent annually, with a farm-gate value that now tops $1 billion. Similar growth-rate gains can be documented for Canada, Great Britain, the Soviet Union, and other developed nations. To this extent, then, we enjoy our daily bread by partial grace of the genetic variability that we find in wild relatives of modern crop plants.

And "we" means each and every one of us. Whether we realize it or not, we enjoy the exceptional productivity of modern corn each time we read a magazine. Since cornstarch is used in the manufacture of sizing for paper, the reader of this book is enjoying corn by virtue of the "finish" of the page he or she is looking at right now. The same cornstarch contributes to our life-styles each time we put on a shirt or a blouse. Cornstarch likewise contributes to glue, so we benefit from corn each time we mail a letter. And the same applies, through different applications of corn products, whenever we wash our face, apply cosmetics, take aspirin or penicillin, chew gum, eat ice cream (or jams, jellies, catsup, pie fillings, salad dressings, marshmallows, or chocolates), and whenever we take a photograph, draw with crayons, or utilize explosives (Watson, 1977). Corn products also turn up in the manufacture of tires, in the molding of plastics, in drilling for oil, in the electroplating of iron, and in the preservation of human blood plasma. Millions of motorists now utilize corn whenever they put gasohol instead of gasoline into their car fuel tanks; by the year 1990, Americans may be using as much as 4 billion gallons of gasohol a year.

Corn even contributes to a highly absorbent material that rejoices in the name of "super slurper." A chemical combination of cornstarch and a kind of plastic resin, the latest version of this material absorbs 5,000 times its weight of distilled water and large amounts of other liquids. It is widely used in such items as bandages and diapers.

So much for genetic contributions to our major crops. Wild species likewise contribute to our health needs. Each time we take a prescription from our doctor to the neighborhood pharmacy, there is one chance in two that the medication we collect owes its origin to start-point materials from wild organisms. The commercial value of these medicines and drugs in the United States now amounts to some $15 billion a year (Farnsworth, 1982). If we extend the arithmetic to all developed nations, and include nonprescription materials plus pharmaceuticals, the commercial value tops $40 billion a year.

In 1960, a child suffering from leukemia had only one chance in five of remission. Now, thanks to drugs prepared from a tropical forest plant, the rosy periwinkle, the child enjoys four chances in five. Commercial sales worldwide of these drugs from this one plant now total around $100 million a year. According to the National Cancer Institute and the Economic Botany Laboratory outside Washington, D.C., the rainforests of Amazonia alone could well contain plants with materials for several further anticancer "superstar" drugs.

Yet these agricultural and medicinal materials from wildlife are small potatoes as compared with the industrial benefits that we reap from wildlife. Plants and animals already serve the needs of the butcher, the baker, the candlestick maker, and many others. As technology advances in a world growing short of many things except shortages, industry's need for new raw materials expands with every tick of the clock. By way of illustration, let us consider the prime example of the rubber tree. In its many shapes and forms, natural rubber supports us, literally and otherwise, in dozens of ways each day. Other specialized materials contribute to industry by way of gums and exudates, essential oils and ethereal oils, resins and oleoresins, dyes, tannins, vegetable fats and waxes, insecticides, and multitudes of other biodynamic compounds. Many wild plants bear oil-rich seeds with potential for the manufacture of fibers, detergents, starch, and general edibles – even for an improved form of golf ball.

Still more important, a few plant species contain hydrocarbons rather than carbohydrates. As every reader knows, hydrocarbons are what make petroleum petroleum. Hence the critical importance of these plants in an OPEC-dominated age. Fortunately the hydrocarbons in wild plants, while very similar to those in fossil petroleum, are practically free of sulphur and other contaminants found in petroleum. So a number of wild plant species appear to be candidates for "petroleum plantations." As luck would have it, certain of these plants can grow in areas that have been rendered useless through, for example, strip-mining. Hence we have the prospect that land that has been degraded by extraction of hydrocarbons from beneath the surface could be rehabilitated by growing hydrocarbons above the surface. And a petroleum plantation need never run dry as an oil well does.

Not only do wild species supply materials for our direct use, but they provide "models" for researchers to draw on when they are devising synthetic medicines or designing industrial products. Scientists would have had a hard time devising synthetic rubber if they had not had a "blueprint" to copy, in the molecular structure of natural rubber. Each time we enter a high-rise office block or apartment building, we might reflect that the edifice has probably been constructed on the principles of metal-beam architecture, a building design that owes its constructional inspiration to the physical makeup of the giant waterlily in the heart of Amazonia (Lovejoy, 1978). This architectural revolution in the advanced world is being matched by a constructional breakthrough in the developing nations, which need to build as many houses in the next two decades as during the whole course of human history to date. Third World builders are learning to utilize special types of grass, bamboo, and other plants of the tropics as reinforcing materials for their buildings.

Still more esoteric purposes are served by wild creatures. The polar bear, for instance: Its hairs are not white, but, being tiny hollow tubes with no pigment, merely appear white by virtue of their rough inner surfaces that, like transparent snowflakes, reflect invisible light. This feature allows the polar bear to funnel ultraviolet light inwards to warm its body – and it is a feature that now enables manufacturers of cold-weather clothing for humans to do a much better job, and may even lead to incorporation of solar-energy "light pipe" collectors for heating our homes and offices (Grojean *et al.*, 1980).

We can likewise learn from "wildlife models" to help our health. Animal physiology affords many clues to the origins and nature of human ailments. Diseases of the heart and circulatory system, for example, can be studied by comparative investigation of long-flying birds such as the stormy petrel and the albatross. These birds feature highly developed hearts, and their circulatory systems are in top-notch state too, in order for them to accomplish their immense annual migrations. It is the superb physical equipment of these birds that has advanced our understanding of cardiomyopathy, a failing in humans caused by overdevelopment of the heart muscle, obstructing blood outflow. Similar clues to our better health may become available from research into hummingbirds, creatures that spend much of their entire waking life in flight. Much the same applies to those butterflies that wander 4,000 kilometers each year, and to locusts and other insects that sustain high levels of activity for weeks if not months on end.

The desert pupfishes of Nevada and California rank among the most threatened creatures on Earth. They reveal a remarkable tolerance to extremes of temperatures and salinity, an evolved attribute that could assist research into human kidney diseases. The Florida manatee, another endangered species, features poorly clotting blood, offering scope for research into hemophilia. Primates, more closely related to humans, are especially valuable for medical research: the cotton-topped marmoset, a species of monkey susceptible to cancer of the lymphatic system, is helping to produce a potent anticancer vaccine. We are even learning important secrets from such an unlikely seeming source as the African lungfish. This fish can aestivate, that is to say it can enter a state of suspended animation that allows it to survive well over one year without food or water. Scientists are tracking down the substance that triggers the aestivation mechanism, and their finding should help simulate a suspension of metabolic processes in humans who undergo lengthy open-heart operations.

It is even true that there are now living examples of monkey work. In Malaysia, the pig-tailed macaque can be trained to pick coconuts off trees, earning its owner $15 per day.

So much for land and freshwater creatures. Still more bounty for us

The giant waterlily of Amazonia, here held by Dr. Ghillean T. Prance in an inverted position to reveal its underside structure, has supplied the design inspiration for the architecture of many modern high-rise buildings, by virtue of the unusual strength of the lily pad's construction. (Credit: G. T. Prance, New York Botanic Garden)

is to be found in the marine realm. When we paddle our toes at the sea's edge, how could we suspect that beneath the waves are vast stocks of materials to enrich our lives? Yet area for area and species for species, offshore waters contain more utilitarian materials than is the case with terrestrial ecosystems. When I have stepped on a sea urchin and felt its spines injecting poison into me, I have not stopped, I confess, to reflect that these toxins could serve crucial needs of modern medicine. But the sea urchin yields holothurin, a substance that may help with treatment of coronary disorders, even cancer. The octopus yields an extract that relieves hypertension; the seasnake produces an anticoagulant; and the menhaden harbors an oil that helps with atherosclerosis. A Caribbean sponge produces a compound that acts against diseases caused by viruses, much as penicillin did for diseases caused by bacteria; this widely hailed discovery offers us the prospect of curing a wide range of viral diseases from the common cold upwards. The skeletons of shrimps, crabs, and lobsters feature a material known as chitin, in which an enzyme, scientifically termed chitosanase, serves as a preventive medicine against fungal infections much like those common among burn victims and often causing such extensive damage to tissues as to result in amputation. Chitosanase can also help to heal other wounds more quickly and to inhibit certain categories of malignant cells. Even the lowly barnacle, that bane of sailors, could soon make life easier for us when we sit in the dentist's chair. The adhesive that enables the animal to cling to ship bottoms could be adapted into a cement for tooth fillings – and it could even replace the binding pins now used to set bone fractures.

In these diverse ways, plus many more that will come to mind as we consider the manifold materials that keep us going between breakfast and bedtime, our welfare is served by the wild species that make up the planetary ecosystem with us. To date, scientists have conducted intensive screening of less than 1 percent of all species with a view to determining their economic potential. Yet these preliminary investigations have thrown up thousands of products of everyday use.

Interestingly enough, the plant kingdom makes many more contributions to us than the animal kingdom, even though plant species total only some 250,000, whereas animal species probably number at least 5 million and could reach 10 million. Why this disproportionate contribution? Only when one stops to think about the situation does an answer start to emerge. Plants, being stationary, have a hard time warding off threats from their environment in the form of plant eaters, too much heat or too much cold, too much water or not enough, and so forth. An animal can cope with these problems by simply walking, crawling, swimming, or flying away from the scene. A plant must fight its battle where it grows. So a plant's survival strategy lies in the chemical compounds it produces in its tissues in order to cause indigestion for herbivorous mammals, insects, and the like, and in order to help it through times of stress from heat, drought, and other adverse conditions. Indeed a plant's life is one long struggle against difficult circumstances. As a result, the plant kingdom presents an extraordinary array of biocompounds of an abundance and diversity that can hardly be visualized until one starts to dabble in biochemistry. Especially productive of these biocompounds are plant communities that live in areas of "biological warfare," notably in areas with climatic extremes such as deserts and rainforests. In deserts, plants have to deal with a hostile environment, and in rainforests they have to deal with exceptional competition from huge numbers of species crowded into relatively confined localities. When scientists go out to search for specialized chemicals in the plant kingdom, they often head for arid lands and jungles.

So varied and numerous are the biocompounds to be found in plants that even if we were to conduct a systematic analysis of all species on

Earth, we might well find that the plant kingdom still produces more beneficial materials for us than the entire animal kingdom.

While marveling at the many benefits that we enjoy from wild creatures, however, let us remember that they are being driven to extinction at alarming rates. Almost certainly we are losing one species per day right now (Myers, 1979). By the end of the century we shall be fortunate if we do not lose 1 million of earth's 5–10 million species. By the middle of the next century, we may even say goodbye to at least one-third and conceivably one-half of the planetary spectrum of species. This megascale extinction of species has been termed one of the great "sleeper issues" of our times, on the grounds that few problems are more profound in their ultimate implications, while less appreciated by political leaders and the general public. By the middle of the next century, too, it looks likely that our known deposits of fossil petroleum will have become exhausted; if, by that same stage, we have lost a sizable share of earth's stock of species, it will be difficult to determine which event will have the greatest repercussions for the fortunes of our children and grandchildren.

Fortunately there is a parallel to this sleeper issue of superscale extinctions. It is the further sleeper issue that lies with an emergent realization: Earth's stock of species represents some of the most valuable natural resources with which we can confront the unknown challenges of the future. All too slowly, but nonetheless steadily, we are coming to learn that birds and reptiles, insects and sea slugs, fishes and mammals, flowers and mosses, even fungi and bacteria, hold all manner of goodies in store for us if only we can ensure their survival. To consider the needs of agriculture, for example, it is becoming plain that the famous Green Revolution is being superseded by a still more revolutionary phenomenon, the "Gene Revolution"—a breakthrough in agricultural technology that may soon enable us to harvest crops from deserts, farm tomatoes in seawater, grow superpotatoes in many new localities, and enjoy entirely new crops such as a "pomato." Genes are the hereditary materials of each species' makeup; we can isolate and manipulate them. The sophisticated techniques of genetic engineering may even be bringing us closer to the day when we can send every citizen on Earth to bed with a full belly. In medicine, we can look forward to one advance after another to match the discovery of penicillin: Medical pioneers foresee more innovative advances during the last two decades of this century than during the previous two centuries. As for industry, our creative applications of the gene reservoirs of wild species may soon make our present industrial scene appear like a hangover from the Stone Age.

In short, we may soon find ourselves becoming more prosperous in our daily welfare, more sophisticated in our technological know-how, and more sensitive in our use of Earth's renewable resources, by virtue of a new "discover nature" movement.

Finally a word about the philosophic underpinnings of this book. It is confined to the utilitarian benefits that we derive from other species. This is not to say – and the point is emphasized – that we do not derive much else from the many species that share the planet with us. We can marvel at the colors of a butterfly, the grace of a giraffe, the power of an elephant, the delicate structure of a diatom, plus many other aesthetic pleasures. Every time a species goes extinct, we are irreversibly impoverished in terms of the striking and beautiful manifestations of life's diversity. This in itself represents a very cogent argument in favor of preserving species.

At the same time, we can consider an ethical argument to support preservation. What right have we, as a single species, to decide that we can eliminate any other species – especially insofar as we are distinctly Johnny-come-latelies on the evolutionary scene as compared with the great bulk of creatures on Earth? Plainly this ethical argument is a powerful weapon in the hands of conservationists.

Several other arguments can be adduced in support of our save-species campaigns, but this book is not concerned with them – only with the utilitarian rationale. The book's aim is to indicate the huge numbers of ways in which wild species help us to live our lives more fully. If the book were to embrace the aesthetic, ethical, and other arguments, it would be a different sort of book. It confines its attention to the material welfare approach.

There are two reasons for the book's particular focus on *wildlife's* contribution to our daily welfare. First is that the utilitarian argument deserves more systematic analysis than it has received in the past. Second, we live, whether we like it or not, in a world where economics, rather than aesthetics or ethics, tends to call the shots. The more we can demonstrate the economic value of wild species, the more we shall add a much-needed weapon to our arsenal of conservation arguments. In the experience of this writer, who has spent the last 25 years roaming around almost 100 countries of the Third World, there is hardly another argument in support of threatened species that carries so much weight as the economic argument – and this is all the more pertinent in that some 70 percent of Earth's species live in developing countries of the tropics.

PART ONE

———————————■———————————

Agriculture

—————————■—————————

CHAPTER ONE

A Tale of a Few
Wild Corn Stalks

Corn, common corn, plays a greater part in our everyday lives than we may be aware of. It appears in our diets as cornflakes, as popcorn, and as a number of other readily recognizable items. But, as we have seen in the previous chapter, corn turns up many other times during our daily rounds. Each time we take a beer or a bourbon or a soft drink, all of which contain corn sugar, we can drink a silent toast to America's 1 million corn growers. Let us also bear in mind that corn is widely used to feed cattle, pigs, and poultry, so we benefit from corn each time we enjoy a breakfast omelette, a lunchtime escalope, or a dinner-table steak.

We can all be grateful, then, for the exceptional productivity of U.S. cornlands. Whereas corn growers could generate no more than 20 or 25 bushels per hectare (nearly 2.5 acres) in 1930, they now easily exceed 100 bushels and frequently achieve 250 bushels per hectare. Together with wheatlands, cornlands make up the Great Grain Belt of America, constituting the most powerful phenomenon on Earth for producing food.

Need for Genetic Variability

Ups and downs have marked the hardwrought agricultural gains, and without regular infusions of fresh germ plasm for genetic variability, America's farmers could not maintain their present lofty levels of corn production, let alone push them still higher. Corn, like all modern crops, needs regular boosts of genetic material to keep it flourishing. Genes, the chemical units of hereditary information that can be passed on from one generation to another, provide the needed variability. Each individual organism possesses thousands of different genes, each of which affects one or more traits such as growth rate, height, weight, and resistance to disease. Genes determine not only an individual's traits (such as the appearance and makeup of a corn plant), but the individual's potential, or the extent to which its traits can respond to its environment. Hence the importance of an abstruse-sounding component of modern agriculture. Any crop is only as good as its genes.

As a rough rule of thumb, U.S. geneticists believe that around one-half of corn's increased productivity during the past half-century can be attributed to rejiggering or altering the crop's genetic constitution. Hence the unremitting premium on "topping up" corn's genetic vigor with new genes, constantly new genes (Beadle, 1980; Duvick, 1977 and 1981; Wilkes, 1972, 1977, and 1979).

Where do the new genes for modern crops come from? There are two main sources. One is wild relatives of modern crops, usually grassy or "weedy" plants that are sufficiently akin to modern types for plant geneticists to achieve crossbreeding. The second source is "primitive cultivars," or cultivated varieties (hence the name "cultivars") that have long been established by peasant farmers and that harbor much more genetic variability than is generally to be found in modern strains of commercial crops. Without these wild and primitive supplies of germ plasm, U.S. crops, and especially the corn crop, would rapidly lose their marvelous productivity.

We can all look with hope, then, to the news of a recent discovery of an obscure plant in a montane forest of southwestern Mexico (Iltis *et al.*, 1979). Known to scientists as *Zea diploperennis*, this plant is the most primitive known relative of modern corn. It survives only in three tiny patches, covering a mere four hectares. Equally to the point, this last relict habitat in Mexico has been threatened by settlement schemes, squatter cultivators, and timber-cutting enterprises. Yet this unimpressive plant, with its few thousand stalks in all, could be worth many millions, even billions, of dollars a year to corn growers and corn consumers in the United States – as in many other corn-growing lands around the world.

What is so special about this abstruse discovery? According to the team of botanical sleuths, led by Ing. M. R. Guzmán of the University of Guadalajara in Mexico, working with his colleagues Professor Hugh H. Iltis and Dr. John Doebley of the University of Wisconsin, plus Dr. B. Pazy of the Hebrew University of Jerusalem, this wild corn possesses short tuberlike rhizomes that make it a perennial – that is, it resprouts from its rhizomes each year. Thus it is fundamentally different from all established types of modern corn, which are annuals. But although the new variety is the most primitive of the near relatives of modern corn, it is a diploid (with paired chromosomes),

Seen in a patch of the wild corn recently discovered in Mexico are, left to right, Dr. John Doebley of the University of Wisconsin, Ing. M. R. Guzman of the University of Guadalajara in Mexico, Dra. Maria Luz Puga, a leading Mexican botanist, and Professor Hugh H. Iltis of the University of Wisconsin. These scientists, together with their colleagues, came across the remnant population of the wild corn and found that its chromosomal makeup allows it to be crossbred with commercial corn types, thus opening up the prospect of greatly improved strains for corn growers and corn consumers around the world. (Credit: H. H. Iltis, University of Wisconsin)

having 10 pairs or a total of 20 chromosomes, the same as in annual forms. So its pollen can fertilize conventional corn flowers to produce fertile fruit. All this means that the wild species can be crossbred with cultivated varieties. It is this breeding potential that points the way to several major breakthroughs for corn growers in the United States and around the world – and for corn consumers, all of us, at a dozen points of our daily rounds.

Corn is grown by more than 1 million U.S. farmers on 280,000 square kilometers of land, or an area equivalent to Arizona and a good deal larger than Great Britain. It thus accounts for about one-fifth of all U.S. cultivation, and in volume it accounts for almost half of all corn grown in the world. Corn ranks as one of the global "big three" cereal grains, the other two being wheat and rice, each making up about one-quarter of world grain production, roughly 400 million metric tons each year. Put another way, corn constitutes one-quarter of all cereal grains and one-sixth of all food.

Through their extraordinary agricultural feat of growing around 200 million metric tons of corn annually, U.S. farmers can feed not only their fellow citizens, but huge numbers of other people in many other nations, including the Soviet Union and dozens of developing nations. The United States now exports almost one-third of its corn crop, accounting for 70 percent of all corn entering international trade. This vast flood of corn leaving U.S. ports not only helps to feed the hungry of the earth but plays a major role in U.S. foreign-exchange accounts, enabling the nation to continue with its evermore expensive imports of petroleum. If we count corn together with wheat, rice, and soybeans, U.S. food exports are worth far more than the nation's technology exports, notably computers and jet planes. All in all, U.S. grain exports are now worth a whopping $40 billion a year.

Yet U.S. farmers are a good way from realizing the full potential of their corn crop. The record output for corn has topped 1,000 bushels a hectare, and agricultural experts believe that the theoretical maximum under optimal conditions could rise even higher. Thus, greatly expanded yields lie ahead of us, provided plant breeders have access to sufficient genetic variability to produce still more abundant harvests. Yet plant breeders have all too little corn germ plasm to work with. They believe that most of their work has been accomplished with only two of the 250 corn-related plants known worldwide, and these two species simply contain too few genes with untapped potential for creating new varieties. Hence the breeders' urgent search for genes from other corn-related species.

Despite their limited supplies of genetic material, corn breeders have produced one of the most versatile crops ever known to humankind. Even though corn's origin lies in tropical America, it flourishes as far as 65°N. in Fairbanks, Alaska, and it can grow at altitudes as high as 3,000 meters above sea level. Having originated in Mexico and Central America, corn made its way into North America, then spread to Europe in the early 1500s, thereafter to West Africa, and to Asia from India around to China and the Philippines. (Only two other New World products, tobacco and syphilis, have spread with similar success.) Today corn flourishes across a wider geographical range and a broader spectrum of environments than any other cereal. Thanks to continuous redesign of its genetic constitution, corn now ranks among the most efficient plants in capturing the sun's energy for conversion into food.

Corn's Vulnerability

Yet for all its vigor and versatility, modern corn is an exceptionally sensitive crop. It is vulnerable to all manner of pests and diseases and to environmental stresses such as unusual cold or aridity. Ironically, the sophisticated breeding processes that have led to modern corn are responsible for the crop's susceptibility to all manner of setbacks. America's cornfields feature billions of individual plants that are almost identical in their genetic makeup, meaning that whatever genetic combination makes one plant susceptible to disease and other problems may make all its genetic siblings equally susceptible. To quote Professor J. Artie Browning of Iowa State University, testifying before the Senate Agriculture Committee, America's cornlands are "like a tinder-dry prairie, waiting for a spark to ignite it."

This delicate situation can be illustrated by a famous occurrence in 1970. At that time, 70 percent of the seed corn grown by U.S. farmers owed its ancestry to six inbred lines. When a leaf fungus blighted cornfields from the Great Lakes to the Gulf of Mexico, America's great Corn Belt almost came unbuckled. The disease eliminated 15 percent of the entire crop and as much as half of the crop in several states of the South, pushing up corn prices by 20 percent and causing losses to farmers, plus increased costs to consumers, worth more than $2 billion. The damage was halted with the aid of blight-resistant germ plasm of various kinds, with a genetic ancestry that originally derived from Mexico (National Academy of Sciences, 1972; Tatum, 1971; Zuber and Darrah, 1979).

Of course we cannot simplistically assert that the critical genetic material was worth $2 billion. Various other factors contributed to the turnaround, including the professional expertise of plant breeders and their research infrastructures, plus management systems, extension and educational services, marketing networks, and many other contributory factors that complement each other to make up "joint products." It is less than accurate to suggest that specific combinations of germ plasm, such as that which overcame the leaf blight, can directly and exclusively lead to expanded yields worth a specific pile of dollars. Nevertheless, it is apparent that the new genes played a major part in confronting the 1970 disaster: Plant geneticists are no better than the genetic material they have to work with. So we can consider the figure of $2 billion as a "ballpark" indication of the dollar values we are concerned with.

The 1970 episode is not the only occasion when corn growers have faced a crisis. There have been other setbacks for U.S. cornlands this century, though not on such a scale. And much further back in history we might note the experience of the Mayas, whose great civilization came to an abrupt end in the year A.D. 900. So far as we can discern, whole communities of farmers suddenly abandoned the rich agricultural lands that had supported their advanced culture for at least 1,000 years. While some observers believe that the Maya catastrope derived from deforestation and soil erosion, others think it may have been due to a corn disaster. A plant virus could have been brought into the Mayas' cornlands by plant-hopper insects, introducing a devastating disease into the 180,000 square kilometers that supported some 2 to 3 million people. Within just a few years, the virus could have inflicted critical damage on the corn crop that underpinned one of the greatest early civilizations to develop in the Americas (Brewbaker, 1979).

A Perennial Hybrid with Extra Disease Resistance

Because modern corn growers are unusually concerned about diseases in their crop, they have been excited by the discovery of the wild corn in a remote Mexican forest. The few weedy stalks have been crossbred with conventional corn, making a perennial hybrid. So farmers could be spared the annual expense of plowing and sowing, since the crop would come up by itself year after year, just like grass. This advance in itself could offer very large savings. Although the parallel is far from exact, we can get an idea of the scale of savings by looking at the economics of no-tillage cultivation, an agricultural technique that is already practiced on several million hectares of U.S. cropland. The amount of diesel fuel saved by elimination of plowing varies, but the figure for corn would almost certainly be at least 5.6 gallons per hectare per year, worth at least $300 million (Myers, 1981). Some observers believe that the savings from a perennial hybrid could be a good deal higher. According to Professor Anthony C. Fisher of the University of California at Berkeley, the overall costs of preparing cornlands and of sowing new seed each year amount, roughly speaking, to $155 per hectare, which means that the annual savings across 28 million hectares could be on the order of $4.375 billion (Fisher, 1982). These theoretical reckonings are probably too high in year-after-year terms, since plowing of the soil and sowing with new seed (introducing upgraded strains from time to time) will be required every few years. All the same, it is plain that the savings could be exceptionally large.

True, the virtues of a perennial hybrid are discounted by a number of experts. They assert that perennial cereals do not generally yield as much as annuals. Annuals tend to direct most of their growing vigor into their seeds, but perennials divert part of it into their roots (in case their seeds "don't make it"); hence perennials tend to produce less grain. Of major grain crops, only one, sorghum, is a perennial; and in only a few instances is it used as a perennial because growing the crop on the same patch of land year after year results in reduced performance, albeit for reasons that we do not properly understand. For one thing, a monoculture perennial grown on the same patch of land year after year makes a first-rate "culture bed" where diseases, insects, and nematodes can prosper.

Thus, in general terms, runs the argument against perennials. The analysis stands up in temperate zones. But in the tropics, where corn growers total many millions of farmers, a perennial hybrid may prove more appropriate. Third World peasants do not necessarily aim for record-breaking harvests of their crops. Rather they hope to grow reasonable-sized crops with as little expense as possible. Put another way, they do not strive for maximum output, but for minimum input. So a perennial hybrid that saves them the seasonal costs of plowing and sowing might appeal to them more than to farmers in advanced nations. Moreover, whereas the perennial corn from Mexico appears to offer no winter hardiness, which could further rule out its prospects in North America and Europe with their frosty months of the year, there could be much potential for it in the tropics with their year-round warmth.

More readily realizable gains may lie with wild corn's capacity to grow in unusual environments and to resist several prominent diseases. The plant has been discovered at elevations between 2,500 and 3,250 meters, where its cool mountainous habitats are often damp. This feature offers the prospect of growing crossbred corn in wet soils beyond the survival capacities of conventional corn, and thereby expanding the cultivation range around the earth by as much as one-tenth. Even if yields in these marginal environments were to average only half of those in more hospitable areas, the additional output could be worth at least $1 billion per year.

Furthermore, and according to preliminary investigations by Dr. Lowell R. Nault and his colleagues at the Ohio Agricultural Research Center, the Mexican variety is immune or tolerant to at least four of eight major viruses and mycoplasmas that are significant to corn growers around the world (Nault and Findley, 1981). The wild corn has probably survived for such a long time in the wild precisely because it offers genetic immunity to sundry diseases (perhaps also to insect pests). Generally speaking, we can reckon that perennials are more resistant to systematic plant diseases than are annuals: they have to be, since their year-after-year growth pattern encourages year-after-year attack by diseases and insects, which can maintain a more sustained assault against these plants than their short-run efforts against annuals.

The corn diseases against which the wild Mexican variety features tolerance or immunity now cause at least a 1 percent loss to the world's corn harvest each year, worth at least $500 million. The wild corn appears to be the sole genetic source of resistance to chlorotic dwarf disease (one of the two most serious viruses to attack corn in the United States) and to strain B of dwarf mosaic virus. It also shows immunity to chlorotic mottle disease and streak viruses, plus virtual immunity to stripe virus. On top of this, the wild strain may supply genes resistant to various nematodes, fungi, and bacteria, notably foliar and root pathogens; and it may help with insect pests such as corn earworms, stalk borers, and rootworms. All these traits will result in yet higher savings to corn farmers. The wild germ plasm could also supply general hybrid vigor, greater strength for the plant's stalks and roots, and other advantageous characteristics (such as more ears per plant) with sizable economic benefits. No wonder that the discovery of the wild corn may eventually rank, to cite several scientists, as the "botanical find of the century."

Of course these speculations remain no more than speculations. No cornfield in North America, or anywhere else on Earth, has been planted with a hybrid variety utilizing germ plasm from the wild Mexican species (though 3-meter-tall specimens have been grown in experimental plots). Equally to the point, however, the wild species could lead to one breeding breakthrough after another, eventually amounting to what farmers in the year 2000 could look back upon as a revolution in corn growing. With every year that goes by, and with every new demand on cornlands around the earth, there is mounting need for as much genetic variability as we can find. It is not going too far to assert that those few thousand stalks of wild corn growing in a Mexican forest could ultimately rival, in dollar terms, the few hundred tree seedlings that were smuggled out of Brazil one century ago and thereafter used to establish the $4-billion rubber-growing industry in Southeast Asia.

Farmers in the year 2000 may find additional cause to look for new corn strains with special adaptability. Scientists now believe that it is certainly possible, if not probable, that the carbon dioxide content of the earth's atmosphere is steadily building up. This could lead to a "greenhouse effect" for the earth's climates, bringing warmer and drier weather to many temperate zones, especially those North American territories that now yield abundant grain harvests. If climatic changes work out as projected by many of the scientists, the temperature at the height of the North American growing season could show an increase by the year 2000, warming up by at least 2°C by about the year 2025. At the same time, rainfall could decline within the next five decades by 20 mm. The costs to corn growers and consumers, if adapted strains of new corn were not available, could, at mid-1970s prices, reach around $300 million per year (Bryson and Murray, 1977; Starr, 1977). Hence the urgency of tracking down further genetic materials that await our discovery in Mexico or in any Central American homeland of ancestral corn. Among recent finds are strains with relatively high protein content, increased vigor, resistance to drought, and tolerance for waterlogged soils. But as is the case with the habitat of the perennial species, the last strongholds of these wild varieties are being taken over by expanding agriculture in the form of hybrid sorghum—and, of all things, strawberry farms that export to the United States (DeWet, 1979; Wilkes, 1972, 1977, and 1979).

Some Conservation Options

Gene Banks

What can be done to save wild genetic materials, such as those found in a remote montane forest of Mexico? One proposal lies in collecting a representative sample of the germ plasm in question and storing it in a gene bank, such as the one at the National Seed Storage Laboratory of the U.S. Department of Agriculture in Fort Collins, Colorado. Seeds of many plant species, especially those with dry, small seeds, can often be stored dormant for long periods at a humidity level of 5 percent and a temperature of −20°C without undergoing physical damage or loss of genetic integrity. Within a small space, a single center can protect many thousands of species. For example, the Fort Collins facility contains 100,000 samples of more than 1,300 plant species, with a capacity for at least 500,000 samples.

There is considerable risk, however, in supposing that gene banks can represent any absolute answer for plant genetic resources in general (Justice and Bass, 1978). First, the technique simply does not work with many seed plants. This applies especially to most vegetatively propagated plants; for example, potato, cassava, members of the orchid family, and tree species such as apples and pears that do not breed true from seeds. In addition, the reservation applies to many tropical plant species, such as the cacao tree, whose seeds can be conserved outside the wild only with great difficulty. For the huge majority of species, botanists simply do not have enough information to say whether seed-bank storage could work or not.

Not that these general problems apply to corn genes. But two other categories of problems certainly do apply to corn genes. First, there are many technical difficulties, including low storage tolerance of many seeds, plus mutability of strains. Barley, for example, undergoes chromosomal damage during seed storage (Murata *et al.*, 1981) and beans are prone to genetic shifts (Roos, 1977). There can be accidents in storage facilities: An entire year's stock of seed potatoes, held at the storage facility at Sturgeon Bay in Wisconsin, was destroyed through a power failure caused by blown fuses. On top of all this, there can be unwitting or deliberate disposal of strains—a far from uncommon occurrence.

As a measure of all the problems involved, we may consider the experience of one of the leading gene banks in the world, the Royal Botanic Garden at Kew in Great Britain. The Garden receives around 2,000 accessions of seeds each year, yet its total holding of around 25,000 species has remained much the same during the past 40 years. As fast as new material is brought in, existing material deteriorates to the point where it must be thrown out.

A similar track record applies to the Fort Collins seed bank. Following a visit by a high-level government inspection team to Fort Collins in 1981, the Comptroller-General of the United States described the facility as providing inadequate security for genetic materials (General Accounting Office of the United States, 1981). Its facilities are viewed as "haphazard," they lack a "sense of direction and purpose," and they risk "the permanent loss of some genetic stocks." Nor are these criticisms confined to Fort Collins. The Comptroller-General's report goes on to state that "most of the nation's primary food crops are grown from only a few plant varieties, increasing the risk of major losses from severe disease, insect infestation, or adverse weather conditions. The Department of Agriculture does not adequately assess the risk or take adequate steps to minimize it"—even though its National Plant Germplasm System has been receiving some $50 million a year in federal funds. Perhaps this sum, large as it may sound, is simply not enough. Many experts believe that much more money is needed—at least five times as much. Not surprisingly, then, the State Department Strategy Conference on Biological Diversity in late 1981 heard the head of the USDA Plant Germplasm Program, Dr.

Quentin Jones, comment that "our present maintenance facilities are generally inadequate in providing storage environments that will maintain seed viability at desirable levels for desirable periods of time."

As for other developed nations and their gene banks, the experience of Denmark parallels that of the United States. Scientists at its International Seed Pathology Institute believe that one-third of Denmark's genetic resources in storage banks may be diseased. When we look at the developed world as a whole, we can reckon that a good one-half of all seed stored may eventually become valueless because of various storage problems, notably technological glitches.

Even if these problems were to be entirely ironed out, a further, and yet more important, problem would remain. This lies with the risk of reduced adaptiveness of stored seeds. When a plant species is "preserved" in refrigerated conditions, evolution is effectively frozen until such time as the genetic material can be grown afresh. Meantime, various threats to which it is subject in natural environments — insects, pathogens, and the like — continue to evolve, producing new forms of attack to which the host plant will not have evolved adequate defenses during its term of refrigerated protection.

In sum, seed collections, whether frozen or cultivated, tend to become genetic ghettos. Storage facilities can serve as no more than a strategem to supplement preservation of genetic variability in the wild, i.e., in species' natural environments. This applies especially if our aim is to safeguard genotypic variability of species over periods of many decades, if not centuries.

Conservation of Native Habitats

If we accept, then, that the only worthwhile approach for the long term is to safeguard genetic stocks in the wild, as in the case of the wild perennial corn in its native environment in Mexico, how shall we tackle the problem of habitat destruction caused by squatter cultivation and the like? The few Mexican farmers who want to put the forest patches to alternative use are doing no more than pursuing their legitimate interests as self-supporting citizens. What inducement can they be offered to do otherwise?

Similarly, what can be done to safeguard the so-called primitive cultivars that are still utilized by certain peasant communities in the tropics? These primitive cultivars tend to vary from community to community, hence they harbor a large amount of genetic variability. In a sense, we can even say that it was Mexican farmers who virtually "invented" corn as a food crop, devising several hundred cultivars before the crop spread north of the Rio Grande. The farmers' achievement is not so surprising when we remember that for a number of millennia the world's farmers have selectively domesticated and diversified their crop plants into numerous "land races" and "folk varieties." This slow process of plant improvement can now be accelerated through the skills of modern geneticists, who combine diverse characteristics from numerous primitive cultivars before hybridizing the results in order to produce today's superproductive crop types. In order to achieve these breeding advances, the geneticists need as much primitive-cultivar variability as they can lay their hands on—just as they need as much wild genetic material as they can track down.

Primitive cultivars present a special problem. They do not produce bumper harvests to rival those of modern commercial strains. Understandably, small-scale farmers are inclined to adopt the improved varieties of Green Revolution crops, with their uniformly high productivity—and with their uniformly narrow genetic base. This adoption of modern varieties tends to eliminate the old established varieties with their much broader array of genetic materials. The paradox has been graphically expressed by Professor H. Garrison Wilkes, a botanist with the University of Massachusetts: "The products of technology are displacing the source upon which the technology is based. It is analogous to taking stones from the foundation to repair the roof." This process of "genetic erosion" can be exceptionally swift. As Wilkes further points out, a Mexican farmer may, when opting for a modern variety, abandon a traditional variety that has fed his forebears for generations, and thereby allow it to become extinct in just a single year—or even less, if he eats all the seeds that he would normally save for replanting. In Wilkes's words, "the genetic heritage of a millennium can disappear in a single bowl of porridge."

How can we respond to this situation? One approach would be to raise a levy on commercial seed companies that sell genetically improved corn seed. To date, germ plasm has been traded internationally at nominal charge, on the grounds that it should be considered a part of the common heritage of humankind, hence to be traded as a "free good" among the community of nations. The trifling trading cost does not fractionally reflect the benefits derived by large numbers of better-fed people. A U.S. company that produces 2 million bushels of hybrid corn seed at $50 per bushel could contribute perhaps 1 percent of its $100 million revenues, or $1 million, toward preservation of corn strains in Mexico or in the other countries where corn varieties still survive. (The same could apply, of course, to commercial sales of other crop seeds: Global sales of the commercial seed industry are now well above $10 billion a year, so a 1 percent tax could produce the $100 million that many agricultural experts believe is needed for a crash budget to finance the urgent conservation of crop genetic resources.) The seed companies would doubtless pass on the costs to their consumers, a move which, while inflationary, would be no more than economically efficient and socially equitable. Should disease repeat the 1970 debacle of a 15 percent loss in the U.S. corn crop, the increased charges for more expensive corn products – a full $2 billion following 1970 – would be passed on to consumers anyway.

The revenues raised through a levy along these lines could be used to subsidize farmers in Mexico, who would thereby be restrained from digging up patches of land with wild forms of corn. Or they could be encouraged, if not required, to continue to farm with traditional sources of genetic variety, that is, nonmodern strains of corn or "primitive cultivars," notably those that are on the verge of extinction. While a Green Revolution farmer in Mexico can grow large amounts of high-yielding corn, another farmer, using a less productive but genetically unique type of native corn, might produce only one-third as much. Thus the latter farmer, supposing he can be persuaded to continue with the old type, would need to be subsidized to an extent three times the national corn price for his crop. But can we "pay people to remain peasants"?

Measures that are parallel in spirit and principle to this proposal are already established between the United States and Mexico, with respect to agricultural practices. The United States has supplied appreciable financial assistance to Mexico in order to keep hoof-and-mouth disease far to the south of the Rio Grande, and thereby safeguard the U.S. livestock industry. So there is already a precedent for the United States to intervene, in constructive fashion, in Mexico's agriculture.

The rationale for compensation measures in support of genetic conservation has been given an airing on repeated occasions, notably at the Stockholm Conference on the Human Environment in 1972, when there was much play with the concept of an "additionality principle." This concept proposes that compensation payments on appreciable scale should be made by the community of nations (meaning mainly those that can afford it) to the developing world, in order to offset adverse repercussions of conservation measures on emergent economies. Developing nations consider that funds for environmental action at international level should be independent of those provided for economic development; that is, these monies should be "additional" to funds already supplied. Hence the emergence of this cardinal principle, recognized at Stockholm by the international community, and a concept of sound practical sense in light of our growing need to safeguard our declining genetic reservoirs. Equally to the point, compensation payments should not be made available as another form of foreign aid, dispensed out of a spirit of charity. Rather they should reflect a recognition of joint responsibility for the deteriorating assets of the common heritage.

True, some observers may consider that subsidies on the part of rich nations for crop gene reservoirs in Mexico (among other tropical nations with rich genetic endowment) amount to a pie-in-the-sky notion—and the same for economic incentives on the part of other developed nations, such as Great Britain, in support of genetic conservation in whatever part of the developing world. But the day may come when we find that, as citizens of the global village, there is not much difference between being idealistic and realistic.

CHAPTER TWO

———————■———————

The Genetic Guts of Modern Agriculture

Many readers will have started their day with a wake-up mug of coffee. They may have breakfasted on fruit (or fruit juice), eggs, and toast; if not, a bowl of cereal probably was their choice. Lunch may have been a salad of one sort or another. Dinner could include meat and vegetables, with perhaps rice or potatoes. In between times, certain readers may have slipped in a cookie or two, a candy or three, and who knows what other snacks. Plus cups of coffee, tea, or occasionally chocolate, and a glass of beer, wine, or bourbon.

A diversified diet is one of the perquisites of living in the late twentieth century. This is a time when most of us eat far better than virtually all persons who have peopled the planet in the past. In fact, our daily intake would have challenged the most experienced palates of history, including those of kings and emperors.

These various items of food and drink derive from the bounty of modern agriculture – a phenomenon we are all familiar with. In fact, growing food is America's most efficient and most productive activity. Yet modern agriculture yields such abundant harvests by virtue of a factor that we rarely think about, but that ranks front and center in productive farming, and that is crop breeding. We sometimes hear that the marvels of modern agriculture are attributable to vast amounts of fertilizers and pesticides, plus sophisticated machinery and other aids that farmers can deploy in their fields. But it is basically through the efforts of plant geneticists that we reap such remarkable harvest from our corn and wheat fields, fruit orchards, vegetable plots, vineyards, and the like. Plant breeders, in turn, owe their achievements to the genetic resources that underpin all aspects of food growing.

Hence we enjoy our daily bread, in its many forms, through primary grace of genetic materials from the plant kingdom with all its

27

wild variety (Day, 1977; Frankel and Hawkes, 1974; Harlan, 1975; Myers, 1981; Office of Technology Assessment, 1981; Prescott-Allen and Prescott-Allen, 1981; Simmonds, 1976; Wittwer, 1982). It has ever been thus, right from the first beginning of agriculture around 8000 B.C. Our earliest farming forebears learned to domesticate the more productive forms of wild food plants; nearly all the staple foods of today, including most cereals, several root crops, and a number of legumes were cultivated during the Stone Age.

Indeed it is not going too far to say that the genetic underpinnings of no more than a couple of dozen major food crops stand between humankind and starvation. This is a sweeping statement, but a realistic one, when we consider the ultimate source of our food. As we sit down to our meal tables, let us consider that what lies before us would not be there but for the "free gifts" of nature's genetic resources.

Americans, together with Britishers, Germans, Japanese, and other well fed citizens of temperate zones, might bear in mind a further critical factor. Almost all the genetic resources in question stem from outside their countries. The earth's stocks of species and their genetic variability are largely located in the tropics and subtropics, zones that, with their year-round warmth and often year-round moisture, plus their variegated topography, represent the main powerhouse of evolution. By contrast, the temperate zones of North America, Europe, and most of the developed world are relatively impoverished in terms of their wildlife endowment and gene pools. For an American, there is no such thing as a "homegrown" meal. Without regular infusions of foreign germ plasm for its crops, the United States' farmlands would produce cranberries, blueberries, strawberries, pecans, sunflower seeds, and little else. Whereas the United States is mainly a nation of immigrants as concerns its human forebears, it is entirely so as concerns the ancestors of its corn, wheat, and all other leading crops.

These circumstances are so critical to our daily lives that it is worthwhile to take a lengthy look at some details. The extraordinary productivity of modern agriculture cannot be maintained, let alone expanded, without constant genetic support from wild relatives of agricultural crops – sometimes supplemented with the primitive cultivars of not-yet-modern farmers. In many instances, germ plasm from the wild makes a direct contribution to modern crops via crossbreeding of wild relatives with commercial strains; this applies particularly to corn, barley, oats, sorghum, pepper, sweet potato, several citrus fruits, and safflower. In certain other instances, germ plasm from the wild makes its contribution to modern agriculture via cultivars – notably in the cases of rice, sugarcane, potato, tomato, cacao, grape, strawberry, tobacco, and cotton, but also, though to a lesser degree, in the cases of wheat, rye, cassava, banana, pineapple, pea, peanut, sugarbeet, oil palm, and rubber.

To be sure, modern agriculture benefits from huge amounts of artificial additives such as fertilizers and pesticides. But these additives work best when used in support of crop varieties that can best exploit them, which means, in turn, that they depend for their impact upon the genetic quality of the crop plant varieties. "Miracle grains," lauded for their superproductivity, are not so much "high-yielding" grains as they are popularly called; rather they are "high-response" grains, able to flourish only when supported by stacks of fertilizer and so forth.

Genetic Gains

In the main, we have to thank the plant geneticists and their skills for the record crop yields of recent years. From 1930 onwards, when plant breeders became sufficiently sophisticated to exploit the genetic variability of wild relatives and of primitive cultivars, the yield of U.S. wheat has increased by 115 percent, that of rice 118 percent, tomatoes 172 percent, peanuts 295 percent, potatoes 312 percent, corn 320 percent, and sorghum 361 percent. Of this expanded productivity, we can reckon that, as a rough rule of thumb, at least 40 percent and sometimes 50 to 60 percent can be attributed to genetic breeding, and hence to the genetic materials on which plant breeders depend (Bertrand, 1980; Dalrymple, 1979 and 1980; Day, 1977; Duckham *et al.*, 1976; Duvick, 1977 and 1981; Frankel and Hawkes, 1974; Nabham, 1979; Office of Technology Assessment, 1981; Oldfield, 1981; Russell, 1974; Silvey, 1981; Sprague, 1979; Sprague *et al.*, 1980; Wittwer, 1980).

The reader who wonders how genetic breeding can contribute so much to modern agriculture may consider an illustrative example from the animal kingdom. The domestic dog contains so much "genetic plasticity" that we now have such canine contrasts as the St. Bernard and the Pekingese, the swift greyhound and the waddling basset. These dog varieties, however differentiated they may appear, are genetically much closer to one another than is the sparrow to the robin. Similar genetic plasticity can be found among the wild relatives and primitive ancestors of modern crop species.

It is this genetic plasticity that holds the best hope for our capacity to feed many more hungry mouths on Earth in the next few decades. Artificial additives such as fertilizer clearly cannot contribute evermore support for expanding agriculture in the future. Plants cannot keep on absorbing more and more fertilizer; on this front, we have reached a point of fast-diminishing returns. This is the main reason for the leveling-out of increases in crop productivity during the 1970s; put another way, the productivity of major food crops has "plateaued." In the United States, several crops, notably corn, wheat, sorghum, soybeans, and potatoes, have scarcely expanded their per-hectare output since 1970 – and the same is true in parts of the Third World for corn, wheat, potatoes, and cassava. In point of fact, grain yields worldwide have actually declined a little, and we manage to produce more grain year after year only by finding new lands to dig up – a pioneering strategy that is rapidly running out of virgin territories. If we are to produce enough food to ensure that everybody on earth is adequately fed by the year 2000, we shall have to increase our present food output by at least 60 to 70 percent (supposing that the present unjust distribution patterns persist, favoring the rich against the poor – for it is easier to improve agricultural technology than to change political postures). But the net increase in croplands that we can realistically expect during the last two decades of this century amounts to a mere 4 percent. So there must be massive emphasis on persuading each hectare of cropland to grow much more food.

It is with genetic improvements, then, that our best hope for the future lies. Fortunately the genetic plasticity of modern crop plants offers us a good deal of maneuvering room. When we consider the average yield of corn in the United States in 1975, some 150–200 bushels per hectare, and compare it with the current world record for corn production, over 1,000 bushels per hectare, we can see what a gap there is between present performance and future potential. Furthermore, the theoretical maximum yield for corn (in conditions of optimum sunlight, carbon dioxide, water, and plant nutrients, and with no diseases and insects or environmental stresses of any kind) is believed to be 2,665 bushels per hectare: Again, we have much ground to make up before we can claim that corn productivity is bumping its head against the ceiling of absolute limits. The figures above indicate that the present world record for corn is 5 to 6 times the average U.S. yield; and similarly large ratios apply to other American crops, namely, 7 times for wheat and cassava, 6.5 for sorghum, 6.2 for oats, 5.8 for rice, 5 for sugarcane, 4.8 for barley, 3.6 for potatoes, 3 for soybeans, and 2.4 for sugar beets (Wittwer, 1979). Most world record yields remain at about one-half of potential maximum yields.

Plainly, the heyday of the plant geneticist lies ahead. The Green Revolution, which has brought us outsize harvests in the past two decades, may shortly give way to a still more remarkable phase in agricultural innovation, the Gene Revolution.

As we have noted, the main genetic reservoirs are located in the tropics, plus a few sectors of the subtropics. The great bulk of these reservoirs are confined to around one dozen so-called "centers of diversity," these being areas of exceptional genetic variability. They were first designated by the Russian geneticist Vavilov, hence are known as the Vavilov Centers. Almost everything we eat can be traced back to these few concentrations of genetic materials: corn to Mexico, Central America, and the northern Andes; wheat and barley to Asia Minor and Ethiopia; rice to Indo-Burma and Southeast Asia; potatoes to the northern Andes; the common bean to Central America; coffee to Ethiopia; sugarcane to Indo-Burma, Southeast Asia, and China; and so forth with the roughly 30 crop plants that supply 95 percent of human nutrition (a mere 8 contribute 75 percent of the carbohydrates that generate human energy).

Genetic Erosion

Should anything happen to reduce the genetic reservoirs of the Vavilov Centers (plus a number of subsidiary centers around the tropics), the potential for a global food crisis would be great indeed. And much is happening. It is ironic that, precisely at a time when we are more dependent than ever on genetic variability, we are pushing Earth's stocks of genetic materials down the tubes at ever-faster rates. With each day that goes by, the germ plasm basis for tomorrow's supper is being destroyed. So serious is the situation that certain leading agriculturalists believe we are on the verge of another "resource snarl-up"—too few resources to meet everybody's needs, and too many of the scarce resources concentrated in a few localities. In other words, we face yet another in the list of emerging resource shortages that now characterize the global community. In this sense, crop genetic resources serve as a further illustration of interdependency relationships among the family of nations. They thereby present another opportunity for international cooperation by which we all gain—or for international squabbling by which we all lose.

The problem of genetic erosion lies in part with the sheer attrition of natural environments through increase in human numbers and in human aspirations. In part too, a major threat lies with a trend for subsistence farming to give way to commercial agriculture, whereupon food plants that over centuries have evolved adaptations to their local ecological conditions are supplanted by more productive varieties, often from foreign sources. In this latter sense, the Green Revolution, while an admirable achievement in many respects, is proving a disaster for local genetic diversity—and this applies to advanced nations of the temperate zones as well as to developing nations of the

tropics. Advanced nations tend to plant their croplands with genetically identical varieties of corn, wheat, barley, and the like, leaving
their crop productivity resting on a critically narrow genetic base. The
prospect for America's agriculture was described one decade ago in
these terms: "The situation is serious, potentially dangerous to the
welfare of the nation, and appears to be getting worse rather than better" (National Academy of Sciences, 1972). More recently, experts
have asserted that the Department of Agriculture's National Plant
Germplasm System, which is responsible for conserving the genetic
base and improving crop varieties, "lacks a sense of direction and purpose . . . [It] does not determine the risks of genetic vulnerability or
adequately perform the housekeeping chores of collection, maintenance, and evaluation of the germplasm stock" (General Accounting
Office, 1981).

True, not all breeding experts agree. Dr. Donald N. Duvick, the
director of plant breeding at a leading commercial enterprise, Pioneer
Hi-Bred International, finds that his corporate colleagues take a more
positive view – but that may be because they are more interested in
immediate scope for breeding, rather than longer-term needs.

As for the main centers of diversity, located as they are in the tropics
and subtropics, the situation is rapidly declining, according to annual
reports of the Food and Agriculture Organization of the United Nations and of the International Board for Plant Genetic Resources. The
previous chapter noted the declining status of corn's genetic materials
in Mexico. Similar threats are overtaking wheat in its countries of
origin, and likewise oats, barley, rye, coffee, beets, olives, oil palm,
cacao, cotton, and several other leading crops.

To quote a leading plant geneticist, Professor Jack Harlan of the
Department of Agronomy, University of Illinois: "Genetic resources
stand between us and catastrophic starvation on a scale that we cannot imagine. In a very real sense, the future of the human race rides
on these materials. Yet most of our so-called world collections [of crop
genetic resources] are sadly deficient in wild races. As we obtain more
and more useful results from incorporating wild genetic resources, the
principal bottleneck lies in the paucity of wild germplasm in our collections" (Harlan, 1976). A similar comment has been offered yet more
recently by the Executive Secretary of the International Board for
Plant Genetic Resources, when he stated, at the Strategy Conference
on Biological Diversity in Washington, D.C., in late 1981, that "genetic
material is being eroded in many parts of the world, to the extent that
in the case of many crops we are facing a crisis situation" (Walsh,
1981).

It is not going too far to say that plant breeders face virtual wipeout
of endemic genetic diversity of several crops. Take barley, for exam-

ple: A high-protein strain has recently been discovered in Ethiopia, just in the nick of time since its native habitat has been scheduled for a settlement scheme. Plant breeders have been trying to upgrade the protein content of sorghum; they have analyzed 9,000 forms before finding two strains from Ethiopia that are rich in an essential protein chemical, an amino acid known as lysine (Shapley, 1973). As a result of this discovery, the nutritional content of sorghum has been improved for millions of sorghum growers, especially in developing countries. Ethiopia is, as we have already noted, a gene center for several crops, but during the course of recent decades, its wild flora has undergone widespread impoverishment through expanding cultivation, overgrazing, and deforestation (Harlan, 1969; Kuru, 1978).

Plant Diseases

Specialist strains of modern crops not only increase general productivity and add to nutritional content, but resist dozens of diseases that afflict agricultural plants. Diseases now cause annual losses to world crops worth around $25 billion. The potential of rice, corn, and wheat is reduced by about 9 percent as a result of diseases. Without regular supplies of resistant genes from the wild, blight could sweep through many of humankind's main food crops.

To gain an idea of the far-reaching repercussions of plant diseases, let us bear in mind the traumatic experiences of the Irish when a blight hit their potato crop way back in the 1840s. During the course of that decade, at least 1 million and possibly 2 million Irish died of outright starvation and associated sicknesses, out of a total population of only 8 million. Another 1.5 to 2 million emigrated, with profound consequences for the New York police, Boston politics, and Notre Dame football.

Nor can the disease problem ever be finally won. In the case of most major crops, plant breeders believe that between 5 and 15 years after they introduce a crop strain with fresh resistance to disease, the resistance collapses in the face of newly evolved forms of the disease agents. So there is constant need to refurbish the plant's genetic constitution with new germ plasm.

To see how these considerations apply to some specific items that appear on our plates during the course of a day, let us take a look at a few leading crops.

Wheat

Wheat deserves our special attention, as one of the "big three" of modern cereal grains that together account for three-quarters of all cereal food grown (Feldman and Sears, 1981; Jensen, 1978). In conjunction with sorghum, these three—wheat, corn, and rice—account for over half of all Earth's croplands; and in conjunction with potatoes, they contribute more food than the next 26 most important crops combined. The United States produces about one-seventh of the world's wheat, almost 60 million metric tons, of which three-fifths is exported; compare with corn, around 200 million metric tons produced by U.S. farmers, with almost one-third exported.

Wheat growers are more dependent than corn growers upon wild sources of germ plasm, on the grounds that there is limited genetic variability in primitive cultivars of wheat. In fact, the genetic material of all cultivated wheats has already been exploited by crop breeders almost to its full capacity. At the same time, the range of genetic variation in cultivated wheats has been decreasing drastically in recent years, as a consequence of the trend toward genetically uniform crops. Fortunately, wheat is able to tolerate "wide crosses" between related species, which means that commercial varieties can readily be bred with wild varieties. In this sense, wheat shares a breeding tolerance that characterizes several other modern crops, notably rice, sugarcane, potato, and many fruits, plus tobacco and cotton, all of which benefit markedly from wild relatives.

The compatibility of domesticated wheats with wild relatives is all the more pertinent in that the crop is unusually susceptible to disease—and it is mainly in wild forms that we find genetic resistance to disease. The history of wheat growing reveals that a disease-resistant variety of commercial wheat may last as little as five years before pathogens and pests devise a way around the variety's defenses (CIMMYT, 1974; Dalrymple, 1979 and 1980; Jensen, 1978; Zeven, 1977). Mexico, for example, has encountered continuing problems with rust diseases and has had to switch wheat varieties six times in 20 years. U.S. farmers, during the past several decades, have utilized as many as 700 varieties in their efforts to steer clear of disease problems.

A prominent type of disease is stripe rust. This blight reached epidemic proportions in northwestern wheatlands of the United States during the 1960s. The situation was saved by germ plasm from a wild wheat found in Turkey, a variety which has likewise supplied resistance to some 50 other races of disease-causing pathogens, including a noted menace called dwarf bunt. As a result of this single genetic infusion from overseas, America's wheat crop has been saved massive damage. In Montana alone, where 30 percent of the crop was being lost, the savings are believed to have amounted to at least $3 million in subsequent years (National Academy of Sciences, 1972). When we consider this wild wheat's contributions across the nation, eliminating all known races of common and dwarf bunts, among several other diseases, the wild strain can be reckoned to be worth around $50 million annually. On top of all this, a pest of America's wheatlands, the hessian fly, has been overcome through fly-resistant varieties, with savings over the decades that have reached $250 million (U.S. Department of Agriculture, 1976).

Of course, wheat breeders aim not only to develop resistance to disease, but to incorporate a lengthy list of other traits. These items can include higher yield, better milling and baking qualities, shorter growing seasons, and capacity to survive drought and winter cold. Thanks to wild genes that offer winter hardiness, the Soviet Union has recently been able to move its spring wheat zone further northward by more than 300 kilometers; and now that new levels of cold tolerance are genetically available, the Russians hope to move their winter wheat zone another 300 kilometers further north within the near future.

At the same time, wheat breeders are tinkering with wheat genes to make each individual plant more productive. They seek to increase the grains per head from 20 to 30; in greenhouse trials, as many as 70 prove possible. They also seek to increase the number of heads growing on each plant. If wheat breeders can achieve breakthroughs on both these fronts, they could accomplish a whopping 50 to 100 percent increase in yields. A mere 20 percent increase by U.S. farmers who grow winter wheat, with their present output of 45 million metric tons (three-quarters of the nation's entire crop), would mean an additional 9 million metric tons—and similar increases could be anticipated in Canada, Australia, Argentina, and other major wheat-growing nations.

But these virtues would bring further problems with them. More grains in more heads per plant would constitute a much heavier load for the plant's stem to support, causing a tendency for the entire plant to bend over, or to "lodge," in the field before it can be harvested. The answer to the problem: develop wheat varieties with shorter and stronger stems, or "dwarf" varieties. This restructuring of the wheat plant's architecture has already been partially achieved through distantly related derivatives of a weedy grass known as *Agropyron* (which also, fortunately, offers many disease-resistant genes) (Zeven, 1977).

These breeding breakthroughs are all the more imperative in that we now appear to have reached a stage where wheat yield increases are "flattening out." The past few years have seen little advance in wheat productivity. Hence there is a premium on finding other wild wheats for diverse supplies of genetic variability, in order to reboost the yield of wheatlands. At the same time, crop breeders constantly seek adaptable germ plasm to counter changing environmental conditions, for example the warmer and drier weather that we may well experience within just a few decades if the carbon dioxide content of the global atmosphere continues to build up, leading, as predicted by many scientists, to the "greenhouse effect" with gross repercussions for major food crops. (For details of this potential climatic dislocation ahead of us, see the previous chapter.)

As an indication of how different environmental conditions can lead to different wheat yields, let us briefly consider the experience of British farmers. During the last three decades, their wheat yields have roughly doubled, from just over 2.5 metric tons per hectare to just over 5.5 metric tons; and during the 1970s, when the "variety effect" has been particularly prominent, output has grown by a massive 3 percent per year. This striking increase could have been achieved only by a combination of factors, including the improved varieties of the crop, plus massive amounts of fertilizers, pesticides, and growth regulators along with better cultivation techniques and improved management all around. A key question: How much of the increase can be attributed to plant breeding, and thus to genetic resources, alone? To come up with an answer, the Plant Breeding Institute and the National Institute of Agricultural Botany in Cambridge have conducted various experiments, finding that modern wheat varieties do not depend so much on fertilizers, pesticides, soil types, and the like as on genetic improvement. In fact, the amount of increased yield that can be assigned to advanced varieties can be reckoned at a solid one-half (Silvey, 1981). The explanation lies with the fact that breeders can redesign the distribution of wheat plants' dry matter, reducing the amount of straw and thereby allowing more "growth energy" to be directed into grain.

As for developing countries, improved varieties of wheat, with their greater productivity and disease resistance, plus their capacity to benefit from artificial additives and improved agronomic techniques, have boosted output to an extent that has been estimated for 1975 to have been worth $2 billion (CIMMYT, 1976 and 1978; Dalrymple, 1979; World Bank, 1978).

In view of the premium that breeders place on wild varieties, we can share the concern of agriculturalists that many wild wheats are disappearing. In extensive sectors of wheat's original range, there is virtual "wipeout" of endemic genetic diversity. From the Atlas mountains through the Mediterranean Basin as far as Ethiopia and Nepal, many wild strains have all but disappeared. Of Greece's native wheats, 95 percent have become extinct during the past 40 years. Even in the remotest valleys, native wheats are becoming rare. Right across Turkey, wild progenitors find sanctuary from grazing animals only in graveyards and castle ruins. According to the Food and Agriculture Organization of the United Nations, the main centers of wheat diversity in the Middle East, Asia Minor, and Ethiopia could become completely lost as primary genetic sources before the end of the 1980s. As for wheat germ plasm collections, they have been described by Dr. J. T. Williams, Executive Secretary of the International Board for Plant Genetic Resources, as "completely inadequate" (Walsh, 1981).

All the more welcome, then, is the recent discovery of a "lost" progenitor of modern wheat, this being one of only three wild wheats that have supplied present-day wheats with their superproductive properties. After lengthy searches in Sumeria, Judea, and the watershed of the River Jordan, scientists have rediscovered this wild progenitor, with its many important genes that confer increased protein content and resistance to drought.

As with corn, the main sources of wheat germ plasm derive from outside the territories of the main wheat growers in the developed world. In the case of the United States, for example, one-quarter of its wheat collections are from southeastern Europe, well over one-third from southwestern Asia, one-twelfth from northeastern Africa, and the rest from scattered localities. The genetic underpinning of a major strain of American wheat, the "soft red winter" wheat, derives mainly from Mediterranean sources; the best resistance to diseases comes from Turkey, Ethiopia, and Palestine; and the main supplies of genes conferring leaf-rust resistance come from Turkey and the Balkans (Reitz and Craddock, 1969).

Rice

Rice is the most important crop in the most populous region of the world, southern and eastern Asia. Yet by the late 1970s, a mere one-third of ricelands were growing genetically improved varieties, meaning there is great scope ahead for the rice geneticist. Plainly a main aim of rice breeding is to expand the productivity of rice.

Rice geneticists also must pay special attention to the depredations of diseases, which are a constant challenge for rice growers. A few years ago, a famous cultivar of rice in the Philippines, IR-8, was hit by tungro disease. So rice growers switched to a further form, IR-20, but this hybrid soon proved fatally vulnerable to grassy stunt virus, a disease spread by brown hopper insects. So potent was this threat that it could have proved devastating for the huge numbers of people in the region who depend on rice as a staple food. Scientists at the International Rice Research Institute in the Philippines searched rice gene collections around the world, totaling some 47,000 items (albeit representing a mere fraction of known rice germ plasm available), looking for genetic resistance. Eventually they came across a single wild species collected from Kerala in the southern part of India, allowing them to transfer the appropriate genes to established rice varieties. But one of these varieties, a superhybrid known as IR-26, while exceptionally resistant to many diseases and insect pests, proved too fragile for the strong winds that characterize the many island environments of eastern Asia, whereupon plant breeders decided to try an original Taiwan strain that had shown unusual capacity to stand up to winds—only to find that it had been all but eliminated by Taiwan farmers as they planted virtually all their ricelands with the original IR-8. So much for the uniformly high productivity of the Green Revolution, with its uniformly narrow genetic base!

As a measure of the benefits from genetically improved rice in Asia, we can reckon that the expanded output amounted to at least 15 million metric tons in 1976, roughly double the harvest in 1971, with an economic value of at least $1.5 billion (Dalrymple, 1979). If, as many geneticists believe is realistic, we assign half of the expanded output to genetic improvement, and the rest to associated factors such as better cultivation, fertilizer, and the like, the dollar value of the genetic contributions has proved sizable. In the Philippines, agricultural economists calculate that every $1 invested in rice research produces an overall benefit to the country of $4—a rate of return comparable in scale with experience in the United States for research in hybrid corn and sorghum (Flores-Moya *et al.*, 1978). In Colombia, several dwarf strains of rice were introduced in the mid-1960s, and by 1975 they had achieved a 2.5-fold increase in output, estimated to be worth $350 million, or more than ten times as much as the research investment (Jennings, 1976; Scobie and Posada, 1977). Of course, not all the return can be credited to genetic contributions. The bulk of the investment expense is accounted for by scientific staff and research and consultant facilities. But these backup services would be useless without genetic variability as a prime component of the entire exercise.

Barley

The main center of diversity for barley is probably Ethiopia, with subsidiary centers in northern Africa, Turkey, parts of Russia, Manchuria, and the Himalayas (Reitz and Craddock, 1969). In California, where the farm-gate value of the barley crop is around $140 million per year, a single barley gene from Ethiopia protects the crop from the devastating effects of yellow dwarf virus (Schaller, 1977). In England and Wales, genetic improvements in the yield of spring barley have averaged 0.84 percent a year between 1953 and 1980; virtually all the yield increase of the 1970s has been due to the introduction of new varieties (Austin, 1978; Riggs *et al.*, 1981). The average yield is now about 4.2 metric tons per hectare, a good way off the 10–11 metric tons per hectare thought feasible under optimal conditions – which places all the greater emphasis on as much genetic variability as barley breeders can lay their hands on.

One of the main products of barley is beer. The best brewer, however, cannot get far without hops, with their alpha-acid content that contributes to the characteristically bitter taste of beer. According to the Hop Research Department at Wye College in England, three wild American ancestors of modern hops underpin the genotype that is grown in almost half of all hoplands around the world. Because these wild American hops have induced a 40 percent increase in the alpha-acid content, their economic contribution can now be reckoned, for England alone, at some £8 million a year within the context of a hop crop valued at £21 million in 1981 (Thompson, 1981).

Potato

The prosaic potato is one of the most efficient crops in converting nature's sunlight and man's sweat into a high-quality food that is popular among many communities around the world. In the Andes, for instance, it is the single most important source of food; and throughout the Third World, the crop is expanding more rapidly than most other major food crops, on the grounds that it yields more nutritious food more quickly on less land and in harsher climates than leading competitors such as corn, wheat, or rice.

In view of the potato's adverse image among weight watchers, we may be surprised to learn that it features a higher ratio of protein to carbohydrate than do other roots and tubers, and many cereals. Moreover, potato protein is of better grade than the protein of most other major food crops. On a "biological value" scale measuring the proportion of nitrogen that the human body retains for growth and maintenance, the potato ranks at 73 (out of 100), ahead of soybean at 72, corn at 54, wheat at 53, and peas and beans at 47. (For comparison, an egg ranks at 96.)

All in all, farmers around the world now grow almost 300 million metric tons of potatoes each year, a crop for which consumers pay well over $100 billion. In the United States, which produces 16 million metric tons a year, consumers eat their way through 2 million metric tons of french fries a year, and almost 2 million metric tons of potato chips, each item being worth roughly $3 billion.

Yet the plant breeder finds that established commercial crops of potatoes no longer possess enough genetic variability to meet current and future breeding needs. Hence the search for alternative sources of genetic variability, in the form of primitive cultivars and wild strains (Glendinning, 1979; Harlan, 1981; Ross, 1979). Fortunately, peasant farmers in the Andes still maintain as many as 3,000 cultivars, including all 8 species of potato utilized worldwide (the genus *Solanum* actually includes more than 2,000 species, of which about 160 bear tubers—meaning that there could be scope for us to develop new types of potato-like crops). As for wild forms, a Mexican plant, rejoicing in the stodgy name of *Solanum demissum* (the well known commercial variety is known as *S. tuberosum*), has yielded genes with resistance to bacterial wilt, to two viruses, to two races of nematodes, and to the Colorado potato beetle, among other threats. Another wild relative, this one from Peru and Bolivia, and known as *S. acaule*, is widely used to help the crop's capacity to withstand frost, even temperatures as chilly as $-8°C$.

Certain wild strains of potato feature sophisticated techniques for resisting insects. Now that several insect pests have acquired immunity to chemical pesticides, potato growers have been casting around for a response strategy. Apparently a variety of wild potato from Bolivia has developed a curious technique. It is nothing so crude as a poisonous chemical; rather it is a technique somewhat akin to the cement overshoes favored by Chicago gangsters in the 1920s. The stem and leaves of the plant are covered with tiny hairs (resembling those of a tomato plant), containing a fluid and an enzyme; when the hairs are disturbed by a sap-sucking aphid crawling across the leaves, the fluid and the enzyme combine with oxygen to produce a quick-setting "cement" (Tingey *et al.*, 1981). Within a few years, we may see a bristly new type of potato plant thriving in potato growers' fields.

Tomato

Partly because of Americans' addiction to ketchup and pizza, the second most widely grown vegetable crop in the United States is the tomato, with an annual value that has now topped $1 billion. As with the potato, the tomato is heavily dependent on wild sources of genetic variability. Thanks to disease resistance from a single gene of a wild tomato relative in Peru, more than 100 commercial types of tomato are now free of a particularly potent form of wilt disease. Other wild relatives offer resistance to diverse blights, leaf mold, and grey leafspot, among other diseases; and they feature increased vitamin C content, plus additional sugar and carotene (Rick, 1979 and 1982).

Coffee

An early morning stimulus for many a reader, coffee is the second most important commodity in international trade (the first is petroleum). It is grown in more than 40 countries of the developing world and is a main form of livelihood for almost three-quarters of a million farmers, together with millions more people who find employment in harvesting, processing, and marketing the coffee.

Coffee growers faced a major setback in 1970 when a rust disease appeared in southern Brazil, with 30 different races or types of the disease. The rust soon spread to Central America, where coffee exports were worth $3 billion. Conventional methods of response, in forms such as fungicides, would have cost $200 per hectare, more than many farmers could afford. Fortunately a rust-resistant strain became available from germ plasm collected in forests of Ethiopia, this country being the original source of genetic variability for coffee (Ferwerda, 1976). Even though a good 80 percent of Ethiopia's original forests have been eliminated, and the rest are facing extreme threat, germ plasm collectors reached the wild gene pools in time – whereupon coffee growers in Latin America were saved from disaster, and coffee drinkers around the world were saved from the $1 cup of coffee.

Even health addicts benefit from wild sources of coffee germ plasm. A new variety of wild coffee that contains not a trace of caffeine has been discovered in the Comoros Islands off eastern Africa.

Dollar Value of Genetic Improvements

What overall economic benefits do we ultimately enjoy from infusions of new crop germ plasm?

It is more than difficult to come up with a worthwhile figure. But we should attempt the task, if only to help us "get a handle" on the value of wild gene reservoirs. As a preliminary evaluation, the U.S. Department of Agriculture believes that the farm-gate value of all U.S. crops can now be put at $100 billion per year. The Department also estimates that increases in productivity due to genetic improvement average around 1 percent per year. This means that advances through infusions of new germ plasm can be set at $1 billion per year for the United States alone.

Let us conclude this chapter with a meditation on an ancient petition: "Give us this day our daily bread" – this being a part of the Lord's prayer that is now taking on a new meaning. We enjoy our daily bread, in its many forms, thanks to the natural bounty of the earth we live on; and this creativity of nature is enhanced by the creativity of the human brain, as expressed through the ingenuity of plant breeders and others involved in the growing of our food. At a time when the skills of crop geneticists are pioneering entirely new territories of agricultural endeavor, it is ironic that the essential elements of their profession, the genetic underpinnings of modern agriculture, are being casually wiped off the face of the earth. So perhaps we might recall the next petition in the Lord's prayer: "And forgive us our trespasses." On top of its many established meanings, this petition is perhaps also taking on a new sense: Let us not trespass so heavy-footedly on the living space of the wild plants that have shared the One Earth home with us for millennia and that can now make a contribution to our daily welfare beyond the dreams of all our forebears.

■

CHAPTER THREE

More Genes for Mealtimes

The last chapter dealt with some obvious applications of genetic materials in support of modern agriculture. Extensive as these applications are, they are far from the whole story. Let us now take a look at some less apparent contributions of genes to our meal tables.

Genetic materials can contribute to several broad areas of improved agriculture. These include photosynthetic efficiency, biological nitrogen fixation, tolerance of environmental stresses, and control of pests.

Photosynthesis

Photosynthesis is the process by which a plant utilizes sunlight to energize water and carbon dioxide before converting them into foods. The plants thus exploit the greatest natural resource that is available to life on earth, but the natural resource that is least efficiently utilized by modern agriculture – sunlight.

Certain plants carry on photosynthesis more efficiently than others. Sugarcane and corn, for example, are markedly more efficient than most cereal grains, soybeans, peanuts, and cotton. In fact most food crops capture only 1 percent, and often less, of the sunlight that illuminates their leaves. Yet we know that photosynthesis can be increased considerably. Whereas the process could theoretically convert as much as 6.6 percent of the sun's energy, the highest yields obtained with the most efficient plant known – 112 metric tons per hectare with sugarcane – correspond to only 3.3 percent.

Despite the scope to improve photosynthesis, there has been little research as yet on ways to enhance the process through photosynthetically positive mutants that are available in wild gene pools

(Bassham, 1977; Marzola and Bartholomew, 1979; Wittwer, 1980; Zelitch, 1975). Yet we know that geneticists can, for instance, rearrange a plant's leaf configuration in order to encourage greater uptake of sunlight. In the tropics, where sunlight is an abundant natural resource, this technique alone could probably double the productivity of several major crops.

In addition, geneticists can work on those factors—hormonal mechanisms, growth regulators, and the like—that control the flowering of plants, the aging of their leaves, and other key functions of photosynthesis. Much of a plant's development is governed by hormonal mechanisms, which in turn are regulated by chemicals. Geneticists are learning to manipulate a plant's chemical makeup to "trigger" hormones into stimulating the plant's growth, its rooting and flowering, and its resistance to pests. For example, when sugarcane is treated with specialized chemicals, the crop ripens earlier, expanding sugar yield by more than 10 percent (Nickell, 1977). Similarly, growth regulators can dramatically alter the shape of the "canopies" of crops such as soybean and cereals, in order to help them take in more light. A hormone stimulant has been used with forest trees that are commercially important, in order to induce flowering at age 4–6 years instead of 10–20 years.

A notable plant regulator, a polypeptide known as phytochrome, serves as a "switch" to alert the plant to changes in its environment. In response to the signals it receives from phytochrome, a plant can adjust its growth patterns. Plant breeders believe that they could learn what makes the switch work if they could investigate the mechanism in a sufficiently broad spectrum of plants, both domestic and wild. Breeders hope that if they once achieve this research breakthrough, they will be able to manipulate the switch device in order to persuade plants to grow at a time that is most convenient to the farmer.

A promising avenue for photosynthesis research lies with the characteristics of C_3 and C_4 plants (Hall and Rao, 1980). Most plants are of C_3 type, and they derive their curious name from the fact that, after fixing carbon dioxide from the atmosphere, they produce a 3-carbon acid that is converted into a 3-carbon sugar (and thereafter into other sugars, plus proteins and fats). Satisfactory as this photosynthetic strategy is, it leaves the plant in something of a "physiological Catch-22 situation." As the plant absorbs carbon dioxide from the atmosphere, it also loses water by transpiration—a moisture loss that the plant can ill afford. This trade-off becomes more critical for the plant's welfare when its photosynthesis is stimulated by a rise in temperature—a change that also encourages photorespiration, an energy-using process that can increase to a rate that moves the plant's carbon economy eventually into deficit. On a day with calm, hot weather, a farmer's crop may actually decline in size.

To overcome these problems of photosynthesis, some plant species take in carbon dioxide only at night. Their carbon dioxide is used in producing a 4-carbon acid that is stored until next day, when, during hours of sunlight, it can be transferred into cytoplasm. These plants are known as C_4 plants. Whereas a C_3 plant may need 500 grams of water to produce one gram of biomass (dry weight), a C_4 plant may need only 200 grams.

As we might expect, most temperate-zone plants are C_3 types, while most C_4 plants can be found in the tropics, plus the warmer localities of temperate zones. Examples of C_3 plants include rice, oats, barley, rye, wheat, sugarbeet, soybean, beans, peas, and potatoes. C_4 plants include corn, sugarcane, millet, sorghum, and papyrus. In addition, a number of tropical grasses, among many other wild species, are C_4 plants, for example *Pennisetum*, which, when used as a pastureland grass, can produce 85 metric tons of forage per hectare per year, by contrast with a typical C_3 forage plant, rye grass in Great Britain, which manages only 30 metric tons. Not surprisingly, Great Britain possesses only a few C_4 species, such as saltmarsh grass, or the prickly saltwort and a few other maritime dicotyledons (literally, two cotyledons or embryonic leaves per seed, as opposed to one in grasses, grains, and other monocotyledons). By contrast, we find that in southern sectors of Florida and California, at least 80 percent of grass species are C_4 plants. In fact, large numbers of the Gramineae family of grasses are C_4 plants, together with many Amaranthaceae (cockscombs and celosias), Compositae (sunflowers), and Euphorbiaceae (many common euphorbias). Altogether the C_4 mechanism has been observed in 19 families of flowering plants, as well as in one fern and one gymnosperm.

In short, C_4 plants tend to photosynthesize faster than C_3 plants. They benefit more from high levels of carbon dioxide in the atmosphere, losing less water. They thrive in the bright light of the tropics. Because their photosynthetic strategies have been discovered only recently, botanists have not yet managed to decipher their precise techniques – not, at least, to the extent that C_3 plants can be manipulated into emulating some of the C_4 characteristics. But as plant physiologists come across more wild species with the C_4 photosynthetic pathway, they can use these "plant models" to decipher the C_4 code. Provided enough wild species offer "design inspiration" to plant physiologists and geneticists, we can look forward to a time when key components of the C_4 code can be introduced into C_3 plants. The growth spurts that we can then expect in our major crops will give a sizable boost to modern agriculture.

So complex and arcane is the C_4 strategy that it would probably not have been visualized by plant physiologists if the plants themselves had not supplied the "template insights." How many more plant species, we might well wonder, are "out there," offering research models of further metabolic processes that could make massive contributions to our field crops?

Biological Nitrogen Fixation

The most frequent limiting factor in agriculture, after water, is nitrogenous fertilizer. Virtually all species on Earth, including humans, all other animals, and all higher plants, are unable to use nitrogen in its free, or "elemental" state in the atmosphere. It must first be "fixed"; that is, it must be combined with other elements such as hydrogen, carbon, or oxygen before it can be assimilated into living tissue.

Crop plants need nitrogen – lots of it. While this comment applies to farmlands everywhere on Earth, it applies especially to tropical farmlands with their often infertile soils. Yet most tropical farmers cannot afford the high prices of chemical nitrogenous fertilizer, dependent for its manufacture on fossil fuels. To produce one metric ton of nitrogenous fertilizer requires natural gas equivalent to six barrels of oil. Not surprisingly, chemically-fixed nitrogen is the single most costly item in modern agriculture.

At the same time, demand for nitrogenous fertilizer is growing fast. At the start of the century, the amount of chemical nitrogen produced was less than 0.5 million metric tons a year. By 1950 it had grown to 3.5 million metric tons a year, and today it has jumped to over 50 million metric tons a year (out of a total for all artificial fertilizers, including potassium and phosphorus, of 80 million metric tons). By the year 2000, according to United Nations projections, our need for nitrogenous fertilizer could soar to 200 million metric tons. At present, developing-world farmers, seeking to support 75 percent of the world's population, consume less than one-fifth of the world's fertilizer, and it costs them $3 billion a year to enjoy this meager share. Generally speaking, one kilogram of fertilizer on a developing-world cereal crop can generate an additional 10 kilograms of grain. If Third World farmers are to increase their food output by almost 4 percent a year, as they must to keep up with their growing human numbers and human aspirations, they will need a full five times as much fertilizer by the year 2000. To date, they use an average of only 30 kg of chemical nutrients for each hectare of cropland, which, while four times more than 20 years ago, is only one-fifth as much as is used in North America and Europe.

Agricultural experts respond to this fertilizer challenge in two main ways (Child, 1977; Franda, 1980; Kovaly, 1979; Wittwer, 1979 and 1980). First, plant geneticists breed varieties of crop plants that do a much better job with the fertilizer they receive. When a farmer applies costly fertilizer to his fields, he may not be aware that less than half of the nitrogen is recovered by his crops, the rest being lost to the atmosphere or leached away from the surface soil. This represents a massive loss, amounting to at least 25–30 million metric tons of nitrogen a year. The waste through nitrification and denitrification (as the "leak" processes are called) can be reduced by genetic improvement of existing crops. Again, plant breeders need as much genetic diversity from the plant kingdom as they can find, in order to incorporate reduced-leak characteristics into crop species.

The second, and probably the more promising, approach lies with an agricultural technique using biological nitrogen fixation (Brewbaker and Wei Hu, 1981; Brill, 1979; Dobereiner *et al.*, 1978; Felker and Bandurski, 1979; Newton and Nyman, 1976; Phillips, 1980). The secret lies with certain bacteria that possess the ability to fix nitrogen from the atmosphere. Generally speaking, these microorganisms set themselves up in nodules, or "nitrogen factories," on the roots of plants. The host plant provides food and energy that the bacteria use, and the bacteria fix nitrogen that the plant uses. So efficient is this process that nitrogen-fixing microorganisms are estimated to fix 175 million metric tons of nitrogen per year. When used as fertilizer, this biologically-fixed nitrogen proves as effective in boosting crop yields as does commercial fertilizer, and it costs only one-tenth as much. At the same time, biologically-fixed nitrogen is a "slow-release" nitrogen, meaning that losses in the field are cut by half.

Biologically fixed nitrogen can be made available in various ways. One is through the use of those leguminous plants that, by virtue of the bacteria-harboring nodules on their roots, can pluck nitrogen from the atmosphere. Legumes, notably species such as alfalfa and clover, fix anywhere between 100 and 600 kg of nitrogen per hectare per year. All the farmer has to do is to "interplant" his conventional crops with legumes (e.g., between rows of corn stalks, or between seasonal crops of corn), enabling a "free" supply of fixed nitrogen to be introduced into the soil. Corn growers in the United States, using a rotation system of alfalfa with corn, find they can cut their use of commercially manufactured nitrogen fertilizer by as much as 60 kg per hectare, for a saving of one-fifth of their costs. (At present, U.S. cornlands absorb a full one-half of all the nitrogen fertilizer that American farmers apply to their crops, or one-eighth of all such fertilizer applied worldwide.) In similar fashion, peasant farmers in Asia find that by using a leguminous tree, the ipilipil (*Leucaena leucocephala*), as a rotational fertilizer crop, they can obtain as much nitrogen from six bags of tree leaves as from one bag of ammonium sulfate.

All told, legumes are estimated to fix at least 35 million metric tons of nitrogen annually. This service is estimated to be worth several billion dollars. Yet we have only begun to explore the potential benefits of the legume-nodule association. The legume family totals at least 13,000 known species, and we utilize only about 100 of them for commercial purposes. Plainly there is much scope to mobilize the nitrogen-fixing services of many wild legumes awaiting the attentions of plant breeders and geneticists.

The bacteria that work a trick with legumes in providing fixed nitrogen are of the genus *Rhizobium*. Other nitrogen-fixing microorganisms known as actinomycetes or *Frankia* species form nodules on nonleguminous plants. At least 145 such plants benefit from the actinomycetes; these plants are mainly trees and woody shrubs, spanning 15 genera in 7 plant families. The red alder–actinomycete association, for example, absorbs 300 kg of nitrogen per hectare per year, while birch-actinomycete associations, important to the timber industry, can fix almost as much. Moreover, these rates of fixation can be greatly improved through genetic selection.

Parallel circumstances exist with *Spirillum*-rhizosphere associations in grasses, especially important for cereal crops that have originated from tropical grasses, as is the case with corn, wheat, barley, rye, millets, sorghum, and rice (also sugarcane). In the early 1970s, a number of grasses were discovered in Brazil with an ability to associate with microorganisms of the genus *Spirillum* that fix nitrogen from the air. These grasses feature a form of intracellular root symbiosis that enables microorganisms to fix almost 2 kg of nitrogen per hectare per day (Dobereiner et al., 1972; Smith et al., 1976; Van Bulow and Dobereiner, 1975). Obviously, much potential lies ahead for us if we can incorporate in our grass-type crops the genes responsible for the nitrogen-fixing associations of these wild grasses.

Still more promising is a technique that depends upon the manipulation of nitrogen-fixing bacteria. As we have noted, only a few genera of bacteria can extract nitrogen from the atmosphere and use it as a nutritional resource. Some of these bacteria are able to "invade" root cells of their main hosts, leguminous plants, where they establish their nitrogen-fixing nodules. Recent research shows that the invasion process is regulated by a segment of bacterial DNA, the hereditary material of genes. It is this insight that offers a key to the genetic engineering of other "infective" bacteria that could set up nitrogen-fixing factories in crop plants' roots. The engineering technique depends upon the emergent science of recombinant DNA, or gene-splicing, by which plant geneticists transfer rhizobia genes into circular pieces of bacterial DNA, or "plasmids" of other bacteria capable of fixing nitrogen. The plasmids, reinserted into the former free-living types of bacteria, instruct the host plant to accept these nitrogen-fixing bacteria.

At this early stage of the sophisticated technique, plant geneticists are working primarily with the protein-rich soybean. Being a legume, the soybean already derives its nitrogen from bacteria in its root nodules. But it does so in inefficient fashion. So scientists are giving the soybean a helping hand. They plant soybean seeds in peat that has been impregnated with "superior" bacteria, and they thereby inoculate the soybean seeds with nitrogen-fixing capacities that should greatly increase crop yields. Preliminary research indicates that less than 1 kg of high-quality inoculant, properly applied to legume seeds, can replace more than 100 kg of nitrogen fertilizer per hectare.

A similar technique is being applied by scientists at the International Crop Research Institute for the Semi-Arid Tropics, at Hyderabad in India. The scientists have recruited the capacities of "super strains" of rhizobia to increase nitrogen fixation in leguminous crops by 300 to 500 percent.

Still more pertinent is the prospect of exploiting a symbiotic relationship between a water fern of the genus *Azolla* and blue-green algae of the genus *Anabaena* (Lumpkin and Plucknett, 1980; Watanabe *et al.*, 1977). Plants of these two genera are already familiar to rice growers as "scum" floating on the surface of water in paddy fields. The algae live in small cavities within the fern leaves, enabling nitrogen production to be 12–20 times higher than is possible for free-living algae. In fact, the symbiotic relationship generates anywhere from 50 to several hundred kg of nitrogen per hectare per year, of which about 80 percent is available for the rice crop. Experiments at the International Rice Research Institute in the Philippines reveal that these two plants in association can double their biomass in only five days, and generate 117 kg of nitrogen per hectare in 106 days, even up to 500 kg in less than one year, allowing the rice farmer to achieve a remarkable increase in his rice crop (Food and Agriculture Organization, 1978; International Rice Research Institute, 1977). According to the Chinese, who have pioneered this agricultural breakthrough, rice yields can be boosted by as much as 158 percent a year.

Plainly these findings mean much to the great rice-growing regions of the developing tropics, which, if they are to double their output by the end of the century (as they must, in order to feed their growing populations), will have to expand their fertilizer use several times. Accordingly scientists are hunting throughout the plant kingdom for other species that, thanks to their associated microorganisms, can, in effect, pull nitrogen out of the air. We can reasonably hope that numerous such species exist in the wild, waiting for botanists to track them down.

Environmental Stresses

Plant breeders can use genetic resources to help crops resist the environmental stresses that they encounter in their habitats (Christiansen and Lewis, 1982; Jung, 1978; Wittwer, 1981 and 1982; Wright, 1976). Of the earth's land surface (discounting Antarctica), almost 90 percent is less than suitable for modern agriculture, due to too little or too much water, excess heat or cold, and soils that are shallow or are infertile because of too few nutrients or too many toxic elements. In various parts of the earth, notably in the tropics, some 29 million square kilometers (km²) of land are limited by mineral stresses (not only nutrient deficiencies and toxicities, but also salinity, acidity, and alkalinity, plus air pollution in the form of acid rain). A further 32 million km² are limited by shallow soils, together with another 37 million that suffer from too little water and 16 million that suffer from too much water. These territories altogether amount to 114 million km², to be compared with our present croplands covering only 15 million km² (an area equivalent to the United States and half of Canada combined). Equally to the point, we stand to lose one-third of our present croplands by the end of the century as a result of our inclination to allow topsoil to be degraded or eroded, or simply paved over.

So we have plenty of incentive, as well as scope, to push the frontiers of agriculture into territories that have hitherto been considered "off limits." This puts pressure on plant geneticists to devise crop varieties that will flourish in areas with pronounced environmental stresses.

Fortunately, this challenge is being met through a new agricultural strategy supported by new breeding techniques. Hitherto our main approach has been to adapt environments to our crops. For example, we have overcome drought by irrigation, and we have used chemicals to counter mineral deficiencies and to control diseases. This approach has worked well enough as long as we could depend on fossil energy to fuel our irrigation pumps, and to supply synthetic fertilizer and pesticidal sprays. From around 1950 until the mid-1970s, our agriculture has been increasingly dependent on fossil fuel—lots of it, at cheap prices. Now, in the wake of OPEC, we have to change direction. Instead of modifying environmental factors to suit our crops, we must manipulate our crops to suit their environments, especially those marginal environments that have hitherto remained beyond the pale of established agriculture.

All in all, this amounts to a reorientation that is revolutionary in its implications. It will mark one of the great advances in our agricultural history. Fortunately we can do the job as long as plant breeders and genetic engineers have enough "tolerant germ plasm" with which to design new crop varieties for new environments. Already we can take heart at the success of hybrid sorghum and millets that prosper in areas that, until very recently, were considered too hot and dry. What if we could come up with a type of wheat that would grow in the lowland humid tropics, territories which, with their many diseases, still defy wheat breeders? Provided there is enough wild wheat germ plasm available, with its multiple forms of disease resistance, we may soon see the emergence of wheat genotypes that can flourish in millions of square kilometers that are currently closed to them. But, as we have noted in Chapter 2, wild wheat germ plasm is becoming a scarce commodity.

With many crops, however, we can help plants to grow more vigorously through mobilizing the support of minute organisms known as mycorrhizae. If we learn how to manipulate mycorrhizae, we shall boost the productivity of many crop species. These fungi can "infect" a plant's roots, whereupon they absorb phosphate and other essential nutrients from the soil, making them available to the plant. Although mycorrhizal fungi probably increase the plant's uptake of all essential elements, they are particularly important in helping with phosphorus. Soils often contain only small amounts of phosphates, and usually in very immobile form. By thrusting out their hyphae strands into the surrounding soil, mycorrhizae greatly increase the amount of soil from which phosphorus can be obtained. So dependent are many plants on mycorrhizal fungi for their nutrients, that if the fungi disappear the plants starve to death.

Mycorrhizae are widespread in two major crop families, the Leguminosae and the Gramineae (grasses). They offer notable benefits to corn, wheat, barley, potato, many vegetables, fruit trees, and pasture and forage legumes, right around the world. In temperate zones, they assist plants with thick fleshy roots and short root hairs, such as onions, citrus, and grapevines, while in the tropics, they assist species such as pineapple, coffee, tea, cocoa, oil palm, pawpaw, rubber, and cassava.

Plant geneticists are discovering ways to inoculate plants with "superior" strains of mycorrhizae. They thereby enable plants to prosper in areas that would otherwise be considered unfavorable due to infertile soils, adverse climate, and other negative factors. For example, cassava can now be grown in soils that have hitherto proven incapable of supporting the crop because of phosphate deficiency.

If "environmental proofing" were to be applied to more crops in more ways, we could open up millions of hectares of land that now remain little utilized. Again, our success on this plant-breeding front will depend on the supplies of germ plasm available from widely differing environments.

Moreover, modern crops must be able to cope with changes in climate, such as unexpected fluctuations in rainfall and temperature. This attribute is all the more significant in that crops today, with their narrow genetic bases, are adapted to what may have been the most moist 30-year period during the past 1,000 years (Bryson and Murray, 1977). The Soviet Union is particularly vulnerable in this respect, in that year-to-year fluctuations in climate cause shortfalls of as much as 20 percent in grain harvests (Slayter and Levin, 1982). This is all the more critical in that the Soviet Union is the world's number one producer of wheat, with 27 percent of the total. By contrast, the United States produces only 11 percent of the world's wheat, but it exports more than half of its crop. Thus wheat's emergent role as a factor in geo-politics.

Climatic dislocations may soon emerge on a far grander scale. Within the next half-century at most, we may witness greater climatic changes than at any period during the past several thousand years, due to carbon dioxide buildup with its "greenhouse effect," and to changes in the earth's albedo (or "shininess" of the planet's surface) associated with forest clearing and other forms of devegetation. An increase in global carbon dioxide could cause U.S. farmers to experience growing-season conditions akin to the heat and drought of 1980, which reduced grain output by a whopping one-fifth. If these climatic changes become more pronounced, and if adaptable crop types are not available, Americans could find themselves facing "dust bowl" conditions. At the same time, of course, we should recognize that warmer weather will allow the range of many major crops to be expanded into areas that have hitherto been too cold. In the United States, an increase of 1°C could allow the Corn Belt to extend 175 km northeastwards. Furthermore, an increase in carbon dioxide may, in certain circumstances, prove beneficial to some crops in some sectors of the world, on the grounds that an "enriched" atmosphere can generate a "fertilizing impact" on photosynthesis.

We still do not know nearly enough to say how agriculture will work out under the changing climates of the foreseeable future. But we do know that massive climatic upheavals could be in store for conventional agriculture. The best way to hedge our bets is by stocking up with as much genetic variability as we can find for all our leading crops. This implies a comprehensive and systematic campaign to evaluate the genetic reservoirs in all sectors of the plant kingdom. This is a task on which we have scarcely made a start – and the task will become all the more daunting as we find that vast stocks of diverse germ plasm are disappearing for good (or, to express it more accurately, are disappearing for bad).

Salt-Tolerant Plants

Many natural environments are too saline for conventional crops. So a major strategy for innovative agriculture lies with salt-tolerant plants. So promising is this strategy that certain agricultural experts believe it offers one of the finest potential advances for the immediate future.

According to the Food and Agriculture Organization, saline soils around the world amount to 9.5 million km², to be compared with total world croplands now covering some 15 million km². Prominent among these salt-dominated environments are desert zones that overlie aquifers (underground water stocks) that are too brackish for established agriculture. There are at least 3.75 million km² of these desert zones, equivalent in size to Australia. Of course not all these arid territories can be brought into production, because of excessively sandy soils among other factors. But under the Sahara, there is reputedly a reservoir of brackish fresh water as large as the world's lakes combined. If this water could be used for irrigation, some non-sandy sectors of the Sahara could be brought into agricultural use. In the United States, the Department of Agriculture believes that more than 600,000 km², or one-fifteenth of the entire country, overlie aquifers with a salinity of 3,000 parts per million, which, while only one-tenth as salty as the oceans, is three times as salty as most conventional crops will tolerate. If U.S. farmers could mobilize those saline underground water stocks that are readily pumpable, they would have access to as much water as would fill Lake Michigan six times over. Right now the nonsaline groundwater stocks of the United States are being depleted so rapidly that American agriculture could face a crisis of water supplies by the late 1980s.

Salt-dominated environments also include those irrigated croplands that, through misuse and overuse, have become too salty for further cultivation. Irrigation water can dump as much as 12 tons of salt on one hectare of cropland each year. In the time since people learned to channel water for intensive agriculture, they have ruined at least one-quarter of all irrigated croplands in this way. Today salinization is a major problem of some 350,000 km², and it claims a further 2,000 km² each year. In Pakistan, 35,000 km² are affected by severe salinity, and another 45,000 km² are at risk (Gasser, 1981). Similar problems affect 70,000 km² of India's croplands. According to the International Rice Research Institute in the Philippines, some 600,000 km² of rice-growing territories in southern and Southeast Asia are subject to salinization, either actual or potential. As for the United States, one-eighth of California's croplands are affected by gross salinization, and in the lower Rio Grande Valley as much as one-quarter. To rehabilitate salinized lands through conventional methods costs as much as $650 a hectare.

In addition to these two major categories of salt-dominated environments, we can consider coastal lands where soils are too dry unless irrigated – and where the only available source of abundant water is the sea. These coastal deserts include much of Baja California, extensive sectors of Peru and Chile, vast tracts of northern and eastern Africa, a great loop around the Arabian Peninsula starting at Suez and extending almost as far as Bombay, and large coastal sectors of Australia. The total length of these desert shorelines is at least 32,000 km, or almost twice as much as the entire U.S. coastline. To date, they have remained among the most unproductive lands on Earth, since irrigation with seawater proves useless for established crops. But if these coastal deserts could be brought into use, a mere 5-km strip would amount to an area equivalent to West Virginia, or to Belgium and Holland combined.

Hence humankind faces a problem in the form of its saline environments – a problem that is growing greater as salinization spreads. Fortunately, however, we may soon be able to look upon the problem as an opportunity, thanks to recent research that highlights the possibilities of salt-tolerant plants – otherwise known as halophytes, from the Greek "halo" meaning salt and "phyte" meaning plant (Brisky, 1981; Cowell, 1979; Epstein and Norlyn, 1976; Epstein *et al.*, 1980; Hollaender *et al.*, 1979; Jury *et al.*, 1978; Maas and Nieman, 1978; Mudie, 1974; Mussell and Staples, 1979; National Academy of Sciences, 1975; Wright, 1976). Several halophytic species could qualify as candidates for this futuristic type of agriculture. Some are wild relatives of commercial barley, wheat, sorghum, rice, several types of millet, sugarbeet, tomato, date palm, and pistachio (a kind of nut that is popular in many parts of the United States and Europe). They also include certain kinds of forage plants that serve the needs of livestock; examples are alfalfa, ladino clover, creeping bentgrass, Bermuda grass, and various reeds and rushes. Any of these salt-tolerant plants could be grown in desert areas through irrigation with brackish water. They could be grown in salinized zones such as the Central Valley of California; they could be grown in those areas where fresh water is becoming a scarce commodity, and where seawater is within easy pumping distance, again as in the Central Valley of California; and they could be grown along coastlines irrigated with seawater. For example, a strain of barley has been discovered that, deriving all its moisture from seawater, produces almost 1.2 metric tons per hectare. A similar prospect appears in store with a number of wheat strains. In Israel, salt water serves the needs of adapted types of sorghum, soybean, and avocado. As for rice, several hundred salt-tolerant varieties have been identified, but their grain yield is low and they prove susceptible to insect pests and diseases. Nonetheless, plant geneticists hope to find salt-tolerant varieties among wild rices that will meet the needs of rice growers.

In addition, a number of wild plants could serve as forage for livestock, these being plants with names that do not yet appear in the lexicon of established agriculture. They include the saltwort, saltbush, pickleweed, mesquite, atriplex, and spineless cacti – all plants that can be grown through irrigation with brackish water or even with seawater. Many other plants surely await our discovery, when scientists get around to checking the many candidates that await their attention in the wild.

Not only can halophytic plants produce food and feed, but they can help to bind sandy soils, notably along coastlines, by virtue of their vigorous runners that help to stabilize the surface of the ground. Equally important, certain halophytes can absorb so much salt from soil that they can be used to rehabilitate salinized irrigation lands. This applies to those species of *Atriplex* that can tolerate water with as much as 39,000 parts per million of salt, a good deal more saline than seawater.

Several wild forms of halophytes are being grown in experimental plantings in Arizona, irrigated with seawater from the Gulf of Mexico. Field trials show that the plants feature a nutritional value that is comparable, or even superior, to established forms of wheat, rice, and alfalfa. Equally important, their productivity can be surprisingly high. For halophytic types of alfalfa, the highest yields are twice as much as

U.S. farmers consider acceptable for established alfalfa varieties grown with fresh water.

For sure, most halophytes cannot grow as well using saline water as they can using fresh water. Handling the salt imposes a penalty. Each time a plant has to pump a salt molecule through its system, it uses energy that could otherwise be used to grow additional plant tissue. The saltbush, for example, grows only about one-third as well using seawater as using fresh water. But so successful is saltgrass that it has been introduced to revegetate 20 km² of arid alkaline lakebed at Lake Texcoco, located 45 km northeast of Mexico City, with a result that the area, formerly considered useless is now supporting livestock. In that sector of the Sonoran Desert that lies in northern Mexico, just south of Arizona, a number of salt-tolerant forage plants are flourishing using seawater, producing a pasture that may shortly support livestock.

Only a few horizons northwest of Arizona, the California tomato industry may soon benefit from a halophytic variety that should serve to extend the crop into areas that have hitherto been too dry and saline for it (Rick, 1977; Rush and Epstein, 1976). The key lies with a wild species of tomato found along the seashore of one of the Galápagos Islands. The wild fruit is small, green, and unpalatable, but when it is crossed with a common tomato, it produces fruit that is large enough to be marketable, is suitably red, and is unusually tasty. In field trials of hybrid tomato plants, two-thirds of plantings can survive using 70 percent seawater and only 30 percent fresh water, producing a worthwhile yield of commercial-quality tomatoes.

Among other halophytic possibilities is a garden beet, able to flourish using water that is 75 percent seawater; genetically bred strains could probably grow direct in the sea (Mudie, 1974). Similar success has been reported with wild varieties of barley, of which selected strains, irrigated with undiluted seawater, yield almost half as much per hectare as the average yield of good-quality conventional barley (Epstein et al., 1980). Agricultural scientists hope that something similar could soon apply to assorted types of wheat, sorghum, and millet. Even a few varieties of rice could qualify in hybridized form, a boon indeed for the vast tracts of salinized paddy lands of southern Asia.

As a final example of a salt-tolerant plant, the leguminous tamarugo tree of the Atacama Desert in Chile can survive in soil covered with salt to a depth of 1 meter. According to the National Academy of Sciences (1975), its highly nutritious pods and leaves allow sheep to be stocked at rates approaching those of the best grasslands anywhere.

The tamarugo trees of Chile can flourish in extremely saline soil, and they supply sufficient forage for sheep to match some of the best grazing lands anywhere. (Credit: M. Sarquis. Courtesy of Dr. N. D. Vietmeyer, National Academy of Sciences)

Resistance to Pests

Crop pests do much damage each year. All in all, we lose an average of 14 percent of our crops to insects and 9 percent to weeds (plus 12 percent to diseases) (Wittwer, 1980). In the case of wheat, we lose 5 percent to insects and 10 percent to weeds (plus 10 percent to diseases); of corn, 13 percent each to insects and weeds (and almost 10 percent to diseases), and of rice 27 percent to insects and 11 percent to weeds (plus 9 percent to diseases). The United States alone loses crops to insects worth more than $5 billion a year.

Fortunately, we can call upon the aid of a number of wild plants, notably tropical species, that produce chemical compounds that repel insects or inhibit their feeding. These toxic compounds occur in two main categories—the pyrethrins from chrysanthemum-type plants and the rotenoids from roots of rainforest legumes. Both categories are biodegradable, and they do not accumulate in organisms, hence they cause little harm to higher animals such as birds and mammals (including humans). Many plants and insects, notably those of tropical zones, have evolved together, so we can expect that many other similar insect-repelling substances must be available in wild plants. At the same time, however, we should remember that insect pests include variations that can multiply in numbers to overcome plant defenses in only ten years, sometimes as little as three years. So there is constant need to derive further genetic combinations of crop plants to stay ahead of immune varieties of insects. Regrettably, very few wild plants have been screened for this purpose (or for any other purpose), so we can surmise little about their potential for controlling insect pests—except that it is surely very large.

As the science of plant genetics becomes more sophisticated, it can resist the onslaught of pests through innovative techniques. Certain crops can now be sprayed with chemical "messages" that stimulate them to generate insect-resistant materials. For example, a number of plants manufacture a hormone that, as it moves through the plant's tissues, can "instruct" cells to make chemicals that give insects indigestion. Many other hormones offer potential of this sort. While there are only a few primary hormones, whose function is to send specific messages and to affect the plant in various ways, the more numerous secondary hormones trigger specialized responses, such as the "on cue" production of pest-resistant chemicals.

A related strategy lies with "allelopathy," or the growing of two species of plants in association with each other, whereby each plant benefits from the pest control provided by the other—a situation akin to that of two persons standing under one umbrella. The roots and shoots of asparagus and sorghum produce toxic compounds. By interplanting these crops with other crops, the farmer can supply his own built-in pest controls. Sorghum can even continue to supply pesticides after it is dead. Residues of the crop yield herbicidal chemicals that keep down weeds. This spin-off benefit of sorghum will probably become increasingly important as farmers around the world go in for minimum-tillage agriculture, a technique that eliminates seasonal plowing and reduces soil erosion. By the end of the century, we can expect that at least half of U.S. croplands will feature limited tillage. But the big snag of limited-tillage agriculture is that it does not get rid of weeds in the established fashion of "plowing them under." If we were to conduct a survey of the plant kingdom, we would surely come up with other species that feature weed-killing toxins like those of sorghum.

Certain strains of alfalfa are resistant to the spotted aphid. This aphid threatened to become a major pest throughout most alfalfa-growing areas of the United States in the mid-1950s, causing annual damage of more than $40 million. Fortunately a few alfalfa strains were found to feature resistance to the aphid, and the problem was relegated to agricultural history (Sprague *et al.*, 1980).

A tiny (2 to 3 mm long) parasitic wasp, *Spalangia endius*, feeds on blood rising to the surface of a wound it has inflicted on the pupa of a housefly. Scientists are evaluating the wasp as a control agent of houseflies. (Credit: U.S. Department of Agriculture)

Still another approach lies with the physiological anti-insect defenses of certain plant species: for example, trichomes, or tiny fishhook-like spines that impale insects. Trichomes are especially effective against sap-sucking insects such as leaf hoppers, a major pest for bean farmers throughout the Americas. How many plant species in the wild, we might ask, feature trichomes or alternative physiological defenses, the genes for which can be bred into our leading crops? We cannot yet offer an answer to that question, except to say that we have hardly started to explore the plant kingdom for candidate species.

Still a further pest-resistant possibility lies with a defense of plants in the Sonoran Desert (Rodriguez, 1981). The tactic most frequently found among desert plants is to deter insects from feeding on their leaves. This is a preferable approach to the more costly and complicated approach of directly killing the insect feeders. Indeed very few plants make chemicals that kill insects; only organic chemists in the profitable pesticide industry do that. All that plants need to do is to keep the insects off their backs. A Sonoran shrub known as the brittle bush (a member of the sunflower family) secretes sticky substances from glandular hairs on its leaf surfaces, thus providing a trap for incautious insects and a deterrent to the more cautious ones. Since desert plants can ill afford to lose any of their tissues to herbivorous insects, they have developed an entire arsenal of biochemical defenses to ward off insects. A good number of these devices are worth investigation, with a view to incorporation into our crop plants.

A major further strategy is to control insects through other insects that act as predators and parasites, and thus limit the populations of plant-eating insects by attacking their eggs, larvae, pupae, and adults (Batra, 1982; DeBach, 1974; Delucchi, 1976; Huffaker, 1980; Huffaker and Messenger, 1976; Marsden *et al.*, 1980; National Academy of Sciences, 1976; Papavizas, 1982; Pimentel *et al.*, 1980; Sailer, 1979 and 1981; Simmonds and Bennett, 1976; Stevens *et al.*, 1975; Van den Bosch, 1978). Since many predators and parasites are highly specific in their choice of prey or host, they are inclined to limit their attentions to target species of other insects, without doing damage to still other insect species. This makes the strategy of biological control of insect pests far preferable to broad-scale use of persistent toxic chemicals. In any case, many insect species are growing resistant to chemcial insecticides; among certain insect species, as few as 15 generations are needed to build up resistance. According to the Food and Agriculture Organization, more than 300 species of insects, mites, and ticks throughout the world are known to have become resistant to one or more pesticides, and an additional 60 or so species are suspected of becoming resistant. In the United States, entomologists in the Department of Agriculture estimate that approximately 700 species of insects do significant damage to crops within the continental limits (not counting Hawaii, where the damage is still more acute); this damage is calculated at $5 billion a year. Of these 700 insect species, around half have developed resistance to at least one pesticide, some to two or more. U.S. farmers now apply 400,000 metric tons of chemical insecticides to their crops each year, ten times as much as in 1950, yet they lose twice as much food to insects.

When we consider both insect pests and weed plants together, we find that there are more than 250 cases on record of partial or complete control accomplished through introduction of predators and parasites that attack troublesome species. In California alone, during the period 1928–1979, seven leading biological-control projects have reduced crop losses to insects and have reduced the need for pesticidal chemicals to an extent of savings worth just over $987 million (at 1979 prices), with a return on investment of 30:1 (Huffaker, 1980; Van den Bosch *et al.*, 1982). In Australia, four biological-control programs are producing benefits that, projected to the year 2000, are expected to exceed the cost of research to develop them by

$286 million (Waterhouse, 1979). The Commonwealth Institute of Biological Control in Trinidad documents eight leading projects that have cost a total of $610,000 and have accrued total benefits, to 1973, of $29,472,000, with a continuing annual benefit of some $2,175,000 (Simmonds and Bennett, 1976).

In the case of the United States, 250 major insect pests, accounting for at least half of all crop losses to insects, have come from outside the country. It is precisely against these pests that foreign introductions offer the greatest promise (Sailer, 1979 and 1981). Conservative estimates by the Agricultural Research Service of the U.S. Department of Agriculture suggest that 1,000 species of foreign organisms — not only insects, but also mites and pathogens — could be profitably introduced into the United States at a cost of less than $40 million over a period of 20 years. Past performance indicates that there may be a $30 return for each $1 expended on importation of beneficial organisms (by contrast with a 4:1 benefit-to-cost ratio for chemical pesticides). In certain instances, the return can be much higher: In Florida, citrus growers have been able to save their industry at least $35 million a year through a one-time outlay of $35,000 for the importation of three types of parasitic insects. Much potential lies ahead of us in the form of, for example, wasps that act as either parasites or predators — notably the chalcid wasps. At least as much potential probably lies with the ichneumonid or braconid wasps whose larvae, like those of many chalcids, are parasitic on insect pest larvae. Still a third group is certain beetles. For example, a parasitic beetle from India shows considerable promise for control of the Mexican bean beetle, a serious pest of legumes in the United States (Stevens *et al.*, 1975). All in all, American pest experts have used natural enemies from abroad to overcome some 200 foreign insect pests.

To quote a former Chairman of the Insect Identification and Beneficial Insect Introduction Institute of the U.S. Department of Agriculture in Beltsville, Maryland, Professor Reece I. Sailer, speaking in 1981: "When the total program of the past ten years is viewed in perspective of resources available to support the work, I am satisfied that in the United States no area of crop protection has yielded benefits comparable to those resulting from importation of natural enemies for control of insect pests" (Sailer, 1981). All the more regrettable, then, is the meager funding allocated to research and development for natural enemies of crop pests. During the period 1888–1972, the U.S. government invested no more than $20 million, a sum that contrasts with the $110 million spent by the U.S. chemical industry in 1973 alone for research and development of synthetic pesticides. Although the amount of pesticides used in the United States more than doubled during the period 1951–1977, crop losses to insects have continued to increase.

Such, then, are some of the innovative techniques being deployed by agriculturalists who draw on wild species and genetic resources to keep our tables stocked with more and better foods. Who would have thought, only ten years ago, that some of the brightest prospects for agriculture could lie with such esoteric techniques as biological nitrogen fixation and halophytic plants? And who knows what innovative strategies will have become commonplace by the end of the century, supposing that our scientists have sufficient wildlife stocks to draw on?

CHAPTER FOUR

———————————————— ■ ————————————————

New Foods Coming on Line

During the course of human history, we have used around 3,000 plants for food. Yet Earth contains at least another 75,000 edible plants. Of this cornucopia of plant foods, only about 150 have ever been cultivated on a large scale, and fewer than 20 now produce 90 percent of our food. We are essentially using the same limited number of plant species that have served humankind for millennia.

Some Underexploited Food Plants

We know of numerous instances of underexploited food plants with proven potential (National Academy of Sciences, 1975; Ritchie, 1979). For instance, Aborigines in Australia have used scores and possibly hundreds of plants, especially fruits and bulbs, as food. They favor certain yams that are well adapted to dry conditions, opening up the possibility that crossbreeds with forms in the tropics could allow this important crop to be extended to several further regions, notably the tropics themselves. Another dryland plant, the yeheb nut bush of Somalia (*Cordeauxia edulis*) grows prolific bunches of pods that contain seeds the size of peanuts (though they taste more like cashew nuts), making a nutritious food that Somalis prefer to staples such as corn and sorghum (Westphal, 1974). In addition, the yeheb's foliage supplies tasty fodder for livestock. Being adapted to arid environments, the yeheb could assist desert dwellers in many parts of the tropics. It is being brought back from the verge of extinction in the wild through domestication efforts in Somalia, and in Kenya as well.

Much the same applies to plants in other ecological zones. A marine plant from the west coast of Mexico, *Zostera marina*, sometimes known as eelgrass, produces grain that the Seri Indians grind into flour. This plant opens up the prospect that we can use the seas to grow bread (Felger and Moser, 1973). From the highlands of Ethiopia, leafy grassy vegetables prove a promising source of plant protein, yielding as much as alfalfa or soybean (Vaughan, 1977). When considering the potential of these Ethiopian vegetables, we might recall that a single wild species of the same genus has provided us, through plant breeding, with cabbage, kale, broccoli, cauliflower, and brussels sprouts.

Many other leafy food plants are important on a local scale while remaining unknown elsewhere (Herklots, 1972; Oomen and Grubben, 1977). Many leafy plants of the tropics, at least 1,650 of them in tropical forests alone, are reputed to contain roughly as much protein as legumes. They also feature from five to ten times more calcium than legumes and fruits, from two to six times as much iron, and ten to one hundred times more carotene (a yellow pigment in the green chlorophyll). In addition, these leafy vegetables often contain as much vitamin C as the best fruits, together with an abundance of vitamin A. The value of vitamin C is well known; vitamin A performs many essential functions in maintaining cellular structures in the human body and in protecting membranous-tissue surfaces that cover most internal body areas, organs, and outer surfaces of the body. Millions of developing-world people suffer from lack of vitamin A, because they do not obtain enough of its principal source foods such as milk and eggs. The number of children who go blind as a result of vitamin A deficiency is estimated by the Food and Agriculture Organization at about 120,000 per year, with many of them dying from associated disorders. A child need take only 100 grams, equivalent to two heaped teaspoonfuls, of cooked green leaves a day from leafy tropical vegetables to increase his protein intake by at least 15 percent, his calcium and iron intake by over 100 percent, and his vitamin A and C intake by 300 percent, as well as to obtain all the folic acid (a nutrient responsible for structure and function of red blood cells) that he needs. It would be difficult to find another common food that supplies such a spectrum of protective materials to the human diet.

Many other examples of wild foods are available. The wax gourd vegetable (*Benincasa hispida*) grows in the Asian tropics, but could be extended to many parts of Africa and Latin America (Morton, 1971). A creeping vine that looks somewhat like a pumpkin, it can be raised more easily than any other cucurbit (pumpkin, squash, melon, etc.). It grows rapidly; one shoot grows 2.3 cm every three hours during the course of four days. This vigorous growth rate allows three or four crops to be grown each year. A full-grown gourd reaches 35 kg in weight and measures 2 meters long by 1 meter in diameter. Fortunately, the fruit's pulp – a thick white flesh that is crisp and juicy – can be eaten at any stage of growth. Possessing a mild flavor, it is used as a cooked vegetable, as a base for soup, as a sweet when mixed with syrup, and as a food extender. A unique feature of the plant that is very pertinent to the humid tropics is that the gourd's waxy coating preserves the food inside from attack by microorganisms, thus allowing the vegetable to be stored for as long as one year without refrigeration.

Another type of gourd vegetable, the buffalo gourd (*Cucurbita foetidissima*), could supply much starch, edible oil, and other foods (Bemis *et al.*, 1975; Johnson and Hinman, 1980). Able to tolerate extreme drought, the buffalo gourd is a potential crop for arid lands, thus offering no competition with conventional agriculture. Experimental plantings of the gourd in the southwestern United States match the performance of traditional sources of protein and oil such as soybeans and peanuts in well-watered lands.

A vigorous perennial, the buffalo gourd survives, even flourishes, in its harsh environments by virtue of its large, fleshy tubers that penetrate as deep as 5 meters to reach groundwater. The main root can grow to 30 kg after just two seasons, whereupon it constitutes 70 percent moisture. An occasional root can reach 45 kg, of which the 25 kg starchy content equals the amount produced by a score of potato plants growing under favorable conditions. So resilient is the buffalo gourd that some plants reportedly live as long as 40 years.

The round yellow fruit, as much as 8 cm in diameter, has earned the buffalo gourd its popular name of "mock orange." Each season the plant produces, through its extensive vine growths, as many as 200 fruits or gourds, each of which contains 200 to 300 seeds. These seeds consist of one-third protein and one-third oil.

A research project at the Arid Lands Agricultural Development Institute in Lebanon is hybridizing wild varieties of the buffalo gourd to obtain seeds that produce plants with faster growth and higher yields. The Institute has found that some of the most productive plants are male-sterile, opening up the prospect of simplified replication. Some plants, moreover, are essentially barren, others prolific. Some produce large fruits in huge numbers; others less than half as much. Certain of these variations are genetic, indicating much scope for the plant breeder to select the best genotypes from wild populations.

In the United States, domestication of the buffalo gourd is being attempted by the Office of Arid Lands Studies at the University of Arizona. This research program is revealing that the buffalo gourd, with seed yields of up to three metric tons per hectare, can generate at least one metric ton of vegetable oil per hectare, which, together with half this much protein and much crude starch, leads to a potential crop value of almost $700 per hectare.

Next, let us review some fruits. Temperate-zone plants have given us only about ten fruit species altogether, whereas the tropics have supplied us with almost 200 species. The main tropical source is the rainforest biome, particularly the Southeast Asian sector (Soepadmo, 1979; Williams *et al.*, 1975). Around 125 species of fruit plants are cultivated in Southeast Asia, many of them having originated in the forests; and more than 100 other fruit trees grow wild in the forests, several of them producing edible fruits, and others offering potential for crossbreeding with established crop species. A notable instance is the durian *(Durio zibethinus)*, with delectable taste and execrable smell; the experience of consuming a durian can be described as eating an almond-flavored custard in a public toilet. Also from Southeast Asia comes the rambutan *(Nephelium lappaceum)*, a table fruit that is bright red and covered with whiskers. Perhaps tastiest of all fruits from Southeast Asia is the mangosteen *(Garcinia mangostana)*, though regrettably the plant appears to offer little genetic variability. For those people who favor citrus fruits such as oranges and tangerines, the pummelo *(Citrus grandis)* offers a suitably stimulating taste. It yields a larger harvest than most citrus crops, and it can grow in saline conditions.

Equally abundant and diverse could be the fruits of South America, when we get around to cataloging them all. The tree tomato *(Cyphomandra betacea)* resembles an elongated tomato, though with much sweeter taste. The Cape gooseberry *(Physalis peruviana)* is a relative of the ground cherry, a fruit that was popular among the *Mayflower* pilgrims. Also from South America come the feijoa *(Feijoa* spp.), a relative of the guava, with a pineapplelike flavor. Perhaps best tasting of all South American fruits is the naranjilla *(Solanum qui-toense)*, a relative of the tomato, with a taste somewhere between a pineapple and a strawberry, and well deserving of its local name of "the golden fruit of the Andes." As a curiosity from South America, we can note the jabaticaba, a grapelike fruit that grows straight from the bark of its vine, with a flavor similar to that of the finest Concord grapes.

Let us now move on to look at a selection of vegetables. Again, Southeast Asia is a principal center, with at least 300 species having been used in native cultures, about 80 of them still growing only in the wild in forest habitats (Soepadmo, 1979; Williams *et al.*, 1975). A notable example is the winged bean *(Psophocarpus tetragonolobus)*, also known as the four-angled bean and the asparagus pea (National Academy of Sciences, 1976). Known to forest tribes of New Guinea for centuries, the plant is not to be decried as a "poor man's crop," to be dismissed as something second-rate for peasant communities. The vinelike plant contains far more protein than potato, cassava, and

The winged bean has been known for decades among peasant communities of Papua New Guinea and a few other parts of Southeast Asia, where it has been grown in more or less "natural" form. Now, through domestication and breeding, it has been developed to a stage where it serves as a splendid crop in more than 50 countries of the developing tropics, supplying surprisingly large amounts of protein. (Credit: National Research Council, Washington D.C.)

several other crops that serve as principal sources of food for millions of people in the tropics. In fact it offers a nutritional value equivalent to soybean, with 40 percent protein and 17 percent edible oil, plus vitamins and other nutrients. Its capacity to match the soybean might remind us that the United States grew sporadic patches of the soybean for at least a century before the plant was finally upgraded into a widespread crop; today the soybean is the premier protein crop in the world, flourishing in dozens of temperate-zone countries. Could not a similar prospect be in store for the winged bean, scheduled to become the long-sought "soybean of the tropics"?

Looking like a pole bean, the winged bean climbs with extraordinary vigor to a height of 5 meters or more. Its leaves are intertwined with tendrils, and the entire plant becomes covered with white or blue flowers that quickly produce pods. These pods, square in cross section, can reach a full 30 cm in length. They feature distinctive flanges at each corner, giving rise to the bean's popular name.

All parts of the winged bean can be eaten – the tubers, seeds, pods, leaves, flowers, stems, the lot. They can be eaten raw or ground into flour. They can even be liquefied into a beverage with a taste rather like coffee (without the caffeine); you drink the "coffee" and then you eat the "grounds." The leaves can be dried and rolled into a low-tar, almost no-nicotine cigarette. The flowers produce a sweet garnish, looking rather like steamed mushrooms. The root, swelling to the size of a small potato, tastes like choice nuts. The tendrils, looking like filamentous asparagus, are unusually succulent. No wonder that the plant has been called "a supermarket on a stalk."

As a result of genetic improvement, the winged bean is now helping to upgrade diets in more than 50 countries of the developing tropics.

Now for a vegetable of the Andes, tarwi (*Lupinus mutabilis*). A lupine that was domesticated by people who preceded the Incas by one and a half millennia, the tarwi is a staple of Ecuador, Peru, and Bolivia. The plant grows as high as 2 meters tall, with abundant foliage and masses of pods with beanlike seeds that, containing 45 percent protein and 5 to 20 percent oil, are more nutritious than peas, beans, or even soybeans or peanuts. Tarwi is an adaptable and hardy plant, able to flourish in a range of soils and climates, and little bothered by pests.

But there is a problem with the tarwi. Without proper treatment, the seeds taste bitter, due to toxic alkaloids in them. The highland dwellers of the Andes eliminate the alkaloids by soaking the seeds in running water for a couple of days. Not everybody in the high-altitude tropics can cleanse the seeds in this way. But plant breeders may be able to overcome the problem by genetic improvement, provided they can find tarwi strains in the wild that do not feature the bitter chemicals.

Another major Andean food crop is the amaranth, three species of a genus of grain plants (*Amaranthus*) (Downton, 1973). When the Aztec empire reached its climax, amaranth was as important as corn. But Cortez and the Spanish suppressed the crop because of its pagan symbolism. Still grown widely by subsistence peasants in the Andes, the crop could become widespread in both tropical and temperate zones, in view of its extremely broad climatic adaptability. A C_4 plant like corn (see previous chapter), it can thrive in dry territories where corn withers away. Even during times of outright drought, amaranth can produce a good 1.7 metric tons per hectare. The grain contains 12–15 percent protein, with a high level of a key amino acid, lysine, that hardly shows up at all in most grain crops. When boiled, amaranth grain can produce a useful thickener for jams and other foods, and when ground and used as flour it can improve the taste and increase the nutritional value of bread, pancakes, and tortillas, among many other foods. Apart from the grains, the young leaves can be eaten; they taste somewhat like spinach. Fortunately the species turns out to feature good genetic diversity, which should further help it to become established far beyond its native lands. In fact it already offers more genetic variability, even in its present undeveloped state, than do most widely grown crops. The broad geographic spread of the three species has led to the evolution of many subspecies in widely separated areas—a situation to bring joy to the hearts of plant geneticists.

A final plant to be reviewed here is a novelty food, spirulina (*Spirulina platensis*) (Protein Advisory Group of the United Nations, 1973). A filamentous blue-green alga, spirulina grows around the shores of Lake Tchad in Africa. Like related species of blue-green algae, it flourishes in saline, often alkaline, waters, making it suited to arid zones. If mutant varieties could be found with tolerance for magnesium, spirulina could even be grown in seawater. At temperatures of 30–35°C, this alga produces at least 12 grams per square meter per day (a trial project in Mexico, using *S. maxima*, produces only three-quarters as much—still a good yield for algae). Spirulina is larger than other microorganisms that have been promoted as protein sources, so villagers around Lake Tchad harvest it by filtering lake water through muslin. The villagers then dry the residue on the sand and eat it as a cooked green vegetable.

As much as 60 to 70 percent of spirulina is good-quality protein, way ahead of the 12 percent protein content of sorghum and 7 percent of rice. In addition, it is rich in vitamins, and it contains nothing harmful to humans. It can be added (up to 10 percent by volume) to cereals and other food products without altering their tastes. When dried, spirulina does not ferment, so it can be easily stored.

The only other locality where spirulina is eaten by local people is at Lake Texcoco near Mexico City. According to the Spanish Conquistadores, the Aztecs used spirulina as their main source of protein. A pilot plant at Lake Texcoco is now producing about one metric ton of dry spirulina daily.

Still other new foods may become available to us through novel means. Geneticists have recently produced a crop plant, named triticale, by crossbreeding wheat and rye; the name derives from the scientific terms for wheat, *Triticum*, and rye, *Secale*. Plant breeders have recognized for over a century that wheat flowers can be fertilized by rye pollen, but the resulting hybrids have remained infertile. Recent research now enables botanists to produce crossbreeds that bear fertile seeds.

The new cereal—a product of scientific expertise and visionary curiosity—proves highly productive. In tests at the International Center for Improvement of Maize and Wheat in Mexico, a single hectare of triticale yielded over 3.8 metric tons of grain, compared with 3.3 metric tons for a hectare of wheat. As a result of these promising trials, triticale is now being planted in some 4,000 km² of croplands in more than 50 countries. The species inherits from rye a capacity to withstand cold and to grow in sandy, infertile soil, these being characteristics that enable farmers to bring marginal lands into use. At the same time, triticale is very nutritious, being rich in lysine, an amino acid essential for making human proteins.

Having worked their trick with triticale, plant geneticists believe they may be able to fabricate other new crops, for example, by crossing wheat or rye with barley.

Some Animals That Could Be Exploited For Food

Let us now move on to take a look at the potential of animals as sources of new foods. Several dozen wild antelopes and other herbivores of African savannas are prime examples (Myers, 1972), as are certain species of Amazonia (Wetterberg *et al.*, 1976). The kouprey is a secretive cowlike creature that inhabits the forests of the Thailand/Kampuchea border. The animal is believed to have been one of the wild ancestors of the humped zebu cattle of southern Asia, suggesting that fresh crossbreeding between the two bovids could boost cattle raising throughout the entire region. Regrettably, the kouprey's survival is doubtful, due to military activities within its habitats dur-

The kouprey is a forest-dwelling bovid along the Thailand/Kampuchea (Cambodia) frontier. Due to military activities in its habitat during the past two decades, the creature has been reduced to remnant numbers. Yet it could contain genetic material to upgrade domestic cattle throughout Southern and Southeast Asia. Thus this species, with perhaps only a few hundred individuals still surviving, could serve to improve the health and productivity of hundreds of millions of cattle. (Credit: Dr. P. Pfeffer; © World Wildlife Fund)

ing the past 20 years. Other wild bovids of Southeast Asia's forests, such as the selatang, the tamarau, and the anoa, could help cattle husbandry. Like the kouprey, their numbers have all been severely reduced through human disruption of their life-support systems.

Current cattle breeds elsewhere can likewise be improved through hybridization with related species from the wild. In California, a crossbreeding of domestic cattle with bison has led to an animal that reputedly produces meat costing less than beef because of the creature's capacity to thrive off grass without the $500 worth of feedstuffs that conventional cattle consume before slaughter. In addition, the "beefalo" can reach a weight of 450 kg in half the time that cattle usually take (Mason, 1975). Similarly, the domestic goose could be improved by an infusion of genes from Arctic-breeding species of wild geese that feature short incubation periods and ultrarapid growth rates (Short, 1976). Temperate-zone breeds could also be helped through tropical species of geese with their capacity to produce eggs right around the year. And let us remember that our domestic chicken, the world's most important bird to humans, is derived from the jungle fowl, a common pheasant of Southeast Asia, where there are many other rainforest birds that could offer further potential for the future.

In similar style, cattle raising in Africa can be assisted through a highly localized breed of cattle that live around Lake Tchad. This Kuri breed of cattle is able to swim, and it feeds off lake-bottom vegetation. The breed is threatened with "genetic swamping" through excessive and haphazard crossbreeding with local zebu cattle. Also in West Africa is a dwarf shorthorn breed of cattle, the N'dama, with tolerance for trypanosomiasis disease that limits cattle raising in some 10 million km² of Africa, or one-third of the continent. Yet the N'dama is in danger of disappearing.

As a measure of what awaits us through improved breeding of livestock strains, we can consider that the world contains at least twice as many domesticated animals as humans, including 3 billion ruminants (cattle, buffalo, sheep, goats, camels, and llamas), at least half a billion pigs, and over 6 billion poultry. Of these animal stocks, around 60 percent occur in developing nations, which nevertheless enjoy only one-fifth of all animal products generated worldwide (Wittwer, 1979). A good part of the problem for developing nations lies with losses from disease and parasites – at least 50 million cattle and buffalo, and 100 million sheep and goats per year (and in the United States, animal diseases cost $20 billion per year). Through selective breeding, drawing notably on gene reservoirs, we could cut these losses by a full one-half. For example, we can draw on obscure strains

of livestock to develop creatures that are more fertile and that can sub-
sist off low-quality diets.

Aquaculture

Finally, let us consider a form of agriculture that may prove to be
one of the fastest-growing sectors of all agriculture in the foreseeable
future. It may also turn out to represent the most promising means for
us to grow large amounts of that critical form of food, animal protein.
It is technically known as aquaculture, a term that refers to, among
other things, the raising of fish in ponds (Ackefors and Rosen, 1979;
Borgese, 1980; Fryer, 1980; Legner, 1978; Lovell, 1979; Pritchard,
1980; Ryther, 1979; Weatherly and Cogger, 1977).

More than 90 percent of the fish we consume is obtained through
"hunting" of wild species. Yet fish have been reared in enclosed structures, usually ponds, in Asia for at least 4,000 years. Of global fish
consumption today, amounting to some 70 million metric tons (60
million from the oceans and 10 million from fresh waters), only a little
over 6 million metric tons are derived from aquaculture, including 4
million of finfish and more than 1 million of mollusks such as oysters,
mussels, clams, and other high-priced gourmet items (plus more than
1 million metric tons of seaweeds). This means that aquaculture accounts for about 40 percent of freshwater output, and 3 percent of
saltwater output. Small as this aquaculture proportion may be, it
represents a marked advance over the mid-1960s when the annual
harvest amounted to no more than 1 million metric tons. Today's
leaders in aquaculture are China with 2 million metric tons and Indonesia and the Philippines with around 1 million each. Aquaculture
supplies 40 percent of fish eaten in China, 22 percent in Indonesia,
and 10 percent in the Philippines. Israel now obtains almost 60 percent of its total catch of both marine and freshwater fish from culture
ponds.

So great is the scope for increasing aquaculture that the Food and
Agriculture Organization believes this practice could contribute, by
the year 2000, at least three times more animal protein than at present, possibly six times more. There are two main reasons for this vast
potential. First, water-dwelling creatures enjoy a distinct advantage
over their terrestrial relatives in that their body density is almost the
same as that of the water they inhabit, so they do not have to direct
energy into supporting their body weight; this means in turn, that
they can allocate more food energy to the business of growing than is
the case for land animals. Second, fishes, as cold-blooded creatures,
do not consume large amounts of energy to keep themselves warm.

Carp, for instance, can convert one unit of assimilated food into flesh one and a half times as quickly as can pigs or chickens, and twice as rapidly as cattle or sheep. The tiny shrimplike crustaceans called *Daphnia* can, when raised in a nutrient-nourished environment, generate almost 20 metric tons of flesh per hectare in just under five weeks, which is ten times the production rate for soybeans – and at one-tenth the cost per unit of protein produced.

Aquaculturalists in various parts of the world have raised more than 300 species of finfish. But of the 4 million metric tons of finfish cultivated in fish ponds right now, 85 percent comes from a few carp species, notably common carp, Chinese carp, and Indian carp. These carp species may soon have to give way, however, to new contenders from the *Tilapia* genus of finfish. Originally raised by the ancient Egyptians, tilapias are now grown widely in eastern Asia. Their production doubled between 1970 and 1975 and is continuing to grow fast. So proliferant are tilapias that a hybrid species raised in garbage-enriched ponds can generate 3 metric tons per hectare in 180 days. This performance may be compared with that of common carp, which yields almost 0.4 metric ton with no supplemental feeding, 1.5 metric tons with grain as a supplement, and 3.3 metric tons with a protein-fortified diet.

True, these figures are for well-managed ponds in the United States, using the computerized efficiency of modern agribusiness. In Cameroon, small-scale farmers' ponds regularly yield 1 to 2 metric tons of tilapias per hectare per year. But experimental farms in Africa, with year-round warmth, produce at least 20 metric tons per hectare using intensive cultivation methods, and pilot projects under optimal conditions reach 50 metric tons per hectare. All this contrasts with production of wild fish species in seas or lakes, a mere 35–60 kg per hectare.

Still other productivity figures demonstrate the capacity of tilapias to grow, grow, grow. In California, experiments reveal that 190 ponds, each measuring 7.6 meters long by 5.5 meters wide and 34 cm deep, with a water surface equivalent to 0.8 hectare, can produce 1 million fish from just nine pairs of parents in 104 days (Legner, 1978). At Mombasa in Kenya, a 20,000-liter tank produces between 2 and 4 metric tons of table-size fish (weighing over one-quarter of a kilogram each).

Much scope, moreover, lies ahead of us when we consider the large numbers of wild *Tilapia* species that we can use for selective breeding. Lake Tanganyika contains 126 endemic species, Lake Victoria 164, and Lake Malawi 196 (Lowe-McConnell, 1977). These totals may eventually rise a good deal higher, since new species are being found all the time. (Altogether, Africa possesses at least 2,000 species of freshwater fish, out of some 7,000 in the world.) These *Tilapia* species differ from one another in their diets and breeding patterns, which suggests that a systematic approach to aquaculture could utilize combinations of *Tilapia* species in order to expand the protein yield. Different species could divide up the food supplies of a pond much as they divide up the food supplies in each of the three great African lakes, efficiently exploiting many food types that would not be consumed by a single species.

Tilapias can serve a further, and unusual, purpose. In California they are starting to be used to clear irrigation canals of weeds (Legner and Pelsue, 1980). The weeds can grow as much as 10 cm a day, choking waterways and even halting water flow altogether during dry seasons. If Californians have to use tractors and other machinery to pull the weeds out of the state's 8,000 kilometers of waterways, the bill can run to $0.5 million a year. Tilapias 7 cm long can do the job just as well, when stocked at a rate of 7,000 per surface hectare.

But just as we are becoming aware of the immense potential of tilapias as a source of that prized food form, animal protein, the wild stocks are running into trouble. Lake Victoria has endured two decades of overfishing, until many species are declining rapidly, and a number could approach extinction within just a few years. In Lake Malawi, a still worse threat could overtake the *Tilapia* community. This lake, like other great lakes of tropical Africa, is made up of an enormous "sink" of oxygenless water, overlaid with a thin surface layer of oxygen-rich water. By contrast with temperate-zone lakes, which are colder, tropical lakes possess a relatively small absolute amount of oxygen per unit of volume. As a consequence, the great lakes of Africa are less able to deal with oxygen-demanding pollution than is the case for temperate-zone lakes of similar size. At the same time, the African sun causes year-round evaporation, with the result that outflows from the lakes are small. The time the lakes need to renew their water bodies is very long. All this leaves the lakes extremely vulnerable to pollution by oxygen-consuming wastes, such as those that are discharged from paper pulp factories. Just such a pulp mill threatens Lake Malawi. The result could be a biological debacle equivalent to a crash of the fish communities in the Great Lakes of North America, almost seven times as large in area as Lake Malawi but possessing fewer species – most of them to be found elsewhere anyway.

CHAPTER FIVE

■

Insect Food of the Future

So far we have looked at approved versions of established foods and some new foods of types akin to established foods. How about some truly new foods – such as insects? There are many more insect species on Earth than all other species combined. And generally speaking, most insect species comprise more individuals than mammals or fishes or plants. Virtually any insect represents first-rate nutrition, packed with animal protein and essential fats. The insect world, then, represents a massive food supply if only we can learn to use it.

Insects come in all shapes and forms. Some small beetles can crawl through the eye of a needle. Some "stick insects" of the tropics measure one third of a meter long. In proportion to the total number of insect species on Earth, relatively few are harmful to us, whether in a direct physical sense or in an indirect economic sense.

If we were to take to eating insects on a large scale, we would in fact be doing nothing so very innovative. Throughout human history, many people, probably most people, have eaten insects. I was first made aware of this when I arrived in Kenya from Britain in 1958. I was astonished, on my first evening in the country, to see the Africans gulping insects. Since that time, I have come across people of all sorts and conditions, in many parts of Africa, Asia, and Latin America, who chew on locusts, delight in dragonflies, and gobble down grubs. I have not only been surprised at the spectacle, I have felt nauseated at it. But the source of revulsion lies, I have discovered, in my prejudices rather than in the food itself.

The first time was in a small township near Lake Victoria. It was at the start of the rainy season, and a late-afternoon thunderstorm had flooded termite nests, causing their residents to swarm out in thousands from each colony. The "sausage flies," as locals deservedly call them, were attracted to street lights, and each lamp post was the center of a thick flurry of buzzing creatures. It was simple for bystanders to catch the insects. All they had to do was reach out their cupped hands, and they could seize a dozen. Whereupon they crammed the insects into their mouths, whole and wriggling, to crunch them up with gusto. Bon appetit!

Whatever the taste—and it must have been good, to judge by the people's readiness to gorge themselves—the insects certainly made fine fare. According to laboratory tests, termites offer 560 calories per 100 grams, so they are high in energy (Taylor, 1975). They also contain 46 percent protein and 44 percent fat, by contrast with a sirloin steak that offers only 23 percent protein and 32 percent fat.

I later witnessed a similar scene in Uganda's sector of Lake Victoria's shoreline, where tribesmen collect huge amounts of a different insect, the lake fly, which they crush into sticky cakelike masses. The result is said, according to local missionaries whose tastes are more esoteric and whose stomachs are less squeamish than mine, to have a flavor akin to that of caviar. A delicacy indeed!

In Tanzania, Zimbabwe, and Botswana, I have come across people who relish crickets and locusts. Forest folk of Cameroon, Madagascar, and Java share a penchant for dragonflies. The Pygmies of eastern Zaire make a specialty of the myriad creepy-crawlies that hide beneath the bark of fallen trees. Aborigines of the Australian outback favor many kinds of moths and caterpillars. As a special treat, Aborigines seek out honey-ants after the ants have fed on the sweet sap of eucalyptus leaves—whereupon the ants' abdomens, swollen with honey, make a notable delicacy. At streetside markets in Kuala Lumpur, Malaysia, I have come across deep-fried grasshoppers; and in downtown Bogotá, Colombia, I have see French-fried ants, a dish that reputedly resembles salted fish with a delicate flavor all its own. Bushmen of the Kalahari Desert enjoy cockroaches, among many other insects; so adapted are they to an insect diet that they even prefer their staple fare to "modern meat" such as beef—a reaction that has been encountered by Professor P. J. Quin of the Witwatersrand University in South Africa during his field work with the Pedi (Quin, 1959). Professor Kenneth Ruddle of the University of California at Los Angeles encountered the same reaction during his sojourn with the Yukpa tribe in Venezuela (Ruddle, 1973).

In Thailand, people have long eaten beetle larvae. When fried with salt, the larvae are reputed to taste rather like a mixture of raw potato and lettuce (Bristowe, 1932). The same creatures are a gourmet delight in Papua New Guinea, where, according to Drs. Michael and Barbara Robinson of the Smithsonian Institution in Washington, D.C., they are sold in market squares in bundles, for all the world like sticks of asparagus. The Robinsons have also seen people in the central highlands of Papua New Guinea consuming 5-cm wood spiders (spiders are not true insects, in that they have eight legs instead of six, as well as other differences). When roasted, the spiders have "a nutty flavor, rather like peanut butter but without the objectionable consistency" (Robinson and Robinson, 1976). In Bali, favorite foods include butterflies and moths, lightly toasted. In Ethiopia, Nigeria, Thailand, China, and even Japan, the praying mantis, a fearsome beast several inches long, with formidable pincer-legs, makes a gourmet delight; according to friends of mine in Bangkok who vainly urged me to try crushed mantis, it reminds one of shrimp-and-mushroom pate. In Malawi, in the experience of local insect expert Dr. Edward J. Chimaliro, people consume several dozen forms of insects, including caterpillars and army worms (not worms at all, but pupae), and even bees and wasps (after being defused). So plentiful and nutritious are insects in Malawi that the Home Economics Section of the Ministry of Community Development encourages people to consume flying ants, termites, and locusts – all creatures that are on sale in country markets. Some Malawi tribes favor insect eggs, fried: anyone for entomological omelette?

It was not until I had spent 20 years in the tropics, watching people stuff insects into their mouths as if the world was about to run short of the creatures, that I finally sampled a morsel in Mexico City. I was at a sidewalk cafe with local scientist colleagues. The insect tidbit on my plate had been sanitized, so far as my prejudices go, by being French-fried until it was distinctly overdone, barely recognizable as whatever entomological entity it had been while alive. Moreover, it was served out of a tin, which made it respectable to my palate.

Fortified with an extra glass of wine, I braved the crunchy thing lying before me. It tasted, surprisingly and pleasantly, like sardines. Whereupon I was shown the label that had been on the tin: I had downed an agave worm (actually not a worm, but the larva of a Mexican butterfly). I decided to miss out on the beetle-burger, the marinated moths, the fricasseed flies, the cricket quiche, and other delicacies on offer, preferring to stick with my bread and wine. I was indifferent to the nutrition arguments of my professional friends who cited local experts, Professors Julietta Conconi and Hector Rodrigues of the National Institute of Nutrition, Mexico City, to the effect that these various items contain protein ranging from 58 to 78 percent, with protein quality of 46 to 58 percent. Statistics to make me throw up!

Our Culinary Prejudices

But why, I reflected later, should I feel repelled by insect food? Could I have become culturally conditioned against insects to an extent where, scientist as I am, I give in to irrational images of maggots gnawing at my guts? Is there not some substance to my instinctive rejection of insect food?

Almost certainly there is no substance to it (Bodenheimer, 1951; Gabel, 1979; Taylor 1975). As long as humans have existed, they have probably been insectivores. During 2 million years of recent development humans have subsisted often, if not mainly, on insects. According to historical records, virtually every major culture has eaten insects, and virtually every large group of insects has been consumed by humans in one place or another. Many of our ancestors occasionally joined John the Baptist in surviving on locusts. According to Aristotle, Pliny, Herodotus, and other ancient writers, the civilized Greeks and Romans were not impartial to dining off insects; the Athens market sold large larvae that had been specially reared for the purpose. In more recent times, Marco Polo records that Chinese restaurants served silkworms, in culinary form similar to shrimp pies.

The insect that has been an out-in-front favorite of people at all periods is the ubiquitous grasshopper—the "grasshopper" being an umbrella term that includes crickets and other kindred creatures such as wild locusts (Uvarov, 1966). Perhaps the grasshopper has proved a front-runner, if not a front-flier, because it is sometimes available in large numbers. A swarm of wild locusts in East Africa can cover 1,500 square kilometers and comprise up to 400 billion creatures, offering almost 100,000 metric tons of protein.

From the Assyrians 2,800 years ago to nineteenth century American Indians, the grasshopper has been a much sought-after item. Today, grasshoppers are part of regular human diets in many parts of the tropics. Indeed, we can probably say that more grasshoppers are eaten now than ever before. Only one major culture seems to be leaving them behind, and that is the Japanese, partly because Japanese grasshoppers have been clobbered by insecticides, so that surviving grasshoppers may taste as much of toxic chemicals as of fleshy insect.

Second ranker in the popularity listing seems to be the termite, a wood-eating insect that is favored in much of the tropics. Presumably it is favored because, like the grasshopper, it is sometimes available in sizable numbers: a single termite colony can contain 3 million members. Equally to the point, the termite is unusually nutritious, comparing favorably with locusts. Locusts contain 50–75 percent protein, plus 5–19 percent fat; termites, when fried, pack in 36–46 percent protein and 36–44 percent fat. Moreover, termite protein contains, according to Professor S.H.W. Cmelik of the University of Zimbabwe, more of the essential amino acids than most animal proteins (Cmelik and Douglas, 1970).

Most insects are similarly nutritious. The lowest protein content recorded among common varieties is a modest 8 percent for the larvae of some butterflies, roughly the same protein content as in rice. At the other end of the scale are roasted spiders and housefly pupae, with a whopping 64 percent protein. Even ants, slender animals though they are, contain more protein than chicken (23 percent), various fish (21 percent), beef (less than 20 percent), and pork or lamb (less than 17 percent). Hence the attraction, in the protein-starved Third World, of items such as smoked caterpillars, with 38 percent protein. Who is for caterpillar cannelloni?

It is plain that our biological inheritance, reaching back to our early hominid days when one of our main sources of sustenance may have been insects, retains the genes that give us our capacity to digest insects. After all, we consume a moderate amount of insects during the course of our lives. The freshest lettuce we buy almost certainly features aphids, while flour and rice are commonly infested with weevils and beetles. Something similar applies to prepared foods – as recognized by the conservative Food and Drug Administration, which permits apple butter to contain five insects or insect parts in every 100 grams, and peanut butter to contain 50 insect fragments per 100 grams.

Nor can we legitimately complain that insects, being lowly forms of life, should lie beneath the purview of our elevated gastronomic preferences. True, insects are mere invertebrates without the same physical appurtenances and behavioral diversity that characterize higher creatures such as mammals and other vertebrates. But we count some of our greatest gourmet treats among invertebrates, notably scallops, clams, and oysters. What could be more repulsive than to swallow an oyster, one of the most loathsome-looking creatures on Earth, which we consume alive, squirming and perhaps "screaming" in its oysterine fashion. And when we come to shrimps, crabs, and lobsters, we are eating animals that are closely related, in a biological sense, to insects. Both lobsters and grasshoppers, for example, feature skeletons on the outside of their bodies, and they use jointed legs to propel their three-segmented frames. Next time you, dear reader, find yourself in a seafood restaurant, take a look at those lobsters crawling around in their tank: What are they in appearance, if not outsize insects?

Lobsters are far more filthy in their foraging habits than any insect, at least according to our human view of the world. A lobster searches around on the seafloor for every kind of foul flesh, whereas grasshoppers and termites, like caterpillars and most other insects, stick entirely to plant material. And what shall we say about our predilection for pork: hogs thrive on garbage! Try throwing a spatter of hog swill over a bunch of whatever insects, and they will promptly try to escape or to clean off every last speck of it.

And how about that prized product of certain insects – that is, honey – being little other than "bee vomit"?

All we have to do is to swallow our prejudices, and the insects will follow. Far from contaminating our intake, they will actually enrich it.

Insect Supplies

There are roughly twice as many different sorts of insects as there are all other forms of life combined. So abundant are insects, not only in species but in overall numbers, that their total weight far surpasses that of all other creatures on our planet.

So here is a vast supply of food, solid and wholesome, not to say clean and nutritious. And insects come readily to hand, living in virtually every kind of environment. They thrive below ground and in the highest forest canopies; in bodies of water such as rivers, streams, ponds, and lakes; and on both living plants and decaying plants – and the same for animals. Practically any place we go on the planet's surface, we shall have stacks of insects within just a few meters of us.

Fortunately, insects flourish best, in both diversity and overall numbers, in the tropics – precisely the zone where food needs are greatest and where animal protein is a key deficiency. It is this zone that features fewest cultural hang-ups about eating insects. Whether as staples of daily diet or as emergency supplies during times of famine, insects already serve many communities in the tropical Third World. We might well ask, why not many more of these communities? The Food and Agriculture Organization of the United Nations is now sponsoring a project in Papua New Guinea for commercial production of spectacular butterflies, to meet the demand of collectors. Other development agencies are investigating the potential for similar insect enterprises in many other countries of the developing world. Why not insect farms for food?

Rearing Insects

Insects offer much scope for "farming," in terms of their capacity to generate progeny. Consider a single pair of North American houseflies. In one April–August season, they can produce offspring that, if they were all to live and reproduce normally, would generate a total of 191,000,000,000,000,000,000 (or 191 quintillion) flies. Or take a female cabbage aphid of New York State, capable of producing, at the start of the April–September season, an average of 41 offspring; if she eventually becomes the progenitor of 16 generations before autumn arrives, she could theoretically generate a posterity numbering 1,560 sextillion – which would, if they all lived, produce a weight by September greater than all humankind. In the South, with its warmer weather, a cotton aphid or a melon fly can produce more generations and at least twice as many offspring as a cabbage aphid of New York State.

Of course, all but a tiny fraction of these progeny fall by the wayside, becoming victims of disease, predation, and adverse environmental conditions. But supposing a businessman were to set up an insect farm, keeping all these mortality factors under control in order to foster systematic harvesting: what a sustained-yield exercise he could embark on! According to some preliminary arithmetic in this direction by Dr. Edwin W. King, of Clemson University, South Carolina, the farming of the facefly – a creature a little larger than the common housefly, and packing protein on a par with low-grade beef – could prove a success story indeed. A key factor lies with its favored habitat: cow dung, a commodity in excessive supply in many cattle feedlot operations. According to Dr. King, a facefly can produce one gram of pupae per 6.25 square centimeters of breeding (manure) surface each day. Looking for economies of scale, Dr. King visualizes a factory with dozens of buildings per hectare, producing just over 1,000 metric tons of pupae, or at least 450 metric tons of edible protein, per year. To generate a protein supply of this order would require the manure of some 3,030 cattle – and, since the same cattle could produce almost 500 metric tons of protein themselves, the faceflies could enable the total protein output of the cattle herd to be virtually doubled (King, 1976).

While Dr. King find that the pupae of the facefly are palatable enough, albeit tasting like sawdust unless they are seasoned (not that many other processed food products do not resemble sawdust), he finds their best use is as stockfeed for chickens. The facefly and many other species could form an admirable protein supplement for stall-fed cattle, hogs, and other livestock.

But what about the Third World, where intensive livestock-raising is a rare phenomenon, and where the greatest protein hunger is in human stomachs? All manner of possibilities arise. Certain insects are already ground up into powder before being used as flour for bread and biscuits. The powder could likewise serve as a protein supplement for maize meal and rice products. The day may even come when certain Third Worlders sip "fly-fortified cola." (And future health-food addicts in the First World may one day take to stuffing insects into a blender and liquefying the mass into an exotic and nutritious beverage.)

As for "insect husbandry," it is already an established practice in certain sectors of the Third World. The Bari people of the Maracaibo Basin in Venezuela, for instance, have hit upon a way to breed larvae. They use the trunks of palm trees (cut down to yield fruit or palm hearts) and convert the rotting logs into nesting places for colonies of palm weevils. Result, a steady supply of plump and juicy larvae.

A similar-spirited idea has been promoted by Professor Achieng Onyango of the University of Kampala, who believes that a prime breeding ground for insects of all sorts and conditions could be found in another type of decomposer habitat – sewage lagoons of the tropics, with their warm-weather conditions promoting growth right around the year. Plainly this would make a first-rate location for an insect farm, utilizing aquatic bugs, mites, and other sewage-savoring creatures. The lagoons could quickly become so filled with insects that the "farmer" could all but walk across the surface.

Insect Rearing in Developed Nations

It is no big deal to raise insects in your backyard, or, better still, in your back room – mealworms, for example, these being larvae of a beetle. As Professor Ronald L. Taylor of the University of Southern California has described (Taylor, 1975), a sound way to culture mealworms is in small pans or trays or in plastic dishpans. But if you don't have the right equipment at hand, a shoebox will do. Spread a few inches of bran meal around, enough to serve 25–50 adult mealworms. Don't forget to add a slice or two of potato or apple for moisture. Forget about the mealworms until you catch sight of emerging pupae. After two weeks or so, the pupae release fully formed beetles, which promptly start to lay, producing as many as 500 eggs in a lifetime. The eggs hatch about two weeks later into small white larvae, which speedily expand until they are 2.5 cm long, whereupon they pupate, leading to adults again.

If you do not feel like going into home growing of mealworms, you can generally buy them across the counter in many parts of the country. You can even obtain them by mail order. In response to demand from the United States' 20 million fishermen, numerous enterprises raise the creatures. A testimonial that mealworms make fine fare for people is offered by Turkish women, who consume large amounts of the mealworms in order to acquire those pneumatic curves that turn on Turkish men.

Also widely available in the United States are honeybees. In fact a sizable stock of insect food could lie with these honeybees. Each fall, beekeepers across the country kill off their bee colonies, with a view to buying new ones the following spring. As a result, somewhere between 600 and 1,500 metric tons of bees are wantonly discarded each year, causing a loss of 100–225 metric tons of protein. If these surplus bees could be marketed as food, thus offering further profit to the apiculturist, there is little doubt that their supply could be expanded many times over.

Similar potential could lie with the screw-worm, which the Department of Agriculture now breeds in huge numbers. At the Screw-Worm Laboratory in Mission, Texas, sterile males are raised to combat the worm's threat to livestock. The sterile males are released into pasturelands, causing female screw-worms to lay unviable eggs. The Screw-Worm Laboratory produces as many as 200 million worms per week, weighing almost 14 metric tons and containing 8.6 metric tons of protein. This represents a 36 percent food-conversion efficiency (compare with a broiler chicken at 40 percent, a turkey at 21, hogs at less than 20, and cattle at about 10).

Plainly there is much to recommend sauteed mealworm, honeybee mousse, or screw-worm souffle. In the course of more culinary research and development, these dainty dishes could be followed by garlic croquette, fly florentine, and cockroach chowder. For dozens of innovative ideas, why not check the proposals of Professor Ronald L. Taylor and Ms. Barbara J. Carter in their book *Entertaining with Insects* (Taylor and Carter, 1979)?

Recipes

With some imagination and less squeamishness, one can produce all manner of dishes. For his entomology class at the University of Southern California, Professor Taylor has served up fried grasshoppers and fried agave worms, both of which have gone down well. He has also tried fried ants, fried bees, and fried beetles, which graded moderately in the gourmet rankings of the students. Fried silkworms, fried butterflies, and roasted caterpillars ranked poorly. As much depends, not surprisingly, on appearance as on content: Almost any insect that is served with a covering of chocolate draws high marks.

So be adventurous with insects. Try, for instance, termite pilaf. According to its originator, Ms. Carol Miller of California State University at San Luis Obispo, you use rice, sesame seeds, onion, beef bouillon, and one cup of termites.

If termites turn you off, how about a cupful of roasted grasshoppers, ground up into flour for crisp-textured bread? Even bee larvae can be used, without the trouble of cooking them; you just freeze-dry them and serve them as suitably crisp croutons in salads.

What prospects await us, if only we can leave behind our irrational prejudices and start to utilize one of the richest food sources on Earth. We may eventually agree with columnist Joseph Alsop, who remarked, after a visit to Japan, that "fried bees in a Tokyo restaurant have a delicious flavor, somewhere between pork crackling and wild honey."

PART TWO

Medicine

CHAPTER SIX

■

Plants and Medicine

In 1970–1971, I took time out in mid-career to study at the University of California at Berkeley for a doctorate in Conservation and Development. While in Berkeley, my wife Dorothy became sick, then severely ill, finally in danger for her life. She had picked up an obscure "bug" that eventually caused fluid to build up in her lungs, which in turn caused her to start "drowning." Her heart objected to the gross strain, and she went into repeated heart failure.

As I sat by her bedside, watching her "pulse blip" on a television monitor screen above her head, I quizzed the doctors about the drugs they were administering to ease her troubles. The main one was digitalis, a material which serves two crucial functions. First, it increases the force of systolic contractions of the heart muscle; and secondly, it provides more rest between contractions. A powerful help in time of trouble.

On the occasion, I did not give the matter further thought. But after Dorothy had defied the doctors' worst fears and had recovered, I thought again about digitalis. Where had I heard the name before? My mind went back to a botany class at the Berkeley campus, where I heard Professor Herbert G. Baker telling of botanocompounds from the purple foxglove (*Digitalis purpurea*), a plant native to Western Europe and Morocco. So, I reflected, a plant that I had admired in the hedgerows of England during my youth had helped to keep my wife alive in the San Francisco Medical Center. I went to talk more with Professor Baker about this plant, and I learned that, as a secondary effect, digitalis lowers blood pressure in hypertension heart disease, and elevates blood pressure when necessary in order to counteract impaired heart functions.

Professor Baker also told me about a closely related plant, the Grecian foxglove (*Digitalis lanata*), a native to central and southern Europe. This plant serves as a source of digoxin, a drug 300 times more powerful than digitalis. Digoxin is also more stable, and is especially valuable because of its prompt action and quick elimination. During the course of subsequent inquiries, I learned from Professor Walter H. Lewis of Washington University in St. Louis that more than 3 million Americans depend on this foxglove for regular doses of cardiotonic compounds to keep them alive; without it, they might find themselves in terminal trouble within as little as 72 hours (Lewis and Elvin-Lewis, 1977). Commercial sales of digoxin in the United States are now in the region of $50 million a year, and we can reckon that for the related drug digitoxin, the figure approaches $35 million (International Marketing Statistics, 1981).

After my wife and I returned to our beloved Kenya, I became increasingly interested in plants as sources of medicines. I discussed the topic with African experts like Dr. John Kokwaro of the East African Herbarium and Professor Njuguna Mogu of the University of Nairobi. These two scientists told me of the many plants used by African medicine men, certain of which demonstrate their efficacy for modern medicine–they stand up to the most rigorous scientific testing. Indeed Dr. Kokwaro told me of his contributions to a World Health Organization campaign to find new drugs from plants around the world; and this connection took me, in turn, to the office of Professor Norman R. Farnsworth of the College of Pharmacy at the University of Illinois in Chicago. Professor Farnsworth described an analysis he had conducted of the dollar value of plant-derived prescription drugs in the United States: at least $3 billion in 1973 (Farnsworth and Morris, 1976). When Professor Farnsworth included nonprescription drugs and pharmaceuticals, the total doubled. Nonprescription items include laxatives, cough and cold preparations, and the like; to consider a single category, plant-derived laxatives (notably sennosides from *Cassia* species), these much-purchased products generated sales in 1980 of about $165 million. (Moreover, when Professor Farnsworth included drugs derived from animals and microbial forms of life in his analysis of prescription drugs, he found that their economic value approached that of plant-derived prescription drugs.) By 1980, the overall value of plant-derived drugs and pharmaceuticals had reached, so far as Professor Farnsworth could estimate, a total of $16 billion (Farnsworth, 1982). By 1982 we can reasonably reckon that this total has reached around $20 billion.

This figure, moreover, is for commercial sales in the United States alone. When we consider the rest of the developed world, the total can fairly be supposed to be double again, reaching $40 billion. The remarkable increase indicated by the U.S. data over the past decade is due only partly to inflation. Primarily it is due to the expanding exploitation of plants for medicinal purposes. In the case of anticancer drugs, for example, the use of plant-derived drugs has been growing by 20–25 percent a year.

Most important of all, Professor Farnsworth believes that the plants that we already use in support of modern medicine represent only a fraction of what could be mobilized into our service. A systematic screening of all wild species could yield whole pharmacopoeias of new drugs and other medicinal preparations. Indeed Professor Farnsworth considers that the plant kingdom, as a vastly diversified source of start-point materials, represents a "sleeping giant" for the American drug industry. To illustrate his point, Professor Farnsworth observes that in 1980 almost all plant-derived drugs prescribed in the United States came from 41 species of higher plants (only five being native to the country); and these 41 plants have been identified after detailed analysis of some 5,000 species of higher plants worldwide. Extrapolating from this experience, we can reasonably anticipate that we shall find one drug-yielding plant out of every 122 species subjected to pharmacological evaluation. When we extend this calculation to the 250,000 plant species on Earth, we come up with a total of almost 2,050 drug-offering species, or 50 times more than we benefit from today.

Three Main Contributions of Plants

Plants support modern medicine and public health in three main ways. They contribute directly, in the form of active therapeutic agents, e.g., reserpine from *Rauwolfia serpentina*, used notably as a tranquilizer and for spot treatment of hypertension, anxiety, and schizophrenia. Second, plants contribute basic materials for drug synthesis, e.g., the steroidal sapogenins from the Mexican yam, used as the start-point materials for manufacture of cortisone, hydrocortisone, androgens, estrogens, progestins, and oral contraceptives. A third contribution lies with "auxiliary agents" such as binders and stabilizers, e.g., algin from seaweeds that is used as a binding agent in pills, pastilles, and ointments.

All in all, the plant kingdom offers a broad range of medicinal and pharmaceutical products. Prime items include analgesics, antibiotics, heart drugs, anticancer agents, enzymes, hormones, diuretics, antiparasite compounds, ulcer cures, dentifrices, laxatives, dysentery treatments, and anticoagulants, among many others (Altschul, 1977; Farnsworth and Cordell, 1976; Franz, 1978; Lewis and Elvin-Lewis, 1977; Morton, 1977; Schultes, 1980; Schultes and Swain, 1976; Swain, 1972; Trease and Evans, 1972; Wagner and Wolff, 1977). Indeed the number of plant-derived items in modern pharmacopoeias amounts to several thousand. Leading items include ipecac, obtained from a Brazilian plant known as *Cephaelis ipecacuanha*, and used against amoebic dysentery; ephedrine, obtained from *Ephedra*, a semidesert shrub known in China for more than 5,000 years, and used as a nasal decongestant and as a stimulant for the central nervous system; ergot, a poisonous substance from a fungus, long used by midwives to speed labor and to reduce bleeding, and now serving not only to assist difficult childbirths but to supply relief from migraine headaches; vincristine, a powerful drug obtained from the rosy periwinkle and used against several types of cancer; and digitalis and related drugs from foxgloves (previously described). Other items include emetine, diosgenin, codeine, morphine, papaverine, atropine, scopolamine, cocaine, quinine, reserpine, pilocarpine, and colchicine.

Some observers may suppose that we can depend on our sophisticated technology to devise "copy products" that amount to synthesized substitutes for natural materials. This takes an overly optimistic view of our technological "muscle." Of 76 major pharmaceutical compounds obtained from plants, only seven can be commercially produced at competitive prices through synthesis. Reserpine, for example, can be commercially prepared from natural sources for a little over $1 per gram, but through synthesis it costs almost $2. Similar circumstances apply to steroids. Despite many efforts at synthesis during the past 25 years, we still obtain 95 percent of our start-point materials from natural sources.

Whereas technology cannot yet stand in for the medicinal materials from plants, it can benefit from "models" supplied by plants in the molecular structure of the plants' biocompounds. Working from nature's models, scientists can determine chemical formulas of natural extracts, and then go on to synthesize "mimic compounds" in the laboratory. Without model compounds derived from nature, many of our most common synthetic drugs could not have been manufactured (Lewis and Elvin-Lewis, 1977). One century ago, aspirin was extracted from the leaves of willow trees (*Salix* spp.); today it is produced artificially, and a good deal more cheaply, through replication of the chemical formula derived from the willow trees' extracts.

If U.S. medicine depends so widely on plants, how about medicine as practiced in other advanced nations? "Green medicine" is used even more widely in some of these nations. In West Germany, for example, twice as many prescription drugs as in the United States, or one-half of all items, are derived from plants (Ayensu, 1978). In the Soviet Union, more than 2,000 species are recognized for potential medicinal applications, and over 100 applications have been approved by the Ministry of Health for prescriptions (Chikov, 1973; Fulder, 1980;

Teteny, 1979). Included among the sources for these leading 100 is a thorny 4-meter tall plant known as Siberian ginseng (*Eleutherococcus senticosus*) belonging to the family Araliaceae, the same family that includes the common ginseng root with its reputed capacities against dozens of diseases. The plant has come to the attention of the Institute of Biologically Active Substances under the USSR Academy of Sciences, and according to experimental findings of the Institute, an extract from the plant could prove useful to athletes, insofar as it reputedly increases stamina and general performance in long-distance runners, with fewer side-effects than any other known stimulant (Soviet athletes are generally recognized to take all manner of performance-enhancing drugs, regardless of whether this complies with laws of international athletics). The plant's extract is also taken by Soviet mountaineers, deep-sea divers, explorers, miners, soldiers, and factory workers, to help them keep going with intense activity under rugged circumstances.

Apart from its boost for sporting prowess, the thorny Siberian ginseng plant serves to support other medicines in fostering cures for a variety of persistent problems such as chronic pneumonia, chronic tuberculosis, and vascular dystonia. It has also supplied a substance that improves the general health of patients with cancer, ostensibly inhibiting the spread of metastes (the development of secondary tumors). Also in the cancer field, the plant materials reduce the debilitating effects of radiotherapy and chemotherapy, permitting cancer sufferers to endure higher doses of treatment (Fulder, 1980).

It is in developing countries that plant medicines really come into their own. In many of these countries, plants often prove to be the predominant source of medicinals (UNESCO, 1981). In China, more than 5,000 suitable plants have been cataloged, and 1,700 of them are in common use (Thorhaug, 1979). Now that China is increasing its trade with the outside world, it uses Hong Kong as a main conduit for its medicinal preparations. In 1979, Hong Kong handled natural drugs, the great bulk of them derived from plants, worth $258 million (modern synthetic drugs accounted for only $105 million); the plant materials totaled more than 1,000 kinds (Kong *et al.*, 1980). Quite a lucrative trade!

In India, at least 2,500 plants, out of 18,000 recorded in the country, are utilized for medicinal purposes (together with other applications, for example, their aromatic properties). In the Himalayan foothills, a number of plants are known collectively as berberis, their roots being an important source of berberin, a biocompound used widely in tropical Asia, and also in Japan, against diarrhea. As a measure of the commercial value of drug-producing plants, a single species, *Strychnos nuxvomica*, is an important source of strychnine and brucine, leading to an export trade worth over half a million dollars a year (Indian Council of Medical Research, 1976; Kempanna, 1974; UNESCO, 1977). All in all, India now exports phytochemical (plant-derived) materials, primarily medicinals and pharmaceuticals, worth over $55 million. This trade has increased fivefold during the 1970s, and India looks forward to a similarly massive expansion in the future (Chatterjee, 1980; Indian Council of Medical Research, 1976; Sen, 1982).

In Pakistan, with its 2,000-plus plant species, at least 400 are used for medicine (Zaman and Khan, 1970). In Turkey, the Regional Agricultural Research Institute at Menemen, Izmir, has recently documented 163 medicinal plant species (UNESCO, 1981).

Probably the region that makes widest use of herbal preparations is Africa, where people reputedly depend on plants, via traditional medicine, for as much as 95 percent of their drug needs (Ekong, 1979; Miller, 1980; Myers, 1982). In Ghana, for example, a plant known as the Ashanti pepper, long recognized as a potent hypertensive, now serves to treat a variety of troubles including mumps, intestinal disorders, and venereal diseases. Dr. Ivan Addae-Mensahe of the University of Ghana believes the pepper's sedative properties may enable it to be used in developed nations as a drug to reduce blood pressure. Another plant, *Cyrtolepis sanguinolenta*, is widely sold in native markets to resist malaria, to reduce fevers, and to cure urinary infections; scientific investigations at the University of Kumasi reveal that these folkloric applications are right on target – and that the plant has promise in yielding a broad-spectrum antibiotic. Other herbal preparations used in Ghana's traditional medicine include skin ointments, purgatives, and worm expellers (Hanlon, 1979). (For details of plant-derived medicinals in other areas, see, for Southeast Asia generally, Soepadmo, 1979, and Williams *et al.*, 1975; for Indonesia, Soedigdo *et al.*, 1980; for the Philippines, de Padua *et al.*, 1977; and for Brazil, Gottlieb and Mors, 1980.)

That the plant kingdom should have yielded so many botanocompounds is scarcely surprising. Plants, by virtue of the extraordinary diversity of their biosynthetic functions, contribute much more than animals to the dynamic workings of ecosystems. Over 50 classes of secondary organic constituents have already been derived from plants. Moreover, these materials stem from only a very small percentage of plants that have been phytochemically investigated, usually for a mere couple of categories of constituents (Schultes and Swain, 1976). Of Earth's 250,000 species of flowering plants, less than 10 percent have been screened for their potential benefits to humankind, and only 1 percent have been subject to intensive investigations.

Principal Plant Sources of Medicinals

Which categories of plants offer the greatest numbers of medicinals? (For further details of the analysis that follows, see Schultes and Swain, 1976.)

Let us start with one of the lowliest forms of plants, fungi, totaling anywhere between 30,000 and 100,000 species, and harboring many dynamic compounds. Many of our antibiotics, plus many other useful medicines, stem from fungi. Furthermore, fungi serve myriad purposes in the pharmaceutical industry – through carrying out specific transformations in the synthesis of steroids, among other activities (Scheuer, 1973; Turner, 1971).

Next let us consider bryophytes (or mosses and liverworts), with some 14,000–25,000 species, mainly in the tropics. To date, they do not seem to have much to offer to modern medicine. Similarly, the gymnosperms (spruces, pines, and other coniferous trees and shrubs), with 675–700 species, appear to have little to contribute beyond the sympathomimetic alkaloid known as ephedrine. But before we dismiss the bryophytes and the gymnosperms, let us bear in mind our experience with lichens, comprising 16,000–20,000 species. Until recently, lichens have been considered a poor source of biodynamic compounds. Now, however, they are revealing all manner of bacteria-inhibiting compounds, plus many chemovars (Asahinat and Schibata, 1971). About half of all temperate-zone lichens harbor acids capable of inhibiting bacteria, even tuberculosis bacilli (Culbertson, 1969). In like manner, the pteridophytes (ferns and their relatives), totaling 12,000–15,000 species, were formerly believed to have little to contribute, but they now reveal a host of compounds of potential interest, including sesquiterpenoid lactones, ecdysones, alkaloids, and cyanogenic glycosides, plus probably many more to come.

Dominating the world's floras are the angiosperms or flowering plants, least 250,000 species, possibly many more. The angiosperms supply us with the great bulk of our plant medicinals, plus many toxins and narcotics. In particular, they are our best source of alkaloids, a category of very valuable botanochemicals; about 94 percent of all known alkaloids are found in angiosperms. Alkaloids are basic organic alkaline compounds, with many medicinal applications (Cordell, 1978; Levin, 1976; Pelletier, 1970; Raffauf, 1970; Schultes and Swain, 1976). These pharmacologically active compounds are thought to serve defensive functions in plants, as in poisoning insect predators. Partly because of the vast variety of insect predators, alkaloids include a widely diversified array of chemical structures; so far we have identified well over 5,000 kinds, even though we have conducted intensive screening of only 2 percent of Earth's higher plants for alkaloids. Plainly we can reckon that many more alkaloids remain to be discovered, making them the largest group of natural products known.

As an indication of their multiple applications in modern medicine, alkaloids include strychnine, cocaine, narcotics such as morphine and nicotine, hallucinogens such as mescaline and LSD, and a host of drugs used as pain-killers, antimalarials, cardiac and respiratory stimulants, blood pressure boosters, pupil dilators, muscle relaxants, local anesthetics, tumor inhibitors, and antileukemic drugs. The glycoside alkaloids are used for cardiac complaints, while certain other alkaloids show therapeutic promise against hypertension. The pyrrolizidine and acronycine alkaloids are likely to prove active against several forms of cancer, while other recently discovered alkaloids help specifically with leukemia (see next chapter). An alkaloid from the lobelia plant is used in antismoking preparations.

Which angiosperms prove to be the best sources of alkaloids? Among the great subclass of monocotyledons, 26 percent of genera reveal alkaloids; and among the dicotyledons, 31 percent. Unusually rich families are the Liliaceae, Amaryllidaceae, Ranunculaceae, Menispermaceae, Lauraceae, Papaveraceae, Leguminosae, Rutaceae, Euphorbiaceae, Loganiaceae, Apocynaceae, Solanaceae, Rubiaceae, and Orchidaceae. In the last-named family, 32 percent of species are alkaloidal, many of them with exceptionally novel forms (Withner, 1974).

In certain instances, an exceedingly minor concentration of a plant alkaloid can supply sizable benefits to medicine. A well-known example is vincristine, obtained from the rosy periwinkle, with leaf material yield of only 4×10^{-6} percent (4 millionths of a single percent). Further details of the exceptionally powerful activity of the periwinkle's alkaloids will be presented in the next chapter (on anticancer drugs).

The Serpentine Root and Reserpine

As an example of what a single species can contribute, let us consider a small shrub that grows in deciduous moist forests extending from India to Southeast Asia—the serpentine root (*Rauwolfia serpentina*). This plant has been used in traditional medicine for 4,000 years as a treatment for snakebite, nervous disorders, dysentery, cholera, and fever (Lewis and Elvin-Lewis, 1977; Woodson *et al.*, 1957). The shrub was named after its root's twisting shape, which first led to its being prescribed against snakebites. In the eyes of Hindu gurus, it has proved especially useful for an array of nervous troubles. By the late

The serpentine root was originally believed by Hindu seers to offer, by virtue of its shape, therapy against snake bites. More recently it has come into widespread use as a material for tranquilizers and for treatment of mental disorders. (Credit: Alain Compost; © World Wildlife Fund)

1940s, Western-world scientists were taking a long look at the plant. Lo and behold, it turned out to yield a fine hypotensive agent, and by 1953 it was being used to relieve hypertension and schizophrenia. Shortly thereafter, a key extract from the plant, reserpine, became the principal source of materials for modern tranquilizers. Until that time, high blood pressure strongly disposed a patient toward stroke, heart failure, and kidney failure. Today, thanks to this one plant, used in conjunction with diuretics, many millions of people lead a reasonably normal and healthy life, partially freed from hypertension, which constitutes the single greatest and fastest-growing source of mortality in advanced societies. The first widespread tranquilizer in advanced-world communities, reserpine, in conjunction with related products whose primary compound is reserpine, now generates sales worth around $260 million a year (Brooke, 1978).

The serpentine root belongs to a genus of the Apocynaceae family, comprising around 100 species. Pharmacologists believe that species closely related to the serpentine root may offer similar, and still more beneficial, drug materials. Insofar as almost 90 percent of drugs used for hypertension originate from higher plants, we can suppose that large stocks of medicinal treatments await discovery in the plant kingdom. According to Professor Farnsworth of Chicago, scientists have investigated 575 plant species by virtue of their folkloric reputation as sedatives, and laboratory tests reveal that these plants do indeed depress the central nervous system in humans. Of the 575, only 17 have yielded promising extracts, but in the case of nine of them, the extracts prove to offer sedative capacity that matches or exceeds that of a major synthetic drug, pentobarbital sodium.

Malaria and Quinine

So much for some answers to a major developed-world health problem. The developing-world disease that is most widespread, and that causes greatest morbidity and mortality, is malaria, afflicting at least 350 million people a year. Synthetic insecticides are no longer as effective as they once were, because at least 57 species of malaria-carrying mosquitoes have developed resistance to the insecticides. (Nor is this the full extent of the problem; mosquitoes also spread several other major diseases, including yellow fever, filariasis, and encephalitis.) As a result, more than half the 100-plus countries that suffer from malaria are now confronted with the challenge of resistant strains of mosquitoes, and at least one-third of their total populations now find themselves at risk again. In many countries there has been a 30-fold increase in malaria cases during the 1970s. India, which reduced its 100 million cases in 1952 to 60,000 in 1962, recorded 50 million cases in 1978, with the result that India's antimalaria campaign today consumes more than half the nation's health budget.

This situation opens up renewed interest in the cinchona tree of Amazonia, whose bark yields the alkaloid quinine. The cinchona is grown in other tropical nations, too, and harbors at least 20 other alkaloids, of which several can likewise be used against malaria (also as cardiac depressants and as antiarrhythmic agents). So important is cinchona now becoming that botanochemicals from the tree are starting to represent a sizable export item for tropical nations. Kenya, for example, exports around 600 metric tons of cinchona bark to Great Britain and Belgium each year, generating revenues to small-scale farmers that total $30 million.

Let us note, moreover, that even if quinine were to be superseded as a naturally-derived drug, its relevance to our welfare would not come to an end. A good number of synthetic drugs against malaria owe their design to the molecular structure, and thus to the "chemical inspiration," of quinine.

In any case, the Chinese may be coming up with a new antimalaria drug. Derived from a plant known as apiaceous wormwood, the drug has been used in China for more than 1,000 years. It is being developed by the Academy of Traditional Chinese Medicine, with support from the International Development Research Centre of Canada. According to scientists in both agencies, this could represent the first major drug breakthrough against malaria since the discovery of quinine.

Antibilharzia Drugs

Another scourge of the developing world is bilharzia or schistosomiasis, also known as "snail fever." Bilharzia has become one of the developing world's most widespread parasitic diseases, affecting more than 250 million people. The parasite—a worm of the genus *Schistosoma*—causes internal bleeding, fever, headaches, and malfunctioning of the liver, intestines, and kidneys, all of which render the victims defenseless against other, even worse diseases.

Bilharzia, moreover, is spreading. As irrigation systems extend their networks in the tropics, the parasite-bearing snails responsible for bilharzia are given expanding habitats. Forty years ago, bilharzia sufferers in Upper Egypt totaled only about one person in thirty, but since the construction of the Aswan High Dam, permitting year-round irrigation in the region, the level has risen to three out of four persons.

The traditional method of countering bilharzia is to attack the snails by spraying watercourses with synthetic molluscicidal chemicals. This is an expensive approach that attacks many nontarget organisms as well as the snails. Now there is prospect of utilizing a snail-killing compound isolated from an Ethiopian plant known as the "soapberry" or Endod (Lemma *et al.*, 1979). The plant is little toxic to mammals, fish are affected by it to only a limited extent, and birds appear immune; so presumably other vertebrates, notably humans, will remain unharmed by it. A 5-year field trial in Ethiopia, involving 17,000 people, has revealed that the plant can reduce transmission of bilharzia by about 75 percent, for a cost of one dime per head per year.

Similar promise lies with an Egyptian plant, known to local people as damassissa (*Ambrosia maritima*). The plant's snail-killing powers were recognized when scientists noticed that Egypt's strongest people came from Upper Egypt, where the plant grows plentifully. When the snail comes into contact with damassissa, it performs a "dance of death," emerging right out of its shell and twisting around so violently that it oozes blood before dying. When farmers grow the plant along their irrigation channels and cut up its leaves in the water, this proliferant "weed" serves as a cheap and effective molluscicide. According to Dr. Mohamed M. El-Sawy of the Department of Tropical Public Health at the Univerisity of Alexandria on the Mediterranean, a tiny amount of plant extract can kill off all snails, plus their larvae and eggs. Yet it does no harm to fish or livestock, so like the Ethiopian plant it should cause no harm to humans.

Antifertility Drugs

Let us also look briefly at a category of drugs that serve as contraceptives and abortifacients. The rhizomes of a climbing vine, the Mexican yam (*Dioscorea mexicana*), have until recently been yielding virtually the world's entire supply of diosgenin, from which a variety of sex-hormone combinations have been prepared, including "the pill" (Applezweig, 1977). (Apart from its role in regulating global population, diosgenin is a start-point material in the manufacture of cortisone and hydrocortisone, which are used against rheumatoid arthritis, rheumatic fever, sciatica, certain allergies, Addison's disease, and several skin diseases or conditions including contact dermatitis.)

By the mid-1970s, the world was using 180 metric tons of diosgenin a year. If we extrapolate recent trends in family planning, we can expect that by 1985 the amount could rise to 500 metric tons. If we look further down the road, to a time when the contraceptive needs of all women of child-bearing age are to be met, we can expect that by 1995 the total could reach 3,000 metric tons. Today, 80 million pills are used each day – though if total needs were recognized and catered to, the figure would be two and one half times higher. Current sales of plant materials for contraceptive pills amount to over $10 million per year; when chemical compounds have been made up, the figure rises to at least $100 million, and when retail sales of final products are totaled, the figure amounts to well over $1 billion. In view of this end-product turnover in the commercial marketplace, and in view of the fact that the yam has not been persuaded to grow anywhere but in tropical moist forests, the Mexican government decided in 1974 to seize a larger part of the action by jacking up export prices. As a result, the price of one kilogram of diosgenin soared from $11.25 in 1970 to $152 in 1976.

Faced with this massive rise in price, diosgenin manufacturers have been looking around for alternative sources of start-point materials. They may have found a promising substitute in certain *Solanum* species (members of the "potato" family) that are cultivated in eastern Europe and in New Zealand (Mann, 1978). Still other plant candidates are being investigated among forest ecosystems of northern India, where more than 50 species of *Dioscorea* grow wild, several of them containing diosgenin (Indian Council of Medical Research, 1976).

Many other plant species have been identified as harboring antifertility compounds—at least 4,000 such species (Bingel and Farnsworth, 1980; Crabbe, 1979; Farnsworth, 1978; Farnsworth and Farley, 1980; Schultes, 1980; Soejarto, 1975; and Soejarto *et al.*, 1978). Of these 4,000 species, at least 370 have been shown to offer special promise for a safer and more effective contraceptive pill, suitable for both males and females. Among plants being studied, notably under the WHO (World Health Organization) Task Force on Plants for Regulation of Human Fertility, are several leading candidates. The first is the Chinese motherwort (*Leonurus artemisia*), reported to have served the contraceptive needs of women for over 2,000 years. The second is the so-called greem flower of India (*Malvaviscus conzattii*), which could lead to a male pill. The third is a small Mexican shrub called the zoapatle (*Montanoa tomentosa*), which may lead to one of the longest sought and most urgently needed pharmaceuticals, a "morning-after pill." The fourth is the "greenheart" tree (*Ocotea rodiei*) that flourishes in the rainforests of Guyana, where women of several tribes use the tree's nut as a traditionally reliable contraceptive. All these plants, however, are still undergoing tests, and they have yet to prove themselves in extensive human use.

A fifth plant has already demonstrated its capacities in practice. It is the "cottonseed plant," with its seed toxin known as gossypol. The contraceptive capacities of this plant were first discovered in the late 1950s, when a doctor in China's eastern province of Jangsu noticed that childlessness was prominent among couples whose diets included a good deal of cottonseed cooking oil. The doctor was also struck by a report from the central province of Hubei, where the cottonseed plant grows abundantly. Women from Hubei who married into communities outside the province produced children at normal rates, whereas those who wed local men remained childless. So the National Coordination Group on Male Anti-Fertility Agents undertook extensive tests during the mid-1970s, recruiting 10,000 males to take part in clinical experiments. The success rate for the oral contraceptive proved to be 99.89 percent, with no appreciable side-effects, no repercussions for potency, and no irreversible consequences. Virtually all volunteers regained their fertility three months after they stopped taking the gossypol pill. Apparently gossypol inhibits an enzyme that is vital to the metabolism of sperm and sperm-generating cells (Peyster and Wang, 1979). But still more extensive tests will be needed before gossypol can be declared "safe" for long-term use.

Many other antifertility plants are being identified from such disparate parts of the earth as Mexico, Haiti, Bangladesh, Papua New Guinea, Fiji, Cameroon, Madagascar, Paraguay, Colombia, and

Brazil—indeed all main sectors of the tropics and subtropics. For an example of a study of a morning-after contraceptive, see Kanjanopothi *et al.,* 1980.

In addition, more than 600 plant species appear to offer potential as abortifacients. A notable instance is a Mexican plant, the cotton root, whose bark is used in folk medicine to terminate early pregnancy (Gold and Cates, 1980). Another is a pretty ornamental plant, *Plumbago indica,* of the rainforests of India, Thailand, and Malaysia that is also widely used to induce abortions (Lee, 1980).

Hallucinogens

A further group of drugs of increasing importance is the hallucinogens (Schultes, 1976; Schultes and Hofmann, 1979). These complex compounds serve a variety of purposes. They can be used to treat mental disorders. They relieve patients with terminal cancer. They meet the needs of experimental psychiatry. Through drawing on the folkloric knowledge of tribal peoples, medical scientists have tracked down at least 150 plant species with hallucinogenic properties.

A number of psychoactive drugs are already familiar to us, e.g., analgesics and euphorics (cocaine and opium), sedatives and tranquilizers (reserpine), and hypnotics. But whereas other psychoactive substances are merely "mood modifiers," hallucinogens produce "deep changes in the sphere of experience, in perception of reality, space and time, and in consciousness of self" (Schultes and Hofmann, 1979). Thus hallucinogens can serve to throw light on research into our perception of the external world, insofar as there seems to be a similarity between psychoactive plant compounds and naturally occurring brain hormones.

Already a number of drugs are used for direct treatment of mental disorders. Mescaline, from a spineless cactus of northern Mexico and the southwestern United States, helps to relieve schizophrenia (Schultes, 1976). Hyoscine from a forest plant in eastern Australia is used to counter several forms of mental illness.

Still another benefit arises with respect to hallucinogenic plants. When preparing pain-killing codeine, our traditional raw material has been the alkaloid morphine. Regrettably, morphine can also serve as a source of heroin. We are now finding that a promising new start-point for codeine lies with the alkaloid thebaine, from the so-called scarlet or blood poppy (*Papaver bracteatum*). This source would satisfy licit medical needs without fostering illicit drugs for narcotic uses. This is a very hopeful initiative, considering that drug abuse and drug-related crime costs over $16 billion each year in the United States alone.

The evening primrose, a colorful plant that is known to many people in North America and Europe, is one of the only two natural sources of abundant supplies of a key nutrient in human health, gamma-linolenic acid (the other source is human milk). The seeds yield an oil that could help us to tackle eczema, coronary heart disease, arthritis, multiple sclerosis, schizophrenia, and possibly even impotence and alcoholic hangovers. (Credit: Dr. Warren Wagner)

The Evening Primrose

Many a reader will be familiar with the evening primrose. Actually it is an entire group of plants, with over 100 species worldwide, about 60 of them in the United States (four of them endangered). These common and colorful plants turn out to be one of only two natural sources that offer abundant supplies of a key nutrient in human health, gamma-linolenic acid; the other natural source is human milk (Horrobin, 1980). The acid is polyunsaturated and is an essential fatty acid; the essential fatty acids (collectively known as vitamin F) form part of the membranes that surround the cells of the body and are essential to the proper functioning of these membranes. In addition, gamma-linolenic acid is a precursor of prostaglandins, or hormones that are produced by every organ of the body and that control the second-by-second regulation of organ functions. Curiously enough, many humans of the modern world are seriously deficient in essential fatty acids, a deficiency that appears to cause many common diseases such as eczema, arterial disorders, arthritis, and multiple sclerosis – all of which are resistant to therapy and defy the best research efforts to unlock their secrets. Of all essential fatty acids known, gamma-linolenic acid is the most active in correcting these deficiencies. In short, the oil from seeds of evening primroses could play a critical part in helping us to avoid eczema, coronary heart disease, arthritis, and multiple sclerosis, among several other afflictions (including possibly schizophrenia and even impotence). In addition to all these virtues, the evening primrose can even supply materials to help us with our alcoholic hangovers.

Overall Potential Value of Plants for Medicine

Plainly the plant kingdom contributes a great deal to our daily lives in the form of medicines, drugs, pharmaceuticals, and related products. Equally plainly, the plant kingdom's capacity to serve us in this manner has hardly been tapped. To reiterate a basic factor, only one plant species in ten has been even cursorily screened for any medicinal purpose, and only one species in one hundred has been intensively investigated.

Most plants, furthermore, harbor defensive chemicals unevenly in their various parts. The roots of a plant may contain several, and the leaves none; or the seeds plenty, and the stems none; or young leaves may possess plenty, old leaves only a few. Even populations of the same species can vary dramatically in their array of chemical defenses. For instance, the leaves of the rosy periwinkle in Jamaica yield ten times more biological activity than leaves of rosy periwinkle plants cultivated elsewhere (Gupta, 1981), and wild yams growing near Kuala Lumpur in Malaysia reveal a far higher concentration of the steroid diosgenin than generally encountered in other wild yams. Hardly any botanist, then, would realistically claim that even a single plant species, at least a relatively widespread species, has been exhaustively evaluated.

Equally plainly again, we are not going to be able to safeguard all plant species through our conservation campaigns. This means there is a premium on identifying those categories of plants that, with least conservation cost, can supply us with the greatest array of medicinal products in the future. The medical profession, more than other economic sectors such as agriculture and industry, has made a substantive start on evaluations of which plants can offer what. But we have a long way to go. If only we can get to the wild plants before the ax and the plow destroy their habitats, we shall find entire treasure chests of materials to enhance our health, if not to save our lives.

CHAPTER SEVEN

——————■——————

Plants as Sources of Anticancer Drugs

In my high school days, while I was still living in a country town of
northern England, I used to know a girl named Anne Murgatroyd. I
knew Anne only from a distance. She was a pleasant, open-spirited
person – one who reminds you that people can be full of both beauty
and splendid good nature.

Along came our last term at the school, and I noticed that Anne was
absent. It turned out that she had fallen ill during the vacation, with
something that sounded serious. When I asked her friends, they did
not know. When I pursued my inquiry with the class teacher, I
gathered that details were not to be forthcoming.

I was sorry, and I missed Anne. But I did not feel concerned until I
heard at half term that she had been taken off to the hospital. Still
nobody seemed to know what the trouble was, only that it was
something she could not shake off. My final exams arrived, followed
by a last round of farewells to my teachers and classmates, together
with whatever other ceremonies in England passed for "commence-
ment." Straightaway at the start of the vacation I headed for London,
where I washed dishes in a restaurant in order to pay for my first
sight-seeing sojourn in the British capital.

A couple of months later I returned to Lancashire, and looked for
my friends. I heard that Anne was dead. I could not believe it. During
the years I had known her she had seemed bursting with zest. Could
that fine person, embarking on womanhood, truly have been snuffed
out? What demonic bug could have overwhelmed her vital spark? I
was deeply saddened and more mystified than by virtually anything
else I had encountered in my young life. Dumbfounded, I struggled to
accept the incomprehensible.

It was not until months afterwards that I heard Anne had died of a
form of cancer that strikes young people. Apparently there was little

The rosy periwinkle turns out to contain two alkaloids that produce exceptionally potent drugs for use against several forms of cancer. Commercial sales of these drugs now top $100 million worldwide each year. (Credit: Dr. Carmine Coscia)

recourse, back in the early 1950s, that could have helped Anne. In fact, the best prospect she faced, according to the statistics, was a one-in-five chance of remission.

For the Annes of this world who now encounter that form of cancer in the 1980s, the prospect for remission has increased to at least four chances out of five. The difference – the massive change for stricken youngsters, as for their parents and friends – lies with two anticancer drugs prepared from a tropical forest plant, the rosy periwinkle. Although these two drugs are used in combination with six or eight other drugs, it is these two that have made the vital difference.

The Rosy Periwinkle

The periwinkle is a pretty flower that was first described by scientists in Madagascar. Nowadays it grows in many parts of the tropics. It is believed, further back still, to have originated in the West Indies.

This colorful tropical forest plant harbors no fewer than 75 alkaloids. Of this extraordinary diversity of alkaloids, two contribute to the two potent compounds – the drugs vincristine and vinblastine – that apparently prevent cancerous cells from dividing. When administered in combination with other materials such as mustard, vincristine and vinblastine supply chemotherapy that achieves 80 percent remission for sufferers from that cancer of the lymph system known as Hodgkins' disease – a major advance over the 19 percent remission before 1960. The drugs likewise achieve 50 to 80 percent remission for several other forms of cancer, and 99 percent remission for acute lymphocytic leukemia. As a measure of how far a single plant can contribute to our welfare, global sales of these two drugs now total around $100 million a year (Brooke, 1978; International Marketing Statistics, 1980).

Each of the two biochemicals in question is synthesized by the rosy periwinkle through a complex process that may involve 20 or more steps. Still more remarkable, each step is controlled by a separate enzyme. Despite massive research efforts, chemists have so far deciphered only the first four and the last two steps in the sequence leading to one compound. So they remain a good way from unraveling the entire process, without which insight they cannot hope for complete understanding of ways to synthesize this alkaloidal material in the laboratory. Thus they continue to depend upon the plant, which yields this precious compound in extremely small amounts. To produce one kilogram of vincristine may require as much as 530 metric tons of plant material; until recently, that one kilogram was worth well over $1 million, placing it among the most valuable products on Earth, roughly on a par with heroin. Now, through a somewhat streamlined process, vincristine can be manufactured for a trifling $200,000 a kilogram.

The U.S. Anticancer Campaign

Right now one American in five is likely to fall a victim to cancer. A similar statistic applies to citizens of other developed nations. According to the U.S. National Cancer Institute, the figure could rise, by the end of the century, to one in three. There can hardly be a more pervasive phenomenon in our personal prospects than the "big C." Which reader's life has not already been touched by cancer striking a relative or friend? In view of this daunting situation, we can be glad that, according to the best scientific opinion, a good bet for the anticancer campaign lies with wild plants and their alkaloids, among other botanochemicals.

The most broad-scale investigation of wild plants' potential has been mounted by two U.S. federal bodies, the National Cancer Institute and the Economic Botany Laboratory, both located just outside Washington, D.C. Since the mid-1950s, these two bodies have pursued a major program to track down those categories of plants that offer most promise of anticancer materials. All in all, this research program represents perhaps the most extensive and methodical effort to investigate wild species for particular benefits. Regrettably, and due to the scale and complexity of the task (Earth harbors at least 250,000 species of wild plants), the program has hitherto been less than comprehensive and systematic.

Still more regrettably, the program has now fallen victim to federal budget cutting in the United States. Although its budget was only some $3 million per year, out of a total anticancer budget of more than $1 billion, and although the minimal costs of cancer to U.S. society each year can be reckoned to top $30 billion, the wild plant investigation has been considered an inappropriate use of public funds. In late 1981 the program became a "terminal case."

Although consigned to the past, the program is worth a brief review here, both for its intrinsic interest and its substantive results. From its start in 1956, the program's principal endeavor had been to screen thousands of plant species (plus a few animal species) for antitumor activity. Because of the program's limited means, investigators could not do more than take a cursory look at most plants they appraised. Thorough evaluations were limited to way under one species in ten. Nonetheless, the investigators managed to screen some 35,000 plant species in all (taken from some 6,000 genera), representing approximately 14 percent of all higher plants on Earth. It appears that roughly one species in ten, and one genus in four, reveals anticancer activity (Barclay and Perdue, 1976; Cassady and Douros, 1980; Cordell, 1978; Douros, 1976; Douros and Suffness, 1978, 1980, and 1981; Duke, 1979 and 1980; Hartwell, 1976; Hudson, 1979; Kupchan, 1976; Spjut and Perdue, 1976; Suffness and Douros, 1979).

Of the thousands of extracts with ostensible promise against cancer, only about 15 have survived numerous laboratory tests and clinical trials. Of these 15, only two compounds, vincristine and vinblastine, have reached the status of "superstar drugs." The question is, how many more are "out there" in the wild, awaiting discovery? If 35,000 plant species can throw up vincristine and vinblastine (counted here as a single drug, insofar as they are very similar in makeup), could not the remaining 215,000 plant species on Earth (minimal estimate) throw up, as a purely statistical prospect, another six superstars? Probably so, though they will take much tracking down. Indeed, a major problem with the 25-year plant-screening program has been its failure to repeat the triumph of vincristine and vinblastine. Yet who is to say, when only one-seventh of Earth's plants have been investigated (at relatively trifling expense), that many millions of cancer sufferers could not gain relief through drugs still kept secret in nature's treasure chest?

Systematic Screening of Plants for Anticancer Materials

The National Cancer Institute and the Economic Botany Laboratory were always aware that they possessed limited funds, staff, and related resources. So how could they have proceeded in order to give themselves the best chance of identifying key candidates among Earth's abundance of plant forms?

For much of the 25 years of the program's course, the selection of plants for screening purposes was random, except insofar as it focused on those species that were easiest to obtain. A strategy of random selection provided the best chance of coming across really novel materials. But it also threw up a low percentage of active leads, which, in terms of costs and benefits, made the program expensive by some standards. At the height of the program, only about 2,000 plant species could be screened per year, because it was necessary to screen several parts of each plant (different chemical constituents are found in leaves, barks, roots, seeds, etc.). So, short of investigating every plant species on Earth—which would be much more costly in terms of research resources and time—was there another, better way to proceed? That is to say, could the cancer researchers go beyond a scatter-gun approach and devise a "silver bullet" approach?

Let us look at some options in a little detail. Experience offers some clues. First off, it is better to evaluate genera than species, in that genera illustrate comparative anticancer activity better than do species; and genera reveal a greater degree of morphologic and chemical relationship than taxonomic groups of plants at and above the next level, namely the family level (where the investigations should be planned in broad scope). As two leading researchers of the National Cancer Institute, Dr. Mathew Suffness and Dr. John Douros, put it (Suffness and Douros, 1979):

> It is logical to assume that some plant families will have higher yields of anti-cancer agents than others, since there is a relationship between the morphological characteristics of a plant and its biochemical characteristics in terms of the secondary metabolites which it produces. Chemical relationships between particular types of secondary metabolites have been used to classify plants (chemotaxonomy), and it is common knowledge to anyone doing natural product research that botanically related plants tend to have similar kinds of chemicals pres-

ent. Therefore, once some background is available on which botanical groups yield active materials, one can select those groups as priority candidates for further collection and screening in order to find more active materials.

Families of Special Interest

This reasoning led to the concept of "families of special interest," known as the FOSI strategy. A program geared to FOSI was begun by the National Cancer Institute in 1972, focusing on the plant families Apocynaceae, Celastraceae, Compositae, Simaroubaceae, Rutaceae, and Thymelaeaceae, together with the families that make up the order Magnoliales. This program not only increased the yield from active plants, but also led to the discovery of a number of interesting and active analogs of compounds in development.

Overall the FOSI approach was helpful, in that anticancer potential can, within limits, prove predictable. At the same time, the approach turned out to be unsatisfactory in that a newly discovered activity may prove to be too similar to that of already-screened taxa. During the plant-screening program, researchers were more interested in moderate activity from new or unknown compounds than in strong activity from old or well known compounds or their close relatives. Hence the scientists continued to place a premium on the concept of investigations and screening programs directed at those families, genera, and species that could throw up new activities.

Nonetheless, the FOSI program revealed that a few families, out of 250–350 plant families on Earth, contain a wealth of compounds, and it is worthwhile to list these families here. Especially notable is the family Compositae, the sunflower family (Bendz and Santesson, 1974; Runeckles, 1975). In the family Simaroubaceae, which includes the ornamental "tree of heaven," at least two species of the genus *Brucea* offer promise (also against dysentery) (Barclay, 1978; Suffness, 1978). In the Boraginaceae family, including the forget-me-not, a small weed (*Heliotropium indicum*) that is widely distributed throughout the tropics is of special interest. The family Celastraceae, featuring many climbers and twiners, contains several *Maytenus* species that yield various forms of the chemical compound maytensine, whose mode of operation is very similar to vincristine. Maytensine was once thought to show promise against pancreatic cancer, for which no drug is currently available (Perdue, 1976), though to date the drug has achieved no success in use.

Four other plant families can be considered generally representative of plants with potential – the Leguminosae (Fabaceae) (legumes), Liliaceae (lilies), Rubiaceae (including gardenias and coffees), and

Rutaceae (citrus fruits). Of 136 Leguminosae species screened, 25 percent have proved active—by contrast with the 10 percent level for across-the-board species. Of 18 Rubiaceae species screened, 6 percent have proved active; and of 21 Rutaceae species screened, 4 percent. Screened species in all these families reveal an average of almost 20 percent activity (weighted by the very high rate for Leguminosae species), or about twice as much as would be identified through a random screen in any sector of the plant kingdom; the genera of these families reveal 52.4 percent activity. Certain other families are good sources of activity—the Apocynaceae (periwinkles and oleanders), Thymelaeaceae (including many ornamentals), and Cephalotaceae (including the fly catcher) (Barclay and Perdue, 1976; Spjut and Perdue, 1976).

At a higher level of categorization, gymnosperms prove to be nearly twice as productive as angiosperms in yield of active extracts. This applies at both the species and genera levels. Around 52 percent of gymnosperm species, and 88 percent of genera, have been screened, by contrast with only 9 percent of the much more numerous Angiosperm species and 39 percent of genera. Among angiosperms, the dicotyledons, with 165,000 species, reveal significantly higher activity than the monocotyledons, with 55,000 species. Among the monocotyledons, the order Liliales, with 28,000 species in 1,200 genera, 18 families and suborders, reveal the greatest promise (Barclay and Perdue, 1976—a paper that presents many further details of interest).

Even though several categories of plants appear to be worthwhile targets for research, the FOSI approach was discarded in 1975, due to the repetitive recurrence of known compounds; that is, most of the active materials were related to those previously found.

Folklore Strategy

Beyond the FOSI concept, what other "silver bullet" approaches could the scientists devise? Another possible line of attack apparently lay with the "folklore strategy" (Farnsworth, 1979; Farnsworth and Farley, 1980; Farnsworth and Kass, 1978; Douros and Suffness, 1978 and 1980; Duke, 1979 and 1980; Suffness and Douros, 1979). When plant species are selected on the basis of having been claimed useful as folkloric anticancer agents, about 20 percent show significant activity. "Witchdoctors" have traditionally used certain plants against warts, moles, and other skin blemishes, now considered by medical experts to be occasional indicators of beneath-the-skin tumors of malignant types.

Furthermore, when plants are selected not only on the basis of their folkloric applications, but also their use as anthelmintics, 30 percent reveal activity in test-tube tests. When they are selected on the basis of their use as fish poisons (frequently advocated for this purpose by the same witchdoctors who identify supposed medicinal applications), around 40 percent reveal activity; and when they are selected on the basis of their alleged use as arrow poisons (through consultations with the same witchdoctors), about 50 percent. Although laboratory success is no guarantee of success with humans, it is a necessary preliminary indicator.

Thus folkloric insights can, by pinpointing a high ratio of activity among the 3,000-plus plant species utilized by tribal peoples throughout the world, reduce research costs and time. Especially promising families appear to be the Apocynaceae (periwinkles and oleanders), Araceae (aroids), Dioscoreaceae (yams), Lauraceae (laurels), Leguminosae (legumes), Rutaceae (citrus fruits) and Zingiberaceae (including many spice and perfume species). Interestingly enough, three of these families – Apocynaceae, Leguminosae, and Rutaceae – have already appeared through the FOSI approach.

All in all, the plant-screening program found that, when the folklore approach was applied for retrospective appraisal, the yield of active anticancer plants investigated could have been increased by between 50 and 100 percent (Spjut and Perdue, 1976). Regrettably, however, the folklore approach was eventually consigned to the sidelines, for several reasons. First of all, there was a major problem with the remoteness of tribal cultures: scientists simply could not find out enough, fast enough, about traditional medicine. Then there was the problem of folk-medicine "psychology," with its distortive interpretations. Then there was a problem of botanical identification: witchdoctors do not use conventional names for plants. Then there were difficulties with complex plant concoctions, incorporating materials from several, if not many, species. Finally, and perhaps worst of all, there emerged only a small number, proportionately speaking, of novel "leads" through the folkloric approach.

Geographic Analysis

What other research strategies could the anticancer scientists devise? A third one appeared to hold promise, in the form of straightforward geographic analysis.

Certain zones and localities of the earth ostensibly prove better bets than others. For example, plants of tropical and subtropical climates show a higher percentage of anticancer activity, sometimes a tenfold greater proportion, than plants from temperate zones, which in turn rank higher than plants from boreal zones (Douros and Suffness, 1980; Suffness and Douros, 1979). The explanation for this finding could lie with the view that the tropics feature pronounced ecological competition, the temperate zones less, and the boreal zones least, resulting in greatest abundance and diversity of botanochemicals in the tropics, declining toward the poles. Put another way, there is a greater quality as well as quantity of botanochemicals in the tropics than elsewhere.

Among the tropical biomes, does any particular one show exceptional potential? As it turns out, there is probably a clear response to this key question: tropical moist forests, including (but not limited to) the rainforests. This one broad biome could well prove to be in a class of its own as a source of anticancer compounds – not only because of the abundance and diversity of its plant taxa, but because of the biome's evolutionary ecology, which has resulted in the highest percentage of alkaloid-bearing plants, plus the highest yield of alkaloids, of all Earth's biomes (Levin, 1976). Of the 3,000 plant species worldwide that are known to possess anticancer properties, at least 70 percent occur in the tropics – and we may eventually find an equal or greater number in tropical moist forests, which to date have been little explored for their potential in anticancer drugs. Meantime we can only speculate on the concentrated stocks of anticancer materials that ostensibly await investigation in this small sector of Earth's land surface, a mere 7 percent. Not surprisingly, researchers at the National Cancer Institute and at the Economic Botany Laboratory believe that the widespread elimination of tropical moist forests could ultimately represent a serious setback to the anticancer campaign.

Curiously enough, the second-most-promising ecological groups of plants are those that are at the opposite end of the climatic spectrum, in the arid zones. The high potential of these zones is thought to be due to the tendency for arid-zone plants, in response to environmental stress and "biological warfare," to produce toxins of many novel kinds – and it is some of these unusual compounds that can kill cancer cells. Moreover, arid-zone plants represent small and isolated families with highly divergent biochemistries; many of these plants occur in monotypic genera and families, again leading to unusually distinctive botanochemicals.

In short, arid-zone plants, with their "oddball" characteristics, offer outstanding promise for anticancer materials. For this reason, arid-zone endemics are of special interest to cancer researchers. So potent and diverse are the botanochemicals of arid-zone plants that if one were to analyze 100 plant species from Egypt and 100 from Brazil, the Egyptian plants could well reveal much more anticancer capacity than the Brazilian ones (Duke, 1979). In the semi-arid and arid lands of southern Africa, about 60 percent of plant species, in eleven families, could possess anticancer activity (Edwards, 1976).

On a country-by-country basis, we have a few clues, based upon a small-scale screen of an unevenly distributed proportion of plant species (Barclay and Perdue, 1976; Duke, 1979 and 1980). Plants of

Mexico and Central America reveal 3.8 percent activity (but Belize 4.9 percent and Costa Rica 5.6 percent); the West Indies 3.6 percent (but Puerto Rico 5.6 percent); tropical Africa, 4.1 percent (but Nigeria 7.5 percent and Ethiopia 8.3 percent); Pakistan 17.6 percent, Sri Lanka 12.4 percent, and India 4.8 percent; Papua New Guinea 7.8 percent, the Philippines 5.8 percent, and Samoa 5.7 percent; Israel 6 percent and Turkey 5.3 percent; the Netherlands 4.6 percent and Italy 4.3 percent; and the United States 2.9 percent.

Costs and Benefits of Cancer-Related Activities

It is appropriate to end this chapter with a brief review of costs and benefits of cancer-related activities. The combined budgets for anticancer work on the part of the National Cancer Institute and the Economic Botany Laboratory amounted to only $3 million per year. Of this sum, only a sixth was spent on collection of plants and materials, the rest on extraction, screening, isolation, and bioassays (Suffness and Douros, 1979). As already mentioned, the total of $3 million should be viewed within a context of the entire anticancer campaign in the United States, running at more than $1 billion per year.

As for the costs of cancer to U.S. society each year, a rough estimate places the figure at over $30 billion—a figure that ignores or denigrates "externalized" costs such as payments for workers' compensation. Although a figure of $30 billion may seem high, we should note that cancer is the only major fatal disease whose incidence is increasing. Adjusted death rates show that, during the period 1933–1970, cancer mortality increased by about 11 percent per year; and during the 1970s the increase was still more striking. A person born today faces a 27 percent probability of contracting cancer by the age of 85, by contrast with a person born in 1950, with about a 20 percent probability.

Viewed in this light, the expenditure for screening plant materials has been cost-effective, and U.S. society should allocate greater expenditures to the collection and screening of anticancer materials from wild plants. If the cost proves high, the return is also high; the market for anticancer drugs is expanding worldwide at around 25 percent per year and is projected to reach $2 billion by the mid-1980s (Brooke, 1978; International Marketing Statistics, 1981).

By the same token, of course, it would be an unusually sound investment for society to assign far greater priority to safeguarding wild plant habitats around the earth.

CHAPTER EIGHT

———————■———————

Animals and Medicine

In the days of my youth, I had the pleasure of spending three years at Oxford University. Even more fortunately, I found while there that I possessed some natural talent as a cross-country runner. I made the Oxford team, I was selected for a British universities team, and I ran against competitors from various countries of Europe – even against teams from Harvard and Yale.

Encouraged by my new-found talent, I took up running in a big way. After I went out to Kenya in the late 1950s, I captured the record (13.5 hours) for the up-and-down run of Kilimanjaro, Africa's highest mountain at 5860 meters (19,340 feet). More recently still, I have become a marathon runner, and at the age of almost 50 I find I can finish in the leading 7 percent of the huge fields at New York and Boston.

But my running career was almost cut short by troubles that arose in my last term at Oxford. I was getting pains in the small of my back. Doctors diagnosed nephritis, a disorder of the kidneys. Could I, they speculated, be producing excessive sweat while logging those dozens of training miles each week right around the year, eventually causing damage to my kidneys? Alarming as this diagnosis was, their prescription was even more worrying. They had no worthwhile treatment to offer for nephritis, and they urged me to lay off running entirely until the discomfort disappeared – which, they warned, it might never do because nephritis can persist throughout a sufferer's lifetime, in some instances even shortening the lifetime. Not, I speculated, a promising prospect.

Fortunately the discomfort faded away, and I was cleared of all further threat to my kidneys. But at the time, the doctors' reading of the situation was frightening, especially in that they could offer no worthwhile treatment for the disorder. Human kidneys are complex organs, and many of their disorders were little understood by the medical profession in those now-distant days of the 1950s.

How different the situation might have been if medical research had achieved more breakthroughs in understanding the human kidneys, by virtue of insights gained from other animals. One unlikely-seeming source is the desert pupfish of arid lands in the southwestern United States. Actually there are 23 species of the pupfish, tiny creatures confined to a few waterholes of California and Nevada. True, the fish is not much in appearance, usually a stubby and pop-eyed creature. So limited in numbers are some of these species that the entire stock of any one of several species could fit into a shoebox. Yet this minute creature contains, in its bodily mechanisms, some of the most remarkable adaptations known in the animal kingdom. It can tolerate temperatures that sink as low as 1 °C or rise as high as 42 °C; and it can survive in water with a salt content of 70 parts per 1,000 – twice as saline as seawater. It can even withstand a dissolved oxygen concentration as low as 0.5 part per million.

These capacities place the 23 pupfish species way ahead of all the other 7,000 species of freshwater fishes in terms of sheer "survival muscle." A pupfish may not offer a charismatic appearance to match that of a panda, nor a spectacular spirit to rival a tiger, and it certainly ranks lower on the scale for "cute" quotient than the koala bear. But milligram for milligram, we must reckon that the pupfish stands as one of the most capable creatures on Earth when it comes to making out in tough circumstances. Because it is so threatened (lots of thirsty people want to drain those waterholes), conservationists have tried to safeguard it in captivity. But because of its refined life-style, the best aquaria are just not good enough for it.

Due to its exceptional capacity to handle salinity, the pupfish is helping medical researchers with the nature of kidney diseases in humans. Hence it may help with an eventual breakthrough for nephritis and other difficult disorders of human kidneys. In addition it may serve researchers who seek ways for humans to withstand extreme temperatures. To quote a National Science Foundation report:

> The extreme conditions of the pupfish habitats tell us something about the creature's extraordinary kidney function and thermoregulatory system. . . . They can serve as useful biological models for future research on the workings of the kidney in humans, and on the prospects for human survival in seemingly hostile environments – and man, in the opinion of many ecologists, will need all the help he can get in understanding and adapting to arid areas that are expanding around the earth (National Science Foundation, 1977).

Such, then, is one of the esoteric ways in which animals can serve the cause of human health. Let us remember the obscure illustration

The desert pupfish, one of the tiniest vertebrates on Earth, can endure some of the most extreme temperatures and most saline water environments known. It thereby contributes a research model for scientists who look for ways to enable humans to adapt to unusual heat and cold, and it throws light on research into human kidney failings. We might well remember these contributions of the pupfish when next we hear someone asking questions like "What good is a snail darter?" (Credit: Prof. Barbara Kingsolver, Office of Arid Lands Studies, University of Arizona, Tucson)

of the pupfish when next we encounter a controversy over the fate of insignificant-seeming creatures such as the snail darter.

Many other animals supply benefits to modern medicine. All in all, however, the animal kingdom does not, thus far at least, supply nearly as much support for modern medicine as does the plant kingdom. In terms of utilitarian applications, the contribution of animals may be only one-twentieth to one-fortieth that of plants. As discussed earlier (see Prologue), there are sound reasons for this state of affairs. Animals have not had to develop nearly so many biodynamic compounds in their body chemistry as is the case with plants, in order to ward off threats from their environments. When an animal encounters a problem, it can simply move away. Plants can't.

Alkaloids in Animals

Predictably, we find that those key compounds that contribute so much to modern medicine, the alkaloids, are not nearly as widespread among animals as among plants. Scientists have found a few alkaloids in the musk deer and in the Canadian beaver, among a few other mammals. They have found a good number in insects. The best source of animal alkaloids, however, appears to be in creatures that may not immediately spring to mind – marine organisms. In their concentrated communities such as tropical coral reefs, marine creatures encounter many of the same environmental threats and ecological stresses that characterize the plant kingdom (see Chapter 9, "Marine Life and Medicine").

As with alkaloids, so with other biochemical compounds. In terms of, for example, the anticancer campaign, animals offer much less potential than plants. To date, the National Cancer Institute outside Washington, D.C., has examined extracts from some 3,000 animals; 547 species, scattered broadly across 402 genera, have yielded 646 instances of confirmed anticancer activity (Douros and Suffness, 1980). Interestingly, it appears that insects, by proportion to overall numbers, may offer great promise among the animals – an encouraging finding in view of the vast numbers of insect species, probably somewhere between 3 and 7 million. Mollusks, including snails, may help with research into the nature and origins of cancer, insofar as they rank among animal groups that do not contract cancer. A similar candidate could be the bison: Not one of 50,000 bison examined has been found to suffer from cancer of whatever form. If immunologists can isolate the factors that seem to keep the bison free of cancer, they may take a solid stride toward understanding what causes cancer – and what could prevent it.

Miscellaneous Medicinals

When we check out all the sundry medicinals that we obtain from animals, we find there are relatively few major items but a sizable stock of minor items. We have already noted in Chapter 6 that as many as one-half of all medicines, drugs, and pharmaceuticals sold in the United States each year, both prescription and nonprescription items, are derived from natural origins. Of this one-half, only around one in eight medicines is derived from animals (excluding microorganisms). Other developed nations show a similar breakdown in their medicinals from natural origins. The overall value of this commerce now amounts to over $40 billion per year, and we can put the animal contribution at just over $5 billion – rather more than a few pennies.

To list just a few animal examples: Blowfly larvae secrete a substance, alantoin, that promotes healing of deep wounds, decaying tissues, and osteomyelitis; the European blister beetle provides cantharidin, used in the treatment of disorders in the urogenital system; the blood-sucking leech contains hirudin, a material that serves as a valuable anticoagulant of human blood. Curiously, the venom of several creatures also can help modern medicine. Bee venom is used to counter arthritis. The venom of several snake species can be utilized as a nonaddictive pain-killer and also offers promise for treatment of thrombotic disorders (Neill, 1974). A snake of Brazil, the jaceracea (about 2 meters long), harbors material in its venom for the drug captopril, which helps many of the 25 million Americans who suffer from high blood pressure and other hypertension problems; captopril is especially helpful for those people who fail to respond to conventional treatments. The venom of a Malaysian pit viper related to the rattlesnake is commonly used as an anticoagulant, an agent that prevents the formation of blood clots that may cause heart attacks. Even toads may assist us. All toads secrete skin substances with toxic chemicals that could one day yield important drugs. An unusually good source could be the Houston toad – one of the most endangered vertebrates in the United States.

Not only can animals yield drugs, but they can help the medical cause in indirect fashions. As we have noted in Chapter 6, malaria ranks among the most widespread diseases on Earth. Reduced to low levels by insecticides during the 1950s, it has bounced back as mosquitoes have become resistant to toxic chemical sprays. So an answer may lie with a larvivorous fish, known scientifically as *Gambusia* and popularly as "the mosquito fish." It gobbles up insect larvae in its native habitats of the eastern Mediterranean (Legner and Fisher, 1980). A similar function is performed in California by certain flatworms of the genus *Mesostoma*, which paralyze mosquito larvae in rice fields (Case and Washino, 1979). These species could be considered for introduction into malarial zones in many parts of the world, provided that they do not conflict with creatures other than mosquitoes in their new environments.

Animals as Models for Medical Research

So much for a selection of animals' contributions to medicine in the form of their biodynamic compounds and life-styles. Numerous and diverse as these are, they are far surpassed by the medical insights that animals give us through their role as models for research.

The physiology of many creatures affords clues to the origins and nature of many human ailments. Butterflies, wasps, mice, salamanders, toads, sea urchins, and fruit flies have helped us with our basic understanding of genetics and embryology in humans. They have thereby supplied us with clues on how to tackle genetic defects such as Down's syndrome and sickle-cell anemia. For example, the African mocker swallowtail butterfly features unusual genetic processes that govern the production of its different color forms; and these genetic charcteristics have enabled scientists to fathom the mysteries of human genetic blood disease that leads to "rhesus babies." Still more important in the long run, the insights afforded by these creatures into our understanding of human genetics and embryology may eventually assist our research on cancer, which in essence amounts to a breakdown in the genetic control of cells.

Diseases of the heart and circulatory system may be illuminated by elephants in Africa (Sikes, 1966). The elephant sometimes deposits fatty substances on its artery walls, causing partial obstruction of its blood passages. This is an ailment that leads to stiffening of the joints and early signs of old age; it can even lead to heart failure, with the occasional elephant apparently succuming to thrombosis. Hitherto, coronary disease has been attributed mainly to animal fats in the diet, leaving the vegetarian elephant an unlikely candidate. A possible secondary factor, however, could lie with environmental tension. Confined elephants, restricted to parks and other limited habitats, could be reacting with much the same symptoms that afflict humans in stress-filled habitats. Elephants in remoter areas, where they still enjoy a very diversified diet and still roam across wide tracts of countryside free of migration barriers and molestation by people, do not show signs of failing health as do elephants of grasslands and scrublands shared with humans. Remarkably enough, certain elephants reveal lesions of the aorta, with highly similar rates for all habitats. Although calcification of the arteries differs from one place to another for confined elephants, the atherosclerosis does not – a finding that suggests the atherosclerosis is a hormonal complication, a reflection of social disruption for the elephant. We can perhaps draw some obvious parallels for human behavior patterns in crowded communities.

Similarly, the cheetah could eventually present benefits for human health. The animal can accelerate from a standing start to 70 kilometers per hour in a few strides, and it can then maintain a 100-kilometer per hour chase for several hundred meters. The creature obviously possesses an efficient heart, together with finely-

The African elephant sometimes suffers from a thickening of the arteries. Since the creature enjoys an entirely vegetarian diet, the blame cannot be laid on cholesterol and other substances in animal products. Scientists believe that the trouble could lie with the social crowding that afflicts certain modern elephant populations as a result of human encroachment on their living space. Hence, research into elephant physiology, especially hormonal reactions, may supply clues to arterial defects in humans. (Credit: Dr. Norman Myers)

tuned respiratory and circulatory systems, that allow it to sustain a sudden and severe oxygen debt. Hence the cheetah could present clues for treatment of heart disease, blood pressure, and circulatory disorders in humans.

One of the longest-standing scourges of humankind, and still one of the most persistent, is Hansen's disease, or leprosy, which afflicts at least 15 million people in developing countries. Despite decades of research efforts, scientists have not properly unraveled the mechanism of the disease. There have been plenty of human sufferers to observe, but that is not the same as saying there are plenty of groups on which to experiment with drugs. Nor, until very recently, have scientists been able to track down an animal species that contracts leprosy: So far as the scientists could discern the disease was confined

The cheetah, one of Africa's more threatened species, can sustain an immense and sudden "oxygen debt" when it launches into its high-speed chase after a gazelle or other prey. To tolerate this oxygen debt, the cheetah must have a very efficient heart, lungs, and blood-transport network. Physiologists believe that research on the cheetah may yield insights into coronary, respiratory, and circulatory systems in humans. (Credit: Dr. Norman Myers)

to humans, making it much harder to devise a treatment. Fortunately, scientists have now come across two animal species that oblige by contracting leprosy. One is the armadillo, which has greatly promoted research in recent years (Convit and Pinardi, 1974; Maugh, 1982). The armadillo's body temperature is 2–5°C lower than that of most other mammals, and because of this feature, or possibly because of its weak immune system, the armadillo serves as a suitable incubator for the bacilli that cause the disease. When a typical armadillo is injected with diseased cells, it can supply sufficient spleen and liver tissue to provide as many as 10^{12} bacilli for each of the 150–250 grams of tissue, an ample quantity for use in production of an antileprosy vaccine.

The second animal to assist is the Mangabey monkey, which also contracts leprosy. As a primate and thus a close relative of humans, the monkey serves as a first-rate research model and is greatly increasing our hopes of coming up with a cure for the dreaded disease (Meyers et al., 1981).

It is because of their close relatedness to humans that primates are especially valuable for medical research, contributing to the development of many drugs and vaccines. For example, the chimpanzee – of which only 50,000 are left in the wild – is the sole creature other than humans on which the safety of antihepatitis vaccines can be tested. The cotton-topped marmoset, a species of monkey susceptible to cancer of the lymphatic system, is used to help produce a potent anticancer vaccine; tests with the monkey show that we can possibly prevent lymphatic cancer by immunization (Laufs and Steinke, 1975). Related work with the marmoset reveals that a virus thought to be implicated in at least some human cancers can occur in the marmoset; the same virus also can occur in the owl monkey. The African green monkey serves as a research model for a virus that causes diarrhea in human infants – with an appalling death rate among babies in developing nations (Wyatt *et al.*, 1980). The baboon assists in resolving urinary incontinence in humans. Various primates at the Penrose Research Laboratory at the Philadelphia Zoo have served in the development of a standard tuberculosis skin test for humans.

We are even learning important secrets from the black bear. The bear hibernates for five months during the winter, relying on hormonal adaptations that are assisting scientists in developing a low-protein and low-fluid diet for humans suffering from kidney failure (Nelson, 1977). Also contributing to kidney research is the springbok, a gazelle of southern Africa. As many as one American in 500 suffers from polycystic disease of the kidneys, an ailment that has not been encountered in any domestic or laboratory animal, making research difficult – until Professors David Senior and Elliott Jacobson of the University of Florida came across it in the springbok.

Other illustrations are legion, too numerous to list here. Let us conclude with the Florida manatee, a species so endangered that only 850 survive in the wild. The manatee possesses blood with poor clotting capabilities, a trait that helps research on hemophilia.

So much, then, for major forms of animal life. We should not overlook those lowly forms of life that are neither plant nor animal, and that are too small for us to see with the naked eye, hence too small for our passing attention. These are the micro-creatures, including viruses. A standard attitude might be to think that we can do without viruses. The sooner they are made extinct, the better for us, and for our children in perpetuity. An obvious example is the smallpox virus, which has been backed into a corner by modern medicine to the extent that no human being suffers from the disease; the organism now exists only in a few flasks in the laboratory. Should we, by conscious and rational decision, obliterate this manifestation of life's diversity? Or should we keep it alive, on the grounds that it does not cost us much to preserve, and that it may one day, one remote day, serve our needs?

In response to the second question, many people might feel that the cornered virus cannot conceivably assist our welfare, whether now or in the indefinite future. But wait a moment. Let us bear in mind that viruses, including many pathogenic species, have been the sources of many of the momentous discoveries in biology during the recent past. If we were to lose, let alone dispatch, a single such species, we could eventually find that we have deprived ourselves of an important asset in our research on comparative biochemistry and genetics, even for basic investigations on the nature and origin of life.

Too vague, some might say. Curiously enough, however, the smallpox virus could offer direct utilitarian benefits for us. Scientists are pretty sure that it will assist our studies on the antigenic relationships among a number of similar viruses, including the monkeypox and other viruses that have emerged into growing prominence as the smallpox virus has given way to our eradication campaigns. If ever these smallpox-related viruses were to threaten our health, the smallpox virus itself could, as a research model, prove exceptionally important to us. In addition to supporting analytic research, the smallpox virus could help us in a still more critical endeavor, to develop a recombinant virus as a basis for an improved vaccine. A strategy along these lines has recently been applied in developing vaccines against influenza, and scientists believe that a parallel approach could be utilized with respect to the smallpox virus (Dixon, 1976).

All forms of animal life, in short, can serve the needs of modern medicine. As in the case of medical research involving the plant kingdom, scientists have made only a bare start on the challenge of tapping our fellow animal species for the many ways in which they can support human health. If researchers could undertake a systematic investigation of all that the animal world has to offer to modern medicine, they could accomplish much more progress than we can realistically envisage now.

CHAPTER NINE

—————————■—————————

Marine Life
and Medicine

One of the delights of my life in Kenya has been to take a trip to our beach cottage on the Indian Ocean just north of Mombasa. There I headed for a marine park offshore, where I would lie in the super-warm water and goggle at wildlife sights that, in color and variety, surpass anything I might see in the game parks on land.

I have often wondered why there should be such spectacular diversity in these coral reef ecosystems. Of course the East African coast, like the eastern coast of any continent, is fed by warm ocean currents—and it is these currents that are the key element supporting coral reef ecosystems with their teeming fish life and myriad other marine organisms. Without warm salt water, coral reefs cannot exist. But why, just why, should the warmth be such a crucial factor? Why should these tropical shores support many more kinds of life, in such concentrated profusion, than any other ecosystem on Earth except for the richest rainforests?

After years of study I have picked up some clues about what makes the undersea world tick with such complexity and color. I have worked out that the marine community develops ways of its own to look after itself—notably in the form of chemical compounds of multitudinous forms. Fortunately for humankind, these compounds supply us with an exceptional array of medicinal and pharmaceutical products to support our health when we are many horizons away from coral reefs and their secluded beauties.

Numbers and Variety of Marine Species

The seas contain, roughly speaking, 200,000 species of animals and plants. This amounts to 2–4 percent of Earth's 5–10 million species. Not many. But these marine species are confined to only a very small part of the 352 million square kilometers of ocean that cover almost three-quarters of the planet. The fact that marine species are restricted to such small sectors of the marine realm is due to two factors. First, only a few thousand of the species are pelagic, i.e., able to live freely in water. The remainder are benthic, i.e., they need to live on or in the seabed. Second, the great bulk of benthic species occur in shallow or intertidal waters, especially those of tropical seas. Less than 0.5 percent of all marine species live in the hadal zone – at a depth of more than 6 kilometers – yet this zone accounts for over two-thirds of the oceans (Cushing and Walsh, 1976).

In short, then, we can say that 90 percent of marine species live in, at most, 50 million km² of the oceans' waters – and the bulk of them in far less. So, although the marine realm as a whole possesses far fewer life forms than terrestrial zones, a relatively small sector of the oceans harbors a remarkably large proportion of their species.

However deficient they may be quantitatively, the seas' species are qualitatively diverse to an exceptional degree. Indeed they tend to reveal a genetic range that often surpasses that of terrestrial organisms. It is by virtue of both their taxonomic diversity and their genetic variability that marine communities supply an abundance of esoteric materials for modern medicine.

Abundance of Biocompounds

How is it, one might ask, that marine organisms often contain proportionately more biologically active compounds than is the case with terrestrial organisms? There appear to be at least two major explanations.

First off, there is the fact that, despite the oceans' relatively small number of species, they harbor some two-thirds of all animal phyla. Something similar applies to plants when algae are included. This means that, whereas taxonomic and anatomical relationships tend to be sparser, they likewise tend to be more distinctive than is the case with species on land. By extension, we encounter greater uniqueness in the biochemistry of marine organisms, especially with respect to their antibiosis.

Second, the overall paucity of species in the marine world is offset by the exceptional concentration of species in one small sector of the realm – tropical shorelines, particularly tropical coral reef ecosystems. A concentration of species in limited localities makes for competition, lots of it – and competition throws up specialist life-styles, often expressed through biocompounds of many unique forms (for defense, etc.). Why there should be this concentration of species along tropical shorelines, we are less than certain, but we have some strong clues. A key factor seems to lie with the phenomenon of environmental stability, notably concerning the seasons of the year – or, in the tropics, lack of seasons, i.e., aseasonality. In tropical zones with plenty of warmth and moisture right around the year, we almost always find plenty of food stocks right around the year. In the temperate zones and in the higher latitudes, by contrast, plant growth tails off for several months of the year, with the result that there is a prolonged famine every little while for animal life.

A situation with food aplenty at all times, and food with lots of variety, generally means that great numbers of species have evolved to take advantage of the unceasing feast. In fact, many more species emerge than in environments that are characterized by seasonality. Thus, at any rate, runs a consensus of scientific thinking (Emlen, 1973; May, 1973; MacArthur, 1972; Schopf, 1972; Valentine, 1973).

To illustrate this line of thinking in practice, let us look at one of the most diverse invertebrate groups of the oceans, the prosobranch gastropods ("fore-gilled" snails, whelks, conchs, limpets, and their relatives). Numerous at the equator, they become steadily sparser as we move toward the poles. Along the continental shelves of the eastern Atlantic, for instance, the predatory gastropod fauna suddenly becomes markedly more diverse as one moves southwards across the line of latitude 40°N (roughly opposite Madrid). Along European shorelines north of this line, there is little gastropod variety, not only at the level of species but also at the levels of genera and families. Further southwards, however, there is much greater variety, again at several levels. Significantly, this 40° line of latitude is roughly the point at which winter no longer appears, allowing plant growth to continue virtually throughout the year. In turn, this means that plant-eaters have a broader choice of food stocks, so they can be more selective and specialized in their diets. Put another way, it means there is more room for more feeders of many sorts. In a word, more "ecological living space" for many more species.

In turn yet again, the abundance of permanent food supplies means that creatures do not have to roam around looking for their next meal. They can afford to stay in one place, since there is almost always enough food at hand. Organisms of this type are sessile (staying in one place, often attached to something, but not immobile – they may have tentacles or other means of whipping up local excitement). Wildlife communities of tropical zones, such as coral reef communities, tend to be dominated by sessile organisms. In point of fact, the corals, sponges, and the majority of other species that live with them are sessile; these species form the "backbone" of coral reefs. In this sense, coral reef communities correspond with plant communities on land, in which individuals are, by definition, "fixed": examples include trees, flowers, and grasses.

Furthermore, most other inhabitants of coral reefs are characterized by low mobility. Creatures such as starfish, sea urchins, polychaete worms, and gastropod mollusks, while being able to move around somewhat, tend to remain within relatively tiny territories and home ranges. True, certain creatures, notably fishes, do not remain in direct physical contact with the substratum—in this case the reef structure. But many fish, not only coral reef fish themselves but anemone fish and "cleaner fish" such as wrasse, are, to introduce another term, "site-attached," which means that they generally stay close to the reef.

All in all, then, we can say that the great majority of coral reef organisms are sessile or otherwise "tied" to the reef structure. This means that they are unusually subject to sundry hazards. Sessile organisms cannot flee from predators, they risk infection by viruses and bacteria, they may become overgrown by their neighbors, and they may even be "settled on" by mobile larvae of sessile species.

How to cope with these hazards? The main response of the sessile organisms is to generate complex biocompounds, particularly toxins, to ward off predators, etc. These toxins, with their extreme variety of forms, assist the life-styles of their producers in other, and not so obvious, ways. A coral reef community, featuring large numbers of species in small areas, is an arena of intense competition for food and space. A sound strategy for a creature such as a sponge to acquire "elbow room" is to produce a toxic compound that inhibits the growth of neighboring creatures.

So widespread is the toxin-producing phenomenon that most major coral reef phyla—not only the vertebrates, but the echinoderms (starfish, sea urchins, and sea cucumbers), mollusks, sponges, and coelenterates (jellyfish, corals, and anemones)—feature numerous toxins as key factors in their mode of life. Many of these toxins, notoriously more potent than more conventional toxins from terrestrial sources, help scientists in their research into basic life processes, illuminating certain physiological phenomena and biochemical activities that occur in living tissue. Hence the importance of the puffer fish, porcupine fish, and the sand fish in enlarging our understanding of evolution; by virtue of their tetrodotoxin, we have been enabled to grasp some basic clues of what makes an organism "work."

We can even derive insights into the many questions of evolution by looking at sponges and their unique biocompounds. Sponges often contain histamines, substances that we are familiar with as drugs. Ac-

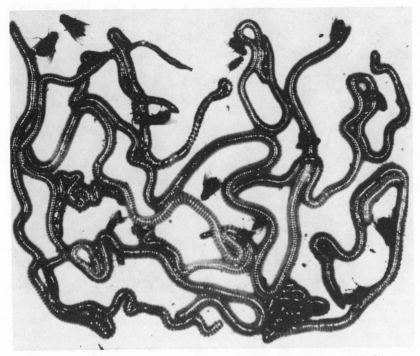

Marine annelids offer support for terrestrial agriculture through biocompounds that assist in the development of an unusually effective insecticide. (Credit: Drs. Yoshiro Hashimoto and Tomotoshi Okaichi, Osborn Laboratories of Marine Sciences, New York)

cording to certain canons of established science, such molecules can hardly be expected to exist in primitive life forms. Yet they do; and this phenomenon substantiates findings of comparative biochemistry, to the effect that fundamental life processes and biochemical metabolic cycles are more or less similar in organisms ranging across the entire phylogenetic spectrum. The lowly sponge thus sheds light on some central functions of life on our planet – to our current knowledge, the only cosmic cinder that supports life.

Lots of other categories of biocompounds are abundant in marine organisms. For instance, hormones and pheromones, complex materials that appear to serve as a mode of "chemical communication," help to maintain dynamic equilibrium among the organisms of their ecosystems (Ruggieri, 1976). Much the same applies to a variety of other metabolites that can serve to inhibit other organisms or to foster symbiotic relationships. We can say something similar about a host of

Many species of sponge, of which a vase-shaped type is featured here, harbor antibacterial substances, and thus make considerable contributions to modern medicine. (Credit: Dr. George D. Ruggieri, Osborn Laboratories of Marine Sciences, New York)

related biological activities that play a salient role in promoting ecological harmony within marine ecosystems.

In sum, we can go so far as to say that marine ecosystems may reveal more complex relationships between species, and more sophisticated organization among their communities, than is the case with terrestrial ecosystems (Anderson *et al.*, 1981; Bakus and Green, 1974; Braekman, 1981; Jackson and Buss, 1975; Kaul, 1979; Ruggieri, 1976; Talbot *et al.*, 1978). As a consequence, many marine organisms contain biocompounds that feature novel types of form and function – distinctively different from the great bulk of biocompounds found in land-based organisms. Such enormous reserves of unusual substances occur in the seas that this realm could prove to be the main source of start-point materials for medicines and drugs in the foreseeable future. To help us get a grasp of this potential, let us take a lengthy look at the ocean's capacity to serve our health needs.

Biomedical Potential of the Oceans

The tiny fraction of marine organisms examined to date has yielded myriad extracts and compounds (Chapman, 1980; Cushing and

Their unprepossessing appearance notwithstanding, sponges, like this "red beard sponge" from Long Island waters, contain antibacterial substances that are in growing demand to meet new medicinal needs. (Credit: Dr. George D. Ruggieri, Osborn Laboratories of Marine Sciences, New York)

Walsh, 1976; Farnsworth, 1969; Kaul, 1979; Kaul and Sinderman, 1978; Piatelli, 1979; Rinehart *et al.* 1981a and b; Ruggieri, 1976; Ruggieri and Rosenberg, 1978; Scheuer, 1979; Wolf, 1978). Their biomedical characteristics are very diverse, including antimicrobial, antiviral, cardioactive, cytotoxic (cell-poisoning, of interest in anticancer treatment), neurophysiologic, and psychotropic – and for blood, both coagulant and anticoagulant activity. Indeed, our experience to date suggests that the marine world could offer us a series of "wonder drugs" to rival antibiotics and tranquilizers.

First of all, let us consider a few categories of biomedical compounds, starting with antibiotics. Although only one group of antibiotics has hitherto been developed from marine life, there are probably antibiotic organisms in every class of marine creatures. This applies especially to algae, whether of red, brown, or green types. An antibiotic compound has been extracted from a fungus gathered in the vicinity of sewage discharge along the coast of Sardinia. The composition of this compound is similar to that of penicillin, and it is effective against a wide spectrum of bacteria, including, notably, those that are resistant to penicillin – a characteristic that it owes to its insensitivity to penicillinase, a bacterial enzyme capable of destroying penicillin (Piatelli, 1979).

As for antiviral drugs, they are rare from whatever source. Just a few broadly useful ones are available to date. Our current antivirals kill only one class of viruses. Fortunately, a promising new product, didemnin, has been derived from sea squirts—gelatinous creatures that cling to rocks. If didemnin proves clinically acceptable, it could be used to attack at least two major classes of viruses (McClure, 1980; Rinehart *et al.*, 1981a and b). According to laboratory tests, didemnin helps against a broad range of DNA and RNA viruses, ranging from cold and influenza viruses to herpes and meningitis viruses. And as revealed in research by Professor Li Hsieng Li of the University of Illinois at Urbana, didemnin can double the life expectancy of animals suffering from leukemia.

Cold-causing viruses can also be inhibited through an active agent derived from several species of seaweed. According to preliminary investigations, the same agent can prove active against several eye infections. At least one type of influenza virus can be resisted by extracts from three species of sea stars, relatives of starfish (Ruggieri and Rosenberg, 1978).

As a result of these widely-hailed discoveries, there are now prospects of curing a wide range of diseases caused by viruses. We could even be on the verge of a breakthrough on a par with what penicillin has achieved against diseases caused by bacteria.

Perhaps the most promising source of antiviral agents is a Caribbean sponge (Schmitz *et al.*, 1981). A compound from this sponge proves effective against herpes encephalitis, a deadly brain infection that strikes many thousands of people each year, and against which there has hitherto been no worthwhile drug available. Indeed herpes, in its various forms, affects 20 million Americans; and one particular strain, genital herpes, is expanding at epidemic rates, from 30,000 cases annually in the mid-1960s to way beyond a quarter of a million annually in the late 1970s. The Caribbean sponge furthermore appears to offer potential against leukemia. Yet more remarkable again, it could even help with organ-transplant operations, insofar as it could suppress the multiplication of white cells that are responsible for organ rejection.

Still other sponges yield compounds that furnish clues to the manufacture of new cortisonelike drugs that could help victims of arthritis (Schmitz *et al.*, 1981). Altogether there are about 5,000 species of marine sponges; one of the largest measures 10 cm long and is able to filter almost 80 liters of water every 24 hours. One particular sponge, the "heavenly blue sponge," has proved deserving of its name by yielding a compound that attacks the bacteria responsible for gastroenteritis—an acute inflammation of the stomach and intestinal linings that poses a severe threat to human infants, accounting for many deaths among them.

Sponges can also serve as abundant sources of antibiotics. At the Osborn Laboratories of Marine Sciences at the New York Aquarium, Drs. George Ruggieri and Ross Nigrelli and their colleagues have investigated more than 120 species of sponges, finding that almost half turn out to contain antibiotic substances (Ruggieri, 1975 and 1976).

Especially useful could be those antibiotics that act against tuberculosis, fungus infection, and staphylococci. The last named are a highly contagious group of bacteria responsible for infections including boils, carbuncles, acne, bladder inflammation, blood poisoning, and bacterial pneumonia. Hospital staff regard staphylococci as an exceptional problem, because they can spread with such dreadful speed and include strains that have become resistant to penicillin and many other antibiotics. Insofar as we have not solved the problem of resistant staphylococci, we can rejoice in the discovery of an extract from clams, oysters, and abalone that, called Paolin I (after the Chinese word for abalone), arrests many other harmful bacteria, including the streptococci that cause painful "strep throat," wound infections, bronchial pneumonia, tonsillitis, and scarlet fever. A related agent, Paolin II, inhibits herpes virus, reduces the incidence of some tumors, and offers promise against influenza, blood poisoning, and polio.

If we were to review all prospective exploitation of marine substances for medicine, there would be enough material for an entire book on this one topic. So let us discuss a few types separately after a quick concluding look at a few further examples that illustrate the extraordinary range of biocompounds available. Several marine algae yield sterols, which reduce cholesterol in the blood; one product from algae keeps blood from clotting, while another hastens coagulation; and a brown alga yields an amino acid with hypertensive properties (Piatelli, 1979). Sand fishes, porcupine fishes, and puffer fishes yield tetrodotoxin, a biocompound that serves as a local anesthetic, as a painkiller, and as a muscle relaxant for cases of terminal cancer; it offers 160,000 times as much potency as cocaine in blocking nerve impulses. The stingray yields a potent cardiac-depressant material. Sea cucumbers harbor a substance that may prove more effective than digitalis in treatment of certain heart conditions. Extracts from the octopus can be used as an anesthetic. (The octopus paralyzes its prey by injecting a secretion from its salivary gland, whereupon, although the victim remains totally insensible, its heart continues to beat normally, thus opening up the prospect that this secretion or "poison" from the octopus could offer much help in the modern surgical theater.) A squid yields an enzyme that neutralizes a type of deadly nerve gas, potentially very important for civil defense measures in times of warfare.

A jellyfish contains a protein that can be stimulated to glow when there is calcium or strontium in the vicinity. This bioluminescent protein, aequorin, provides a very sensitive means of detecting calcium changes in humans—these changes serving as indicators of cellular disfunctions, some of which may signal the start of cancers and cardiac troubles.

Anticancer Drugs from the Seas

Perhaps the most important of all drugs from the seas will prove to be anticancer materials. The marine realm has already supplied us with many start-point materials for anticancer drugs, in compounds derived from corals, sea anemones, sharks, stingrays, mollusks, segmented worms, sponges, sea squirts, sea cucumbers, proboscis worms, and the horseshoe crab (Braekman, 1981; Cushing and Walsh, 1976; Farnsworth, 1969; Kaul, 1979; Kaul and Sindermann, 1978; Piatelli, 1979; Rinehart *et al.*, 1981a and b; Ruggieri, 1976; Ruggieri and Rosenberg, 1978; Scheuer, 1973; Wolf, 1978). For example, the horseshoe crab possesses a serum that serves to isolate tumor cells and white blood cells from the whole blood of cancer patients. Sharks' livers contain lipids that enhance human resistance to cancer. Certain clams yield extracts that delay or prevent the development of cancer in mice. All in all, more than 500 marine animals yield extracts with anticancer activity. The toxins of both the porcupine fish and the puffer fish, as already noted, offer a palliative for terminal cancer. Even seaweeds produce compounds that help in cancer therapy. Patients treated with these compounds find their appetites improve, they are relieved of nausea, and they suffer less pain following surgery and radiation.

One of the most promising anticancer products to be discovered in the marine realm is holothurin, derived primarily from sea cucumbers, starfish, and other spine-spiked creatures known collectively as echinoderms (Ruggieri, 1975). Holothurin may offer a further contribution in its treatment of coronary disorders, administered in conjunction with digitalis and other heart stimulants.

Of more than 2,000 species tested by the U.S. National Cancer Institute, around 40 percent of active species turn out to belong to a single phylum, Coelenterata—the hydroids, jellyfish, sea anemones, and corals. Corals in particular, and especially the gorgonian species in the Caribbean, yield pure cytotoxic compounds, notably crassin acetate (Braekman, 1981; Kaul, 1979). In across-the-board terms, however, it appears that every major marine phylum except for the algae feature natural products with anticancer properties. Equally interesting, the materials occur regularly in most if not all sectors of each phylum. Overall the yield from confirmed active species amounts to 10.9 percent – with a yield around Puerto Rico 15.1 percent, around Fiji 16.2 percent, off the coast of Australia 16.5 percent, and around Grand Cayman 21.2 percent (Rinehart *et al.*, 1981a and b; Siegel *et al.*, 1970; Weinheimer *et al.*, 1978). Significantly, all these marine zones are subject to varying degrees of pollution (which we will consider as a separate topic).

Contraceptive Materials

At a time of urgent search for a safer and more effective contraceptive pill, especially one of the "morning after" type, a breakthrough may have been achieved with a hormonelike prostaglandin extracted from a coral (Kaul, 1979). When first isolated , the compound did not prove to be biologically active after the manner of most naturally occurring prostaglandins. Nonetheless it attracted much interest, for obvious reasons, from the academic profession and from drug enterprises. Eventually, an eight-step synthetic procedure has converted the prostaglandin into physiologically active form.

This prostaglandin, or prostaglandin precursor, has stimulated further search for natural occurring, active prostaglandins. As a result, one has come to light with the capacity to supply large amounts of a much-needed hormonal substance that is otherwise obtainable from mammalian tissues only in trace amounts (Kaul, 1979).

A promising source of prostaglandins, according to Dr. Gustavo A. Garcia de la Mora of the University of Mexico, lies with corals of the Caribbean. Along the coast of the Yucatan Peninsula, a form of black coral grows over 1 meter high, producing larger quantities and higher concentrations of a type of prostaglandin than hitherto discovered elsewhere. (Conservationists need not worry about the prospect of corals being exploited for their biocompounds, provided that it is done on a sustainable basis. When a coral "tree" loses a single branch to a harvester, it can regenerate quite quickly.) Altogether, along its Caribbean coast, Mexico possesses 300 kilometers of barrier reef, which, according to preliminary research, look like a very rich source of biologically active compounds – but look equally likely to become a site of some of the worst marine pollution known.

Marine Organisms as Research Models for Biomedicine

The female octopus, with its specialized glandular mechanisms, offers clues to the aging process of body cells in humans. Similarly, a number of marine fishes can serve as models for the aging process. Salient examples include the Pacific salmon and the steelhead trout. When the salmon migrates from the open sea into fresh water for spawning, it starts to feature progressive and irreversible hyperactivity of the adrenal cortex, excessive circulating body lipids (fats), and fatal arteriosclerosis. By contrast, the steelhead trout develops arteriosclerotic lesions upon migration into fresh water, but these lesions can sometimes be reversed when the trout returns to the open sea.

A host of other marine organisms supply us with research models. The hagfish, with no thymus gland, also has no immune system that could cause rejection of grafts – a trait that makes it an excellent subject for the study of skin grafts in humans. The anglerfish may also serve to foster research into problems associated with the rejection of human grafts and organ transplants. Sea urchins, with their relatively simple life cycles, allow researchers to observe the teratological effects of drugs, since adverse reactions can be noted in a matter of days instead of weeks or months as is generally the case with conventional laboratory animals.

Squids and the sea hare, with their specialized nervous systems, are especially valuable to neuroscientists for their crucial insights into our own nervous system. Research has distinguished 55 individual nerve cells in the sea hare, and has recognized about 1,000 more cells as members of "characteristic-sharing" clusters. The human nervous system, on the other hand, has proved too complex to be resolved into individual cells, although *some* cells can be identified. We have added to our knowledge of the human nervous system by investigating the giant axons of squids (these nerve fibers are up to 1,000-fold larger in cross section than any mammalian nerve fiber) and the neuronal apparatus of the electric eel; and we have added to our understanding of interrelationships between basic behavior and certain nerve circuits by examination of the sea hare's neuronal organization. It is not going too far to say that a useful step in understanding the human brain would be to understand first the simple neuronal circuits found in marine invertebrates (Kandel, 1979; Kaul, 1979).

Of special value as a model for scientific investigations is the liver of the shark (Wolf, 1978). The organ reveals a design and function that have apparently changed little in 400 million years. Architecturally

Many species of shark—a sand tiger shark is shown here—serve to assist the health of humans, notably through their usefulness in research into liver ailments and certain cancers. (Credit: New York Zoological Society)

similar to that of man, the shark's liver appears to perform more of a storage than a metabolic processing function. Some of the biosynthetic activities carried out in the enormously complex human liver are undertaken in the shark by the stomach and intestine, leaving the liver as a somewhat simpler "chemical laboratory" for study. Such biochemical transformations as take place in the shark's liver seem similar to some of those that occur in the human liver, but research on the shark's liver is more straightforward. For example, the shark's liver synthesizes a substance, trimethylamine oxide, for use in controlling osmotic pressure; the substance is manufactured with the aid of an enzyme that is akin to the human enzyme responsible for the detoxification of many foreign chemicals that make their way into the body. Thus an understanding of the regulatory processes of the shark's liver offers key insights into human pathophysiology. Furthermore, the shark's liver can sometimes manufacture albumin, a chemical that has marked relevance to hepatic disease in humans.

The liver of the dogfish, a small shark, also serves as a model for research (Kaul, 1979; Ronsivalli, 1978). The organ excretes bile pigments directly, by contrast with the bile pigments of a human that are conjugated before being expelled (and in which disorders of the conjugation process can cause jaundice in newborn infants). Studies of the dogfish liver could indicate how molecular mechanisms serve to transport materials across the membranes of liver cells. In addition, almost all bodily parts of this small shark feature heparinlike compounds, with potencies far beyond that of commercial heparin and with fewer undesirable side-effects. Thus these compounds offer much potential for use against blood clotting in the human circulatory system.

A species of clam serves as a first-rate model for study of abnormalities in mucus production; it also helps our insights into cystic fibrosis and other diseases of connective tissue (Kaul, 1979). On the basis of a structural model found in a sponge, pharmacologists can now synthesize algenic acid and other compounds for use against leukemia. The common starfish can serve as a "blueprint" for research into potential regrowth of human limbs. The starfish possesses an ability to regenerate body parts after injury; this capacity may teach us, according to Professor H. Eugene Lehman of the University of North Carolina, how to bring about more regeneration of human tissues and organs than the limited amount that occurs naturally.

Even the lowly horseshoe crab, a creature that has remained little changed for 200 million years, can serve the research needs of modern medicine (Cohen, 1979; Pearson, 1978; Pearson and Weary, 1980; Thomson, 1975). An armor-plated creature with a spiny tail, and as broad as a large saucepan, it is not a true crab at all, nor is it closely related to any other creature in the seas. So unique is it among the arthropods (animals with jointed bodies and jointed legs), that it ranks somewhere between the crustaceans and the spiders. In fact its closest relative must be reckoned a land-living spider.

The horseshoe crab can tolerate extremes of temperature and salinity. It can survive doses of radiation that would kill a human. Presumably able to last a year without eating, it consumes vast quantities of mollusks and mussels when it can; ten horseshoe crabs can clean out one square meter of crowded clam flat in a day, or the equivalent of 600 platefuls of fried clams in one year. Because of this appetite, the horseshoe crab has been widely persecuted, notably along the Atlantic seaboard of North America.

But the most curious characteristic of the horseshoe crab is the color of its blood. Of a hue to match the delicate aquamarine coloring of some tidal pools, the crab's blood is blue because of the copper-containing molecules that carry oxygen around the creature's circulatory system. More remarkable still, the blood quickly clots when it is exposed to bacterial endotoxins (chemical poisons released by some bacteria). It is this trait that makes the crab's blood an exceedingly sensitive diagnostic tool for modern medicine. Endotoxins surround us in all our daily activities, occurring in food and water, on our skin, and in our intestines. They do us no harm until they enter our bloodstream (which they can do through shock or severe illness or burns), whereupon even the slightest amount of endotoxin can bring severe illness or even death. Little wonder, then, that medical practitioners take great care with materials injected into patients in the form of intravenous fluids – for a trace of endotoxin could be disastrous. Using extracts from the horseshoe crab's blood, we can now detect endotoxin contamination at a level of one billionth of a gram per milliliter. Not only is the diagnostic test important for standard injections, but it is uniquely valuable in identifying a type of meningitis in children that proves fatal unless appropriate chemotherapy can be prescribed promptly.

Degradation of Marine Ecosystems

Marine ecosystems, and especially close-to-shore ecosystems, are undergoing much degradation (Chapman, 1977 and 1980; Council on Environmental Quality, 1980; Ehrlich *et al.*, 1977; Ray, 1981; Yanchinski, 1981). Notable examples include not only coral reefs of the tropics, but estuaries and intertidal salt marshes of both tropical and temperate zones.

We have already seen how coral reef ecosystems comprise some of the most diversified wildlife communities on Earth. Not quite so rich but still worthy rivals are tropical mangrove communities. Each of these two ecological zones covers roughly half a million square kilometers. They provide food and shelter for about one-third of all fish species on Earth, and for very large numbers of invertebrate species (Connell, 1978; Ehrlich, 1975). Since many present-day tropical coral reefs are ancient ecosystems – some originated 70 million years ago, with continuous growth observable for the past 7,000 years – they have undergone lengthy development under circumstances of general environmental stability. This means that they feature certain characteristics of "K-selected" communities, i.e., they continue to flourish under "normal" circumstances but are unduly vulnerable to the "instant disruption" that large-scale human activities can impose.

Yet coral reef and mangrove ecosystems, like estuaries and intertidal salt marshes, not only constitute a "crossroads" for several interrelated ecosystems of both terrestrial and marine realms, but are invariably in the midst of major zones of human activities. As a result they can undergo greater degradation at a faster rate than virtually any other ecosystems on Earth. They suffer from sedimentation and siltation from land sources, and from pollution from coastal industries. Moreover, many of the nearby zones of human activities support some of the densest human populations on Earth. Of the United States' populace, for example, one-third lives and works in regions surrounding estuaries, and almost another third (or almost two-thirds in all) also lives in coastal territories (this total proportion likely to become three-quarters by the year 1990). Of the ten largest metropolitan areas in the world, seven are located on estuaries – New York, Tokyo, London, Shanghai, Buenos Aires, Osaka, and Los Angeles – and of the 50-plus cities that are projected to grow to more than 5 million people each by the year 2000, half are located on estuaries. As one indication of the human-derived pollution that may overtake these ecosystems in the years immediately ahead, marine transportation systems, which now account for one-third of all marine pollution, are projected to increase some 3 to 7 times before the year 2000. This will mean a great expansion of port facilities along coastlines, together with secondary economic activities and human settlements in coastal zones.

To gain an idea of the disruptive land-use patterns that are overtaking coastal zones, let us briefly review the recent experience of the United States (Hester, 1976; Kumpf, 1977). According to the National Estuary Study of the Department of Interior in 1970, the United States suffers an annual loss of estuarine environments of almost 0.5 percent per year. Small as this amount may sound, it has led to a cumulative loss between 1960 and 1980 of 4,000 square kilometers. Not counting Alaska and Hawaii, the 48 remaining states feature just over 80,000 km² of estuarine waters, of which two-thirds are classified as commercial shellfish waters – and 27 percent of these waters are now closed to shellfishing because of pollution. A recent report from the Fish and Wildlife Service estimates that almost one-quarter of the country's estuaries have become severely degraded, and another 50 percent moderately so, through pollution from oil refineries and other industrial complexes along coastlines. In the foreseeable future there may well be a rapid increase in offshore oil spills, such as the 560 million-liter oil blowout in 1979–1980 off the Mexican coastline. The Gulf of Mexico, one of the busiest petroindustry areas in the world, features 670 km² of exceptional-value estuarine territories. According to the recently established Energy Mobilization Board under the Federal Government of the United States, at least 100 new fossil fuel and nuclear plants are scheduled to be built within the next fifteen years in U.S. coastal zones.

As for coastal ecosystems of the tropics, many coral reefs and mangrove communities have been degraded or destroyed along extensive sectors of coasts of the Americas, Africa, India, east and west Malaysia, Thailand, Indonesia, Vietnam, the Philippines, and eastern Australia (UNESCO, 1978). Highly disruptive dredging operations have damaged or eliminated coral reefs in the Virgin Islands,

Micronesia, Seychelles, Puerto Rico, the Bahamas, Hawaii, and Florida (Chapman, 1977 and 1980; Schmitz *et al.*, 1981; Swift, 1979). This is all the more regrettable in that certain of these areas, notably the Indo-Malay archipelago, the Caribbean, the Gulf of California, and the Gulf of Mexico feature exceptionally diverse coral reef ecosystems. Other extremely rich biotic communities, not yet so impoverished, are located in the Red Sea, the western Pacific, and the southeast Pacific.

Especially critical is the Caribbean, perhaps the richest region of tropical seas. Over 135 million people live in the 29 countries of the Caribbean. Each day the region yields about 8 million barrels of crude oil, 3 million of them from offshore rigs (Yanchinski, 1981). Equally to the point, the refineries in the region now have a total capacity of more than 12 million barrels per day. From 1973 onwards, more than one-sixth of the world's oil has been produced in the Caribbean, or shipped through it; right around the clock, at least 100 oil-carrying vessels are in Caribbean waters, 25 of them supertankers. Not surprisingly, though very regrettably, oil spills in coastal waters of the sea have been steadily increasing until they now approach 100 million barrels a year.

Conservation of marine ecosystems has been disrupted by all these sources of pollution at precisely the locations where the great majority of marine organisms live. The consequences to human use of these ecosystems for medicinal substances, as well as for food, are only just beginning to be felt in posted bans against fishing, shellfishing, and even bathing in the surf.

PART THREE

———————————— ■ ————————————

Industry

CHAPTER 10

———————■———————

Plants and Industry

I have spent a good ten years in poking away at the topic of how wildlife contributes evermore richly to our lives. During most of that time, however, I have supposed that wild species contribute primarily to agriculture and medicine, the first being an obvious form of exploitation and the second a well-established application. I have not realized that plants make a major contribution to industry.

Then came a day in November 1979, when I visited the laboratories of the Agricultural Research Service of the U.S. Department of Agriculture at Peoria, Illinois. What an off-the-beaten-track place, I thought, as I took a plane from Chicago on a freezing fall day, out into the boonies of Illinois. Was I wasting my time? But the day turned out to be one of the most revealing of my professional life. In all my travels to almost 100 countries, with visits to hundreds of research centers, I have rarely put so few hours to such good purpose. As I flew on the evening plane back to Chicago, I reflected that I had been shown an entire new world of wildlife's benefits. I felt as I did after my first glimpse of the Victoria Falls and the Grand Canyon, and after my first visit to China: I had entered a new realm of experience. In many more ways each day than is the case with agriculture and medicine, plants contribute to industrial products that sustain our well-being.

My guide into these unfolding landscapes was Dr. Lambertus H. Princen. It did not take Bert long to show me that many of the chemicals that turn up in our daily lives are not synthetic products of the laboratory. They originate in nature. How wrong I had been, I mused, in my belief that the white-coated scientist with his test tubes is the primary source of our "wonder chemicals." A far greater inventor is the world of plant life, growing wild in areas far removed from laboratories – and with a cornucopia of new products awaiting our investigation.

In fact, wild plants now serve the needs of the textile manufacturer, the toilet-goods producer, and the ice cream maker. In hundreds of forms, we enjoy biochemical products of the plant kingdom (Buchanan and Otey, 1979; Duke, 1979 and 1981; Duke et al., 1975; Gibbs, 1974; Miller, 1973; Oldfield, 1979; Pelletier, 1970; Princen, 1979 and 1982; Pryde, 1977 and 1979; Pryde et al., 1981; Richie, 1979; Robinson, 1975; Schultes, 1980; Schultes and Swain, 1976). Unaware as we may be, we benefit from plant materials every time we apply a shampoo or sunscreen lotion, every time we paint a wall or varnish a table, every time we use a golf ball or a jet engine or oil-drilling equipment, every time we employ goods containing tinplate or glycerine, and every time we allow the dentist to make a mold of our teeth or get the doctor to give us a vaccination or an immunization shot.

To use the technical terms of the biochemist, these plant-derived materials include fats, oils, waxes, latexes, pectins, resins and oleoresins, gums and other exudates, vegetable dyes and tannins, lignin, cellulose, starch, hydrocarbons, and many other biochemical compounds. On top of all these are numerous secondary compounds and chemical intermediates that have been isolated from plants, including sterols, alcohols, alkaloids, rosins, and esters. So abundant and diverse are some of these materials that industrial scientists can choose among 2,500 terpenoids (including 400 carotenoids), 1,500 flavonoids and related phenolic compounds, 700 acetylenes, 500 polyketides, 200 fatty acids, and up to 1,000 other compounds such as quinones and purines.

These various categories are almost certain to expand as scientific research comes up with more plant products – not only more numerous items but materials with greater complexity and novelty. In light of the speedy expansion of the global chemical industry, it is clear that we shall need many additional supplies of organic chemicals. As technology advances in a world that is growing short of just about everything except shortages, innovative industry will be on the lookout for fresh sources of renewable materials, as numerous and diversified as possible. So there will be increasing emphasis on every new material that we can derive from the 250,000 plant species that share our One Earth home.

The global chemical industry is already large, worth $300 billion per year. In the United States alone, production of synthetic organic chemicals totals around 85 million metric tons a year, of which plastics account for 15 million metric tons. Worldwide we now use 60 million metric tons of plastics each year (one-quarter of this total going into packaging materials), together with many other types of plastics ranging from ultrasuede to football-field turf. On top of our hefty appetites for plastics, we also consume large quantities of lubricants, adhesives, surfactants, coatings, and thickeners, among many other types of materials.

The chemical industry continues to derive most of its feedstocks from fossil petroleum. Almost one decade after OPEC started up business, American chemical corporations derive only 3 percent of their raw materials from alternative sources such as vegetable fats and oils. An American citizen now consumes around 230 kg of petrochemical products each year out of his or her total petroleum consumption of around 3,500 kg. Of these chemical products, roughly 40 percent are polymers (for adhesives, thickeners, flocculating agents, and coatings), 27 percent are plastics, 22 percent are lubricants, 6 percent are elastomers, and 5 percent are surfactants. But whereas many petrochemicals in 1973 cost a mere $0.07 per kg, they now cost, in the wake of OPEC, around $0.50 per kg. By contrast, vegetable fats and oils, which cost around $0.22 in 1973, have not even doubled in price. So there is strong incentive for the chemical industry to move beyond its petroleum-dominated era.

Fortunately, almost all petrochemicals in question can be replaced by phytochemicals. Already we use many vegetable oils exclusively for industrial products, notably castor, linseed, tung, and tall oil. In addition, a number of oils that are best known as edible oils in our daily diets contribute as well to industry, notably soybean oil, coconut oil, palm oil, peanut oil, and safflower oil.

Of all the nonedible oils that are used strictly for industrial purposes, only linseed oil is produced within the United States in substantial amounts. (Similar considerations apply to other advanced nations, such as Japan and nations of Western Europe; but for convenience, this chapter confines its attention to the United States.) The United States now imports around 5,500 metric tons of rapeseed oil a year, 5,200 metric tons of waxes (carnauba, candelilla, etc.), 16,000 metric tons of tung oil, 45,000 metric tons of castor oil, 70,000 metric tons of palm kernel oil, 500,000 metric tons of coconut oil, and 750,000 metric tons of natural rubber. Many of these items are expensive: imports of waxes, for example, at around $4 per kg., for a total of over $20 million; and imports of essential oils, 7,816 metric tons for $83 million (as of 1977). Moreover, many vegetable oils are imported from developing nations, with all the political problems that potentially implies. Almost half the developed nations' needs of groundnut oil come from developing nations, along with virtually all copra oil and all palm oil and palm kernel oil.

Clearly the United States, like other developed nations, is going to need growing supplies of these key plant materials. To meet this new challenge, the U.S. government is drawing on the 23 years of experience of its Agricultural Research Service at Peoria, Illinois, supported by the Economic Botany Laboratory at Beltsville, Maryland, and several other cooperating institutions – all of which have been undertaking a systematic search for plant materials to take the place of petrochemicals.

During the course of this botanical investigation, the research team has conducted chemical screenings of almost 8,000 plant species. The main focus of research has been directed at vegetable oils and plant fibers, for which there are serious shortages throughout the industrialized world. In addition, a subsidiary program has looked at further categories of botanochemicals that are increasingly important to industry, notably waxes and hydrocarbons. The scientists also have screened over 5,000 plant species for fibers as substitute sources of paper pulp, plus some 300 species for amino acids and proteins, and almost 100 species for pesticides (plus large numbers of species for antitumor agents, as indicated in Chapter 6). To date this major research effort has yielded 75 new fatty acids and many other high-value chemicals – a major research breakthrough. Equally important, several plant species with valuable components have been upgraded through breeding efforts and agronomic research to the stage where they can now be used as crops.

Broadly speaking, there are three main categories of botanochemicals that are in short supply. First is a group of fats and oils – materials that are generally plentiful for purposes of food and feed but that are generally scarce for crucial applications in industry. Second are waxes, invariably scarce for whatever purpose. Third is a catch-all category that we can call "natural rubber," not just rubber from the rubber tree but rubber from various shrubs and plants. Let us take a look at each of these categories in turn, then at a number of other plant materials.

Fats and Oils

Industrial fats and oils have traditionally been derived from three main sources, these being inedible tallow or lard, fish and whale oil, and a few oil-bearing plants. The animal sources tend to be overexploited, whereas the plants offer greater future supplies. Oil-bearing plants produce an especially valuable category of commodity – the fatty acids, complex mixtures of liquids and semi-solids that melt at low temperature. Fatty acids are highly desirable for many industrial purposes, including (in conjunction with other raw materials) a number of nitrogen derivatives, alcohols, sulfates, sulfonates, and the like – and these derivatives find a multitude of end-uses as polymers, plasticizers, detergents, surfactants, and lubricants (Princen, 1979 and 1982; Pryde, 1979; Pryde *et al.*, 1981). Important applications include cosmetics, adhesives, ore floatation materials, printing inks, corrosion inhibitors, and fabric conditioners. So we use vegetable fats and oils each time we apply skin cream, put on a suit or dress, pen a drawing, and seal up an envelope. The United States now uses around 3 million metric tons of vegetable fats and oils a year for industrial purposes, a total that could increase several times over by the end of the century. Not only will Americans make more use of these traditional applications, but they will use many new products as phytochemicals start to replace petrochemicals.

So important are these materials that it is worthwhile to look at several industrial uses of vegetable fats and oils.

First are coatings, which represent the main outlet for vegetable oils, notably from linseed, tung, soybean, safflower, coconut, and dehydrated castor. In the mid-1970s, the United States produced 545,000 metric tons of coatings, representing 40 percent of the paint-binding market. As petrochemicals become more expensive, manufacturers of enamel paints will shift to plant-derived coatings.

Second are surface-active agents. These constitute by far the largest use of fatty-derived materials, mainly because they are so useful in detergents. U.S. production of surface-active agents now totals well over 2 million metric tons, of which fatty materials account for over 1 million.

Third is glycerol. One-third of the total U.S. supply is derived from natural sources, notably from coconut oil. Obscure as the name glycerol may sound to us, we benefit from glycerol in many forms, including in drugs, cosmetics, foods, beverages, tobacco products, cellophane, and explosives. The United States now manufactures 75,000 metric tons of glycerol products a year.

Fourth are plasticizers, especially for vinyl plastics. In the United States, fatty derivatives contribute a good 15 percent of the total supply. A prime source of plant-derived plasticizers is epoxidized soybean oil, which contributed 100,000 metric tons to U.S. production in 1980.

Fifth are lubricants. Those of U.S. manufacture that contain important constituents of fatty materials from plants include transmission and high-pressure fluids from sulfurized oils, 27,000 metric tons per year; jet-engine ester lubricants, 14,000 metric tons per year (ester lubricants from fatty materials offer improved fuel consumption, reduced wear, longer life, and better high-temperature performance than do ordinary lubricants); crankcase and other oils from ester lubricants, 14,000 metric tons per year; and grease additives, 14,000 metric tons per year. In addition, lubricant additives are essential as

The meadowfoam presents a virtually continuous canopy of light-colored flowers in full bloom, hence its name. The plant contains an oil with more long-chain fatty acids than are found anywhere else in nature. This unique oil serves as a lubricant in high-speed and high-temperature machinery that generates extreme pressures, making it suitable for precision instruments such as those used in medicine and space technology. (Credit: Agricultural Experiment Station, Oregon State University, Eugene)

processing aids for the manufacture of several types of plastics, with a market of 23,000 metric tons a year.

Finally we come to nylons and other polyamides. Vegetable-oil products contribute to several types of polyamides. Fatty-derived materials now account for just over 10,000 metric tons, or 15 percent of the nylon-plastics market, in the United States.

In light of these many expanding applications of fatty materials, the U.S. Department of Agriculture believes it has come up with several promising plant candidates for seed-oil crops, especially for crops rich in long-chain fatty acids. Two front-runners are meadowfoam (*Limnanthes alba*) and crambe (*Crambe abyssinica*), both of which appear, on the basis of experimental plantings, as if they could make economically competitive use of cropland (the only crop that yields a better return is corn).

The meadowfoam, named for the almost solid canopy of light-colored flowers that characterize the plant in full bloom, is a herbaceous annual found along the Pacific Northwest coast. It yields an oil with at least 95 percent of its fatty acids made up of long-chain acids – three of which have not been found elsewhere (Brown *et al.*, 1979; Jalliff *et al.*, 1981). This unique oil serves as a lubricant with two sets of specialized applications. It can be used in high-speed and high-temperature machinery that generates extreme pressures, and it can be used for precision instruments, as in medicine and space technology. The oil may also serve as a raw material in the manufacture of plastics, textile sizing, waxes, soaps, and numerous cosmetics.

Limnanthes alba is the leading candidate for this high-value oil, and several other species of the *Limnanthes* genus, which extends in nature from southern California to British Columbia, are supplying genetic materials. One such species is *L. macounii*, which has greater resistance to disease than *L. alba*, and may thereby contribute to the crop's success through crossbreeding with *L. alba*. But *L. macounii* survives in only a few localities on Vancouver Island; more than once it has been reckoned to be extinct. Through exploiting the genetic variability of these related species, botanists have been able to breed a strain of meadowfoam that grows more upright than the usual wild forms, making the plant much easier to harvest with conventional machinery. Thus we have a prime example of a threatened species that can potentially make a marked contribution to our daily welfare.

As for the crambe, a member of the mustard family, its native habitats are located around the Mediterranean. The plant offers an oil rich in erucic acid, a commodity that is coming into increasingly strong demand in industry. Erucic acid is a key material in lubricants for casting of steel and for manufacture of plastics and rubber additives. Oils with high erucic acid content tend to increase the "oiliness" of mineral oil, improving its durability and its capacity to serve in high-pressure and high-speed operations, such as in jet engines. In addition, mineral oil mixed with erucic acid–rich oil forms stable emulsions with salt water, allowing the oil mixture to be used as a lubricant in marine operations.

The principal source of erucic acid in the past has been rapeseed oil. But rapeseed is now being diverted for food and feed, causing severe shortages for industry. So the U.S. Department of Agriculture is now looking at crambe, a member of the same family to which rapeseed belongs. Crambe seeds contain 30–40 percent oil, and the oil is 60 percent erucic acid, a higher proportion than in rapeseed oil. So great is U.S. demand for oil high in erucic acid that if crambe were to supply the 6,800 metric tons required, crambe growers could anticipate a price of more than $13,000 per metric ton for the oil.

So much for certain major fatty acids. Hydroxy fatty acids, an important subgroup, are generally derived from castor oil and are used for lubricants, coatings, adhesives, and plastics. At least eight wild plants could serve as additional sources, for example, several species of *Lesquerella*, with seeds containing 20–40 percent oil (the oil, in turn, is 50–74 percent hydroxy fatty acids). A further subgroup is the epoxy fatty acids, increasingly important in the manufacture of plastics and coatings. These fatty acids are currently derived from soybean oil, but because the derivation process consumes a lot of energy, epoxidized soybean oil costs more than three times as much as regular soybean oil. Fortunately the U.S. Department of Agriculture now finds that epoxy fatty acids can be derived biochemically from a number of wild plants that produce seed oils. A notable candidate is *Vernonia anthelmintica*, an Indian plant with seeds containing 23–31 percent oil made up of 68–75 percent epoxy acids. Fortunately, the plant reveals plenty of genetic variability in its wild stocks. Another candidate could be *Vernonia galamensis*, a wild plant from East Africa, with 40–42 percent seed oil made up of 73–80 percent epoxy acids. Unlike *V. anthelmintica*, whose ripe seeds shatter all too readily, and thus make harvesting difficult, *V. galamensis* possesses seeds without this disadvantage – hence, a further illustration of the key benefits that we can derive from obscure-seeming wild plants. The two species of *Vernonia* supply an oil for coatings that offers excellent qualities of adhesion, toughness, and chemical resistance.

Yet another candidate for epoxy fatty acids could be Stokes' aster, or *Stokesia laevis*, a wild perennial of the southeastern United States that is often grown as an ornamental. Its seeds contain 36–49 percent oil; the oil, in turn, is 75 percent epoxy acids. Stokes' aster could supply a good part of the U.S. annual demand of 68,000 metric tons of epoxy oils a year, currently worth $1,320 per ton.

Waxes

Waxes make a key contribution to modern industry. They supply much more than materials to polish the floor and the automobile. Little though we realize it, we use industrial waxes each time we read a book, make a carbon copy of a letter, and feed the cat.

Much industrial wax in the past has come from a single source, the sperm whale. This unfortunate creature has supplied a highly specialized type of wax, liquid wax, which is in great industrial demand due to its special "oiliness," its metallic wetting properties, and its nondrying characteristics that prevent "gumming" and "tackiness." Despite many research efforts, liquid wax still cannot be synthesized at commercially acceptable costs, even though it serves numerous industrial processes, including the manufacture of textiles, leather, electrical insulation, paper coatings, polishes, carbon paper, lubricants, pet foods, pharmaceuticals, and cosmetics. Due to rapidly expanding demand for these products, the price of liquid wax has reached one record level after another during the past two decades, until it is now worth around $15 a kilogram.

Because of the prized material that the sperm whale carries around in its head, the unfortunate creature has been hunted almost to the verge of extinction. Happily it is now protected through endangered species laws, and most advanced countries refuse to import sperm whale oil. The United States, for example, which was purchasing at least 27,000 metric tons of whale oil per year in the early 1970s, no longer imports a drop. But American industry still needs liquid wax. So the nation has been taking a long look at a wild plant that may provide a liquid wax of quality equivalent to that of sperm whale oil.

The plant is an obscure desert shrub of the southwestern United States and northern Mexico, the jojoba (*Simmondsia chinensis*) (Johnson and Hinman, 1980; National Academy of Sciences, 1975). The shrub is so adapted to its arid environment that it can thrive in desert areas with as little as 7.4 cm of rainfall a year. Its tap root grows as much as 2.5 cm a day during its early months, eventually reaching a length of 30 meters. The jojoba's seeds contain liquid wax in such abundance that it comprises 50 percent of the seeds by weight. Extensive tests show that the jojoba's wax is equivalent in its lubricant capacities to sperm oil, and that it is superior insofar as it contains no glycerides and few other chemical impurities. It requires little refining for most industrial applications, and it can be stored for long periods of time.

Jojoba wax proves suitable for a range of purposes. It can withstand repeated heatings to high temperatures without changes in its viscosity. It requires little refining before being used as a high-quality lubricant; and when added to other lubricants, it serves as a fine oil for use in cutting or grinding operations. It can be used as a transformer oil, and as an oil for precision instruments and delicate mechanisms. When combined with sulfur, it can contribute to the manufacture of high-performance lubricants, linoleum, printing ink, varnishes, and adhesives. It can be used for hair oil, shampoo, soap, face creams, lipsticks, perfumes, and sunscreen compounds, among many other cosmetics. In pharmaceuticals, it serves as a stabilizer of penicillin products and other coatings for medicinal preparations. When hardened by hydrogenation (the same process that produces margarine from vegetable oils), jojoba oil becomes a dense solid of sparkling white crystals, resembling spermaceti (also from the sperm whale)

The jojoba is so adapted to its desert habitats that it needs as little as 75 mm (three inches) of rainfall a year. The shrub's seeds contain liquid wax, a commodity much in demand by industry – and the only alternative source of this exceptional-quality oil has hitherto been the sperm whale, a highly threatened species. (Credit: Prof. Barbara Kingsolver, Office of Arid Lands Studies, University of Arizona)

and beeswax; the wax's hardness and high melting point (70°C) make it a rival of carnauba, the "king of waxes," that, deriving from a difficult-to-harvest Brazilian palm, is rising rapidly in price. Jojoba wax has further potential uses in polishes for floors, furniture, and automobiles; as a protective coating on fruit, fruit preparations, and paper containers; in candles; as a sizing for textiles; and as high-dielectric-constant material for electrical insulators.

Jojoba oil now sells to Japan for $3,000 a barrel – though as jojoba plantations come "on-stream" by the mid-1980s, the price will drop somewhat. To meet projected world demand for jojoba oil and wax, plantations covering 100,000 hectares and yielding 2,500 kg of nuts per hectare will be required, laying the foundations of what could be a $250 million industry annually. A mature jojoba plant can produce 15 kg of seed or more each year, which suggests that, at present prices, a one-hectare plantation can bring a return of over $60,000. Already commercial plantings have been established in the United States,

Mexico, Australia, Israel, Saudi Arabia, Iran, Jordan, Egypt, Sudan, Kenya, and Ghana.

A further source of hard wax could lie with the candelilla (*Euphorbia antisyphilitica*) (Hodge and Sineheh, 1956; National Academy of Sciences, 1975). A desert shrub of North America, the candelilla exudes a white wax that has so much industrial potential that, at a cost of around $3 per kilogram, it, too, could replace carnauba wax, which costs around $4 per kilogram. Candelilla wax is an amorphous solid, yellowish-brown in color. When refined, it serves as a hardener for soft waxes (such as paraffin wax) and contributes to the manufacture of candles, polishes, chewing gum, leather goods, varnishes and lacquers, paper sizing, dental molds, and electrical insulating materials.

A third source of industrial wax could be the cauassu (*Calathea lutea*)(Mors and Rizzini, 1966). This tall, large-leafed herb grows wild along semi-flooded zones of river courses in Central and South America. Its leaves are coated with a waxy material that reveals qualities at least as good as those of carnauba wax. Because its native habitats are located in rainforest territories, cauassu could be developed as a plantation crop for several sectors of tropical moist Africa and Southeast Asia. And because the plant is a secondary-growth species that readily colonizes disturbed forest ecosystems, it could thrive in areas that have been heavily logged.

In addition to the cauassu, several other species of the same family, the Marantaceae, produce specialized waxes of even greater quantity and quality than cauassu wax. Though more restricted in their natural range than cauassu, they could, with research, offer potential for plantation crops in many parts of the tropics.

In the case of all these wax-producing plants, the chemical composition of the waxes is generally so complex as to defy efforts to synthesize them in the laboratory. So the natural products are likely to retain a strong competitive edge in the industrial marketplace.

Natural Rubber

When Christopher Columbus arrived in the Americas in 1492, he found local people playing with bouncy balls made of plant material. Taking some samples back to Europe, he found they could be used to rub out pencil marks on paper. So the material came to be called "rubber."

The stuff that Columbus encountered may have been derived from a shrub or a tree similar to a desert bush, guayule (*Parthenium argentatum*), of northern Mexico and the southwestern United States—a

The guayule is another desert shrub that serves as a high-quality source of natural rubber, and complements the rubber tree plantations of Southeast Asia. Given the special characteristics of natural rubber, making it superior for certain applications over synthetic rubber, we can expect demand for natural rubber to grow faster than demand for rubber overall, and the guayule should be assured of good marketplace prospects. (Credit: Prof. Barbara Kingsolver, Office of Arid Lands Studies, University of Arizona)

plant that is now attracting much attention from industry. The guayule could prove to be a further source of natural rubber, to go with the well known rubber tree that now flourishes in thousands of plantations of Southeast Asia. In point of fact, the rubber tree is not keeping pace with industry's needs. Given the growing demand of people in all parts of the world for natural rubber, it is likely that the Southeast Asia plantations will not be able to produce sufficient rubber to meet the demand by the end of the 1980s. Hence the special significance of the guayule bush.

Natural rubber is one of the most important products that underpin our daily lives. A moment's thought indicates that we use rubber in dozens, if not hundreds, of ways each day. These widespread applications have led to natural rubber becoming a major cash crop for Malaysia and a handful of other developing nations. In fact, natural rubber is now the fourth largest agricultural export from the Third World, totaling some 3.5 million metric tons a year, worth over $3 billion. According to projections by the World Bank (Imle, 1978; Man and Blandford, 1980), global demand for natural rubber could grow to 6 million metric tons by 1990, if not well before.

Consumers cannot look for relief to synthetic rubber for two reasons. During the era of cheap petroleum, synthetic substitutes for natural rubber captured 70 percent of the entire rubber market. But petroleum-derived synthetics are becoming increasingly expensive. More important still, many of our daily needs cannot be met by synthetic rubber. Certain products are highly dependent on natural rubber because of its elasticity and heat resistance. For instance, lorry and bus tires, also automobile radial tires, use up to 40 percent natural rubber, otherwise they will not be able to withstand large pot holes in the road or dissipate the heat generated in screeching halts. Aircraft and bulldozer tires consist almost entirely of natural rubber; the tires of the space shuttle Columbia are 95–98 percent natural rubber. In fact, the tire industry absorbs more than two-thirds of all natural rubber available. So present consumption patterns are likely to maintain pressure on supplies of natural rubber – and a number of new applications of natural rubber, making use of its particular qualities, will boost this pressure still further. We can expect that the price of natural rubber will double during the 1980s, after which it could go through the roof as market demand steadily outgrows the expected production of the rubber plantations in Southeast Asia.

The number one consumer of natural rubber is the United States, accounting for almost 25 percent of the world's total. The nation now spends around $1 billion a year on natural rubber, making the commodity worth around 5 percent of the overall value of all imported agricultural products. In view of tightening supplies from Southeast Asia, the U.S. Congress has recently authorized an intensive effort to develop a domestic source of rubber. Although natural rubber occurs in some 2,000 species of plants, the leading candidate for the United States is guayule because it is a desert plant that grows within the U.S. borders.

Certainly the guayule appears to offer much potential (Johnson and Hinman, 1980; McGinnies and Haase, 1975; National Research Council, 1977). Seldom reaching more than half a meter high, the shrub sports stiff grey branches with silvery-grey leaves. so adapted is guayule to its desert habitats that it can thrive in areas where no rain falls for months or even years. For its rubber to be extracted, the whole shrub must be disintegrated (after the manner we pulp logs for paper), whereupon the rubber floats away from the waterlogged vegetation or is extracted by solvents. The rubber, which may amount to 10–25 percent of the entire plant, reveals chemical and physical properties virtually identical to those of rubber from the rubber tree.

Remarkably for a plant species, and fortunately for rubber consumers, the genetic diversity of guayule is extreme. Almost every
bush in the wild appears to be something of a separate strain. The extraordinary variability expresses itself not only through the plant's
rubber content, but also through its rate of growth, resistance to
disease, ability to compete with weeds, and tolerance of drought and
cold. With plenty of genetic breeding and agronomic improvement,
guayule may be able to match the achievements of the rubber tree,
whose growers have boosted output by 2,000 percent during the past
three decades.

Kenaf for Paper

If paper pulp is not already scarce, it is sure to become so. Year by
year, we use more and more paper. In 1981, we consumed around 180
million metric tons of paper (together with paperboard products). If
our consumption continues to grow at recent rates, twice as fast as
population increase, we can expect to be using 400 million metric tons
a year by the end of the century.

By far the great bulk of paper use is accounted for by developed nations, where an average citizen now consumes more than 150 kg of
paper a year, and a U.S. citizen twice as much. By contrast, a
developing-world citizen is unlikely to account for more than 5 kg and
may not even account for 1 kg (or roughly half of one copy of the Sun-
day edition of the *New York Times*). By the year 2000, we can expect
that the United States will increase its present share of consumption of
world output, around 75 out of 180 million metric tons, to at least 200
out of 400 million metric tons. At the same time, Africa will expand
from a mere 3–5 to 10 million metric tons, Asia (excluding Japan) from
9 to 24.5 million metric tons, and Latin America from 7 to 14.4 million
metric tons. This all means that while developing countries are likely
to expand their consumption roughly three times over, as compared
with a two and three-quarters times increase on the part of the
developed nations, the largest share of total consumption will remain
with the developed nations.

What is the prospect that the developed nations can find alternative
sources of paper pulp? At present we derive 97 percent of our paper
pulp from wood – and forests everywhere are coming under exploitation pressures that will probably prove unsustainable. It appears that
a suitable source of paper pulp can be found in a wild plant known as
kenaf (*Hibiscus cannabinus*) (Bagby, 1977; Hardy, 1980; International
Paper Sales, 1980; Princen, 1977). Native to eastern Africa, kenaf is a
herbaceous annual that can grow as high as 5 meters tall. It is canelike

When the outer fibers from a kenaf stalk are peeled back, they expose the light-colored inner core of short, woody fibers. (Credit: U.S. Department of Agriculture)

Kenaf shows promise as a source of paper pulp. It can be readily harvested as indicated in this demonstration project near Gainesville, Florida. (Credit: U.S. Department of Agriculture)

in structure, having a single fibrous stem topped by an "umbrella" of spikey leaves. A distant relative of cotton and okra, kenaf has been cultivated for centuries in Asia for making burlap bags. Unlike many related plants, and fortunately for the pulp-maker, kenaf's straight slender stem, about 5 cm thick at ground level, features no side-stems, leaving the harvesting and processing jobs a simple affair. Furthermore, the fact that the plant has to support no branches means that it does not harbor the resins and lignins that must be eliminated during the pulping of wood. Yet according to research by the Northern Regional Research Center under the U.S. Department of Agriculture at Peoria, Illinois, and by the International Paper Sales Corporation at Atlanta, Georgia, kenaf pulp proves a match for prime wood pulps, as measured by its capacity to be handled and bleached easily, and by its strength and durability.

Kenaf grows so fast that its fiber yield beats that of any tree species. Planted and cultivated like corn, it is ready for harvesting within four months. Trial plantings show that it can produce 27 metric tons of material per hectare per season in Georgia, and 45 metric tons in Florida. These yields enable kenaf to produce at least five times more pulp per hectare than a pine tree plantation can achieve in the same time – and kenaf can be grown and pulped at half the cost of wood pulp. With a gross return of $1,000 per hectare, kenaf is marginally more economic than corn, and well over twice as profitable as wheat, soybeans, barley, or sorghum. In light of these virtues, kenaf has been selected as the most promising plant out of 506 species investigated by the U.S. Department of Agriculture. Of course the proof of the pulp is in the reading. Kenaf has already proved acceptable to readers of experimental issues of a dozen newspapers, including *The Miami Herald* and *The Wall Street Journal*. It also produces acceptable bank notes.

Regrettably, kenaf proves susceptible to nematodes, or small soil worms that burrow into its roots. When this problem can be solved, probably through genetic breeding of resistant strains, the plant could be brought into widespread use as a new source of paper pulp.

Natural Fibers for Building Construction

By the year 2000, the developing world will need at least 500 million new dwellings. This is many more than have been constructed throughout the world since the start of human history. To help us face this daunting prospect, we can call on the services of some of the commonest natural fibers available in the developing tropics.

Of all construction materials used around the world, by far the most common is mud. Present-day mud bricks, such as a traveler sees used for houses in most countries of Asia, Africa, and Latin America, are the same basic building blocks that were produced by the Israelites under the Egyptian Pharoahs. Mud has a long tradition, then, and with good reason. It is cheap, easy to work with, and when reinforced with other materials, it endures. At Aswan in Egypt, thousands of visitors each year admire a Coptic church that was built of mud bricks in the tenth century. In Morocco, mud fortresses have lasted still longer. And let us bear in mind that in the southwestern United States today, the latest status symbol is a home built of adobe.

Of course the mud brick construction in these various buildings requires the help of strengthening materials, sometimes expensive ones. By contrast, the poor of many nations still try to make do with the same simple mud that has served humankind for at least five millennia – which means that each tropical rainy season leaves their houses in urgent need of repair. If we can somehow improve the general strength and durability of mud bricks, we shall achieve a giant advance in our efforts to house the impoverished billions of the Third World.

Fortunately, a recent research breakthrough has been achieved at the University of Zambia in Lusaka (Lewis, 1979). Thanks to a simple and cheap technology, a house of mud bricks can be upgraded into a much more permanent affair. The key component is natural fiber, used to strengthen both the bricks that constitute the main structure and to supply a thin cement covering for the walls. All the house builder has to do is chop plenty of elephant grass or sisal into small pieces and mix it into both the mud and the cement plaster, whereupon the two adhere together well. The plaster needs to be only half as thick as unreinforced concrete to make a durable surface, while proving five times tougher. Moreover, a building constructed of mixed mud and fibers remains drier, cooler, and cleaner than a building made of simple mud bricks, and it keeps out insects and vermin better. In addition, the builder can use fiber-reinforced cement for the roof, a less expensive technique than using corrugated iron or asbestos sheets. The result is a building that costs only a fraction as much as one using more modern materials – and a building that meets the needs of the homeless, who require serviceable shelter rather than the latest-style house.

The walls of a typical Third Worlder's house can be constructed from two bags of cement, two wheelbarrows of sand, and five kg of the plant fiber most available locally, often sisal or elephant grass. Together with the roof sheets, a durable home can be built for the equivalent of a few hundred dollars. If sisal or elephant grass is not in plentiful supply, several other plant fibers serve as well, for instance water reeds or plantain. Generally speaking, however, elephant grass is the most popular, since it is a tough plant that grows 3 meters tall, flourishing along water courses. Not only is its fiber unusually strong, but it is slow to rot – a key factor in view of the destructive alkalis contained in cement.

Research in India suggests that another fine reinforcement is bamboo. According to a research project on new fibers and composites in New Delhi, India, split bamboo can be mixed with cement-sand plaster to form "bamboocrete," allowing a durable house to be built for about $600. Another strengthening material is jute, which makes a simple dwelling able to withstand heavy monsoon rains, cyclone-force winds, and prolonged exposure to the tropical sun. Even coconut shells and rice hulls can be used as aggregate.

All this means that Third World house builders can continue to use the traditional material of mud in combination with only trifling amounts of strengthening materials. The "modern" alternatives of concrete and steel are simply beyond the means of most Third Worlders. Whereas a worker in Europe or North America can buy ten bags of cement with one day's wages, a rural Third Worlder must often work ten days to buy one bag. To quote President Julius Nyerere of Tanzania, "The widespread addiction to concrete and metal is a kind of mental paralysis. We are still thinking in terms of international standards instead of what we can afford to do ourselves."

So much, then, for five categories of industrial materials that we derive from plants. Let us now go on to consider a short miscellany of materials from further plants of promise.

Further Promising Plants

All manner of other raw materials are available to us from the plant kingdom, if only we can take advantage of them before the species and their genetic resources disappear. A couple of instances can serve to illustrate the cornucopia of industrial products that await our scientific research.

First of all, let us consider the guar (*Cyanopsis tetragonoloba*) (Whistler and Hymowitz, 1976). This leguminous herb grows mainly in India and Pakistan, but also in southern sectors of the United States. It is related to the soybean, which it resembles in appearance. Its seeds contain 23 percent gum and 40 percent oil, the gum offering between five and eight times the thickening capacity of starch. It is this thickening trait that has brought the gum in high demand as a thickening agent for cosmetics, hand lotions, and creams, plus many pharmaceuticals; as a stabilizer for salad dressings, bakery products, and ice cream; and as a strengthening agent for paper making. The gum also serves as a filter aid in mining operations. The United States now produces some 25,000 metric tons of this gum a year, not nearly enough to keep up with fast-growing demand. Apart from the applications listed, guar seeds also contain 34 percent protein for use as food and feed.

The guar is much in demand for oil-drilling muds and as a food emulsion. It also serves to rehabilitate soil that has been overworked through growing of food crops. (Credit: U.S. Department of Agriculture)

The guar grows well in areas with little rainfall, and it tolerates a moderate amount of salinity in the soil. The plant can be harvested with an ordinary grain harvester. If it can be developed through research, the guar could become a top-ranking agricultural crop in many countries of the tropics and subtropics.

Second, consider ramie, or China grass (*Boehmeria nivea*) (Ghosh and Ghosh, 1971). A slender herb that grows 3 meters high, ramie is native to eastern Asia, where it has been moderately exploited for centuries.It proves capable of thriving in many other parts of the earth, in both tropical and temperate zones. The plant's bast layer contains fibers that are lustrous, durable, and 20–40 cm long, with seven times the tensile strength of silk and eight times that of cotton—characteristics that make the fibers superior to other vegetable fibers in both length and strength. In addition, the fibers are more resistant than most other fibers are to natural decay and chemical degradation. By virtue of these qualities, ramie offers much potential for clothing, fabrics, upholstery, and paper. When it is blended with wool in a 25/75 percent mixture, it greatly improves the wearing properties of clothing and eliminates any tendency of the wool to stretch or shrink. Like both wool and cotton, ramie fibers can "breathe," making the clothing comfortable for the wearer. When ramie is mixed with wool in a 50/50 mixture for carpet material, the carpet's life is doubled.

One problem arises. Unlike other stem fibers such as jute, flax, and hemp, ramie fiber cannot be extracted by the usual retting method, i.e., soaking the fibers in water until the plant tissues disintegrate save for the crude fiber. Not only is the gum too strong, but the bast structure is too complex. To date the fiber has been extracted through processes that involve much tedious manual labor. If research manages to overcome this problem, ramie could become an important crop in many parts of the world.

Natural Sweeteners

Among economic plants of unexploited potential are those that offer a product of increasing importance, natural sweeteners. They deserve consideration on their own.

In the wake of the cyclamate and saccharin controversies, there is urgent need for us to find a non-nutritive sweetening agent—one that does not add calories to our diet and centimeters to our waist lines. We cannot revert to sugar, since we already consume far too much—100 million metric tons, or almost 20 kg per person per year. The average American consumes at least 45 kg per year, making sugar a major factor in overweight problems and associated diseases such as heart disorders in the United States.

Many plant pigments, such as carotenoids in sweet-tasting fruits, serve to attract birds, insects, and other herbivores in nature. Almost certainly, then, they are not toxic to mammals, including humans. The problem with the natural sweeteners of fruits that we use is that they are nutritive sugars—glucose, fructose, and sucrose—and we use them to excess. Fortunately we are finding, however, that certain natural sweeteners in fruits are made up of protein compounds (Higginbotham *et al.*, 1979; Inglett, 1981). These materials, identified only during the last ten years, make up an entirely new class of natural sweeteners. They are all 1,000 times sweeter than sucrose, and at least 300 times sweeter than saccharin.

A leading example of a source of protein sweeteners is the so-called miracle fruit (*Synsepalum dulcificum*), a berry from West African forests. It causes sour foods to taste splendidly sweet, as anyone can tell by merely chewing on a berry at the same time he or she is eating lemons, limes, rhubarb, or grapefruit. The principal sweetening ingredient is a protein known as monellin. Another fruit from West Africa's forests, known as the serendipity berry (*Dioscoreophyllum cumminsii*), features a sweetness 3,000 times greater than that of sucrose. The red, grapelike berry derives its curious name from an occasion in 1965 when an American scientist, Dr. George Inglett, was exploring West African forests for sweet fruits. Coming across the plant by chance, he was surprised to find that its berries tasted so sweet; he had derived no clue about it from scientific reports.

Still more important than these two is a third fruit from West Africa. The katemfe (*Thaumatococcus danielli*) contains two sweet-tasting proteins, thaumatin I and II, each of which is 1,600 times sweeter than sucrose. Thaumatin is now widely marketed by the noted sugar corporation in Great Britain, Tate and Lyle Limited, under the trade name Talin. It is becoming strongly established in Japan, where it is used as a sweetener in such diverse products as candies, chewing gum, dressings, coffee drinks, soups, jellies, pickles, frozen desserts, fish and meat products, and table-top sachets.

And more candidates are waiting in the wings. One is a Paraguay herb (*Stevia rebaudiana*), whose leaves contain stevioside, now well established in Japan as a food additive. Another plant deserving greater exploitation is a fruit of southern China (*Momordica grosvenori*), available in markets of southern China and Hong Kong.

By now it must appear that there is no end of promising plants and their products for almost any industrial need that arises. But let us conclude this chapter anyway with a brief look at one more group of plants, the palms, and the broad array of products they yield.

Palms

Palms, with their 2,800 species, serve an increasing number of innovative uses (Balick, 1979; Hodge, 1975; Kitzke and Johnson, 1975; Moore, 1978; Schultes, 1980). Although only a few palm species have been investigated for their industrial products, and then for only a few types of products, the family has already yielded at least 100 distinctive materials, making the Palmae second in economic importance to the Gramineae (grasses) and way ahead of the Leguminosae.

Many persons are readily acquainted with those palm species that have become major plantation crops, such as oil palm, coconut palm, and date palm. Edible oils from these palms turn up at many points in our daily rounds, in the form of margarine, ice cream, mayonnaise, cooking oil, and bakery products. But apart from well-known items such as edible oils, palms yield many other products, notably wax, sugar, alcohol, and fiber. Thus palm materials contribute to the manufacture of candles, detergents, tinplate, glycerine, and lubricants for jet engines and other precision machinery.

For an illustration of the multiple applications that we can enjoy from a single species, let us consider the Babassu palm (*Orbignya martiana*) that grows wild in some 140,000 km² of Amazonia – a mere 3 percent of the region, but an area almost the size of Florida (Balick, 1979; Smith, 1974). Its many products have earned for the Babassu a local name of "vegetable cow." Reaching a height of 20 meters, the Babassu features elegant curved leaves around 9 meters long, of a majestic fan-shape appearance. The fruit grows in bunches that reach up to a meter in length and can weigh anywhere from 15 to 90 kg. Each bunch contains some 200–600 fruits, and each fruit resembles a small coconut, with 3–8 kernels that contain 60–70 percent of an almost colorless oil – a higher proportion than the coconut palm produces. Since the oil is very similar in makeup to coconut oil, it can be used for margarine, shortening, general edibles, fatty acids, toilet soap, and detergents; and the Babassu may be the only plant that could replace the coconut as a source of olein and stearin. The prolific oil output of the Babassu translates into a yield of 40 kg of oil per tree per year, or the equivalent of one barrel of oil from every four trees. This means that a stand of 500 trees on one hectare could produce 125 barrels of oil per year. After the oil has been extracted from the kernel, the remaining seed-cake, containing 27 percent protein, makes an excellent animal feed. So the same stand of 500 trees could produce 5.7 metric tons of edible protein – plus 250 barrels of ethanol as a further byproduct. As a final bonus, the leaves can yield waxes and steroids.

Plainly this single species of palm offers exceptional prospects for industry if, through research, it can be developed into a plantation crop. Fortunately the Babassu, like many other palm species, reveals great diversity among its populations, with some populations starting to produce fruit earlier, and then producing much larger yields, than other populations. The diversity of traits should prove important for genetic breeding and agronomic improvement. Regrettably the Babassu is undergoing loss of habitat in its Amazonia environments, which probably means that the species is already suffering genetic attrition.

Another little known palm of Amazonia is the Buriti (*Mauritia flexuosa*) (Braun, 1968). More widespread than the Babassu, the Buriti is known to Indian tribes as "the tree of life," on the grounds that it supplies them with many forms of food, drink, clothing, and shelter. Potential products for modern economies include oil and starch for food and wine, and industrial fiber for twine, sacking, and nets.

Next, the Seje palm (*Jessenia polycarpa*) (Uphof, 1968). Growing abundantly in parts of Amazonia within Venezuela and Colombia, the Seje produces an edible oil that is very similar to olive oil. The palm's fruit clusters are so large and heavy that they stand comparison with those of the African oil palm. The fruit's pulp, constituting almost 40 percent (dry weight) of the whole fruit, contains around 50 percent oil. A mature tree can produce 22 kg, or 24 liters of oil per year. According to preliminary research, the oil can be used not only for food, but for soap and cosmetics; and when the species is subject to systematic investigations, it could prove to offer as much industrial potential as the Babassu.

Finally, the Caryocar group of palms comprises another 15 species (Prance and da Silva, 1973). Growing abundantly in Amazonia and a few other parts of tropical South America, these palms reach a height of 10 meters, with a canopy of the same diameter, making for an impressive appearance. Their fruits, like the fruit of the oil palm, yield two edible oils, one from the pericarp and the other from the kernel. So tasty is the meat of the kernel that the Caryocar nut is considered to be the most edible nut of the entire tropics.

CHAPTER ELEVEN

———————————————■———————————————

Growing Gasoline

We may now be entering an era of "green gasoline." In the wake of OPEC, scientists are looking for energy in forms less expensive than fossil fuels. They hope to find some answers in the capacities of the plant kingdom to produce "bio-energy." Ancient plants supplied the start-point materials that led to geologic formation of oil, natural gas, and coal, a process that originated more than a third of a billion years ago. How can we telescope the process, by harvesting the solar energy that plants are photosynthesizing right today? In other words, how can we replace petroleum with "phytoleum"?

Our efforts to grow gasoline will mark a quantum advance in our approach to fuel supplies. To date, we have been inclined to scrabble around in the ground for oil, gas, and coal—an approach that resembles the hunter-gatherer's life-style before agriculture. Perhaps we are now ready to "domesticate" wild plants to produce the same sorts of materials that have generated our fossil fuel stocks in the past, and that could now generate bio-fuels on energy farms. After all, there seems to be little doubt about demand for green gasoline: the Volkswagen Corporation estimates that by the end of the century, more than one car in three will be powered with bio-fuel.

There are various possibilities. Energy farms can range from plantations producing alcohol fuels, to weeds in wetlands producing crude oil, to aquatic plants in sewage lagoons generating ethanol and methanol, to tree species that directly produce hydrocarbons, to crop plants that yield vegetable-oil substitutes for diesel fuel (Bente, 1981; Buvet et al., 1977; Hall, 1981; Hall et al., 1982; Lipinsky et al., 1980; Mitsui and Black, 1982; Office of Technology Assessment, 1980; Slesser and Lewis, 1979; Ward, 1981; Weisz and Marshall, 1979; World Bank, 1980). Plenty of theoretical options are available. Which ones will work best in practice?

Biomass Supplies

A major strategy lies with conversion of biomass, or plant material of any kind, into fuels of various types. The key factor is to accumulate biomass in a single locality—lots of it, continuously. Thereafter it can be processed anaerobically (in the absence of oxygen) using a range of conversion techniques. One technique is biomethanation, or "anaerobic digestion," which produces a fuel gas composed of methane and carbon dioxide, otherwise known as biogas. A second one is fermentation, also anaerobic, to produce liquid fuel in the form of the alcohol called ethanol. A third is pyrolysis, or thermal decomposition of carbonaceous materials in oxygen-free containers, to produce gaseous, solid, or liquid hydrocarbons. These various techniques yield energy-rich products of types that are suitable for different purposes. Biogas is suitable for small-scale operations, notably at the village level in the Third World. Ethanol can be mixed with ordinary gasoline, at a 10–20 percent level for the ethanol, to produce gasohol. Pyrolysis releases an oil akin to crude petroleum, with 75 percent of crude's caloric value—as well as a mixture of gases and a flaky char.

Where shall we look for suitable supplies of biomass? A number of fast-growing plants are well suited, notably starch crops such as corn and cassava, and sugar crops such as cane and beet. They underpin the gasohol programs of Brazil, the United States, and several other nations. Less well known are plants such as Napier grass, Bermuda grass, Sudan grass, and big bluestem (Saterson *et al.*, 1979; University of Puerto Rico, 1978). When grown year-round in the warmth of the tropics, Napier grass can generate a whopping 88 metric tons (dry weight) of biomass per hectare per year, better even than sugarcane, which rarely exceeds 65 metric tons. A number of tropical swamp reeds can yield almost 60 metric tons. When pyrolyzed, the vegetable matter releases a hydrocarbon liquid fuel. (By contrast, a tropical rainforest generates only 35–50 metric tons of biomass per hectare per year, and a deciduous forest in temperate Europe or America, only 15 metric tons.) Among the plethora of wild plants, especially wild grasses, that flourish in the tropics, which ones, we might wonder, are waiting only for our attention before being developed as bio-fuels?

Not that the tropics are the only area on Earth where one can grow enough biomass to be worthwhile. Certain sectors of the temperate zone can produce exceptional amounts of biomass. For example, wetlands are some of the most productive ecosystems anywhere (Andrews and Pratt, 1978; Benemann, 1979; Pratt and Andrews, 1980). In North American wetlands, cattail species (*Typha*) thrive with exceptional vigor, as do the common reed (*Phragmites communis*), bullrushes (*Scirpus* spp.), reed-canary grass (*Phalaris arundinacea*), and sedges (*Carex* spp). The cattail features a "canopy architecture" that enables it to collect solar energy with unusual efficiency. Being a perennial, the plant tolerates a wide range of temperatures; and it is resistant to most insect pests. In the wild, it regularly produces 40 metric tons of biomass per hectare per year, with levels over 50 metric tons recorded in southern Mississippi. Domesticated in plantations, it reaches 97 metric tons per hectare during a seven-month growing season; and with cultivation under ideal conditions, it could presumably sustain an output of well over 100 metric tons. On the basis of these figures, one hectare of cattails could generate at least 20,000 cubic meters (m^3) of methane. True, wetlands are limited in supply, and they tend to be drained for industrial installations and other "more useful" purposes. Here, perhaps, is a way to exploit their natural productivity, while retaining their environmental amenities as habitats for waterfowl and other wetland species.

Swamp-dwelling plants would not compete for land with conventional agricultural crops. Neither would plants that flourish in open bodies of water such as lakes and rivers. The water hyacinth is famous, or infamous, for its capacity to cover a water surface at superswift rates (Chin and Gohj, 1978; Dynatech Research and Development Corporation, 1978; Goldman *et al.*, 1977; National Academy of Sciences, 1976; Ryther *et al.*, 1979; Wolverton and McDonald, 1979). Wild hyacinths on lakes can double their numbers in a mere three weeks, and on sewage lagoons in half as much time. In the southern United States, hyacinths produce 70–100 metric tons of dry-weight biomass per hectare per year, and in the tropics as much as 120 metric tons; hyacinths cultivated with nutrients, as from sewage, can exceed 150 metric tons. Through anaerobic fermentation, the water hyacinth biomass yields methane at a rate of at least 30,000 m^3 per hectare of hyacinths per year.

Other large floating plants can qualify for energy farms. Some of them, for instance the pennywort (*Hydrocotyle umbellata*) and water lettuce (*Pistia stratiotes*), tolerate cold fairly well, so they should suit temperate areas further away from the tropics.

In similar style, certain plant species of the oceans can be exploited for energy. According to research trials in California, various seaweeds can be processed to produce methane. Especially promising is the giant kelp, which, according to the California Institute of Technology and the General Electric Corporation, can be grown in "ocean farms" a few kilometers offshore from southern California (North, 1979; Wilcox, 1980). The kelp usually attaches itself to subsurface rocks, takes nutrients from the mineral-rich seawater, and grows a full half-meter in length per day. If the plants were to be attached to ropes on large radial booms, anchored in several hundred meters of water, they could produce vast volumes of biomass on a sustainable basis, yielding plentiful methane.

So much for nonwoody plants. Biomass is equally acceptable from trees. Generally speaking, one ton of pyrolyzed wood can be expected to yield at least 12 liters of methanol (so-called wood alcohol), 35 liters of wood oil and light tar, 330 kg of charcoal, and 140 m^3 of gas (used to energize the production processes), together with 25 liters of acetic acid, almost 12 liters of creosote oil, more than 7 liters of esters, and 33 kg of pitch (Inman, 1977; Tatom, 1981). Again, the key question is, which tree species provide the greatest stocks of biomass?

Several trees grow fast enough to yield wood in suitably large amounts – for example, several eucalyptus and pine species, grown on numerous plantations in both the temperate and tropical zones. But perhaps the most promising species available to us is one that has gained prominence in just the last few years, the giant ipilipil (*Leucaena leucocephala*) (National Academy of Sciences, 1979). This evergreen tropical legume, a native of Central America, has spread to become one of the most versatile plants on Earth. It can grow to 4 meters in height in six months, almost 10 meters in two years, and more than 15 meters in six years. A one-hectare plantation can easily produce 35 m^3 of wood per year for pyrolysis into liquid fuels (or for direct use in electricity generators and industrial boilers). Ipilipil's basic growth rate matches that of virtually any other fast-growing tree, and experimental plantings show that it can grow twice and even three times as fast under suitable conditions. In order to generate an estimated energy equivalent of 1 million barrels of oil per year, we need to think in terms of a 12,000-hectare plantation, or an area 12 km by 10 km, about twice as large as New York's Manhattan Island.

We might note in passing that the ipilipil can serve our needs in other ways. A one-hectare stand yields huge amounts of palatable forage for livestock. The dry leaves contain 27–34 percent protein, with a balance of amino acids much as in alfalfa, and with one of the highest vitamin A contents ever reported in plants. When cattle are fed on a mixture of grass and leaves from young ipilipil trees, they put on weight as fast as cattle on the best pastures anywhere. Alternatively, the foliage can be used for green manure, whereupon the leaves from one hectare supply 600 kg of nitrogen, 500 kg of potash, and 200 kg of phosphorus fertilizer. A versatile tree indeed.

What counts with this tree crop, as with grain crops and other wild plants scheduled for domestication, is the extent to which plant breeders can improve the genetic content. To date, most ipilipil plantations are scarcely more than wild trees planted in rows. If we can track down enough genetic diversity among ipilipil trees in natural forests, we shall surely come up with tree varieties whose productivity will exceed today's levels, remarkable as they already are.

So much for a notable tree of the tropics. In temperate zones, certain species can exploit the long summer days when photosynthesis continues for at least three-quarters of the 24-hour cycle. Experiments in North America and Western Europe indicate that short-rotation forestry with fast-growing species such as poplars and willows may be able to produce up to 20 metric tons dry weight per hectare per year. Best suited are trees that can be harvested at frequent intervals, no more than four years and sometimes as little as one and a half years. Some sycamore plantations in the southeastern United States are close-planted like a corn crop, whereupon they grow vigorously until they are 3 or 4 meters tall, then are harvested with a giant mowing machine that cuts the trees off at the stump in broad swathes, just like a combine moving through a corn field. The trees then copice, i.e., they regrow from the stump.

Similar systems are being tried in Sweden, which now derives about 8 percent of its energy needs from biomass. The most suitable species for short-rotation forestry turns out to be the willow. Each year the government asks its citizens to look out for the tallest-growing shoots of willow that they can find, offering prices for the best samples. As a result of this experiment, Swedish scientists have now produced nine clones of superstrain willows that yield twice as much as ordinary willows, with a wood output of 10 metric tons of oil equivalent (approximating more than 60 barrels of oil) per hectare per year (Söderman, 1980).

As with the ipilipil, a premium exists on selecting the genetic strains that are best adapted to "petroleum plantations." Among factors that the plant breeder needs to consider are growth rate, wood density, resistance to disease, and tolerance to environmental stress. In Sweden, as many as 2,000 genetic strains of poplar and willow have been examined, and only ten of them appear to meet the geneticist's criteria. Again, we find there is a premium on as much genetic variability as possible, to be derived from wild populations of the trees.

Hydrocarbon Trees

Still another strategy for energy farming involves plant species that do not produce carbohydrates like sugar in their tissues, but hydrocarbons that are akin to oil (Benedict *et al.*, 1979; Buchanan *et al.*, 1978; Calvin, 1977; Johnson and Hinman, 1980; Jones *et al.*, 1979). Carbohydrates have to be converted into fuel via microbial or thermochemical processes, but plant hydrocarbons are sometimes suitable for direct use as fuel.

Plant hydrocarbons come in various types. We have long used two of them—turpentine and rubber. The rubber is from a tree (*Hevea* spp.) of the family Euphorbiaceae; several other members of the family produce significant amounts of milklike sap, or latex, that is actually an emulsion of 30 percent hydrocarbons in water. These hydrocarbons are similar to those produced by the rubber tree, though of much lower molecular weight, in fact of a weight order that is favored by oil engineers. The hydrocarbons have a size distribution, furthermore, that resembles that of the hydrocarbons in petroleum. They are even superior to those of crude oil in that they are practically free of sulfur and other contaminants.

All in all, at least 30,000 species of plants produce latex. But the family Euphorbiaceae, with some 5,000 species, could prove specially suitable for growing gasoline. These plants range in size from small herbs that hug the ground so closely they can easily be overlooked, to trees more than 30 meters tall. At least one dozen species appear to be leading candidates, and the front-runner is probably *Euphorbia lathyris* (Calvin, 1980; Johnson and Hinman, 1980; Kingsolver, 1982; Nemethy *et al.*, 1981; Peoples *et al.*, 1981). This bright green shrub, usually growing between 0.5 meter and 2 meters tall, flourishes in many parts of both the tropical and temperate zones. In one of its better-known habitats, California, it is popularly known as the "gopher plant," on the grounds that its roots, with their highly toxic sap, repel gophers and other rodents. When you break a twig or a leaf off the gopher plant, it exudes a white, sticky, isoprenoid-rich latex that can be extracted with solvents from dry-plant material and converted into compounds akin to those of fossil petroleum.

Some early experiments in the mid-1970s came up with euphoric results for the gopher plant. Professor Melvin Calvin, a Nobel Prize-winning biochemist at the University of California at Berkeley, found in his test plots (albeit rather specialized ones) that about 10 percent of the dried gopher plant is made up of hydrocarbons. So Calvin concluded, albeit on very limited evidence, that a one-hectare plantation could produce at least 25, and conceivably as much as 125, barrels of oil per year. The production costs would run to about $25 per barrel, or way below the OPEC price of oil.

A gopher plantation would produce more than "bio-crude." The hydrocarbons contain a high proportion of compounds such as terpene trimers, which yield products similar to those derived from naphtha, one of the principal raw materials that the chemical industry extracts from petroleum. At the 1982 price of $50 for one barrel of naphtha, hydrocarbons from a gopher plantation are already competitive.

Calvin and his colleagues believe, furthermore, that the productivity of the gopher plant could be increased, perhaps greatly. They invoke the experience of rubber breeders, who have boosted output of the rubber tree by 2,000 percent during the past three decades. So Calvin and his associates suggest that gopher productivity could surely be doubled within just a few years. In point of fact, the prospect for a productivity advance of this scale could turn out to be fairly founded. The gopher plant grows in many parts of the Americas, Europe, the Soviet Union, and Africa, which means that there could be sufficient genetic variability in the wild to select strains with improved oil yield, plus best resistance to diseases such as root rot, and with other key characteristics.

Not only has the University of California shown interest, but the University of Arizona, in conjunction with the Diamond Shamrock Corporation, has engaged in field trials. Professor Jack Johnson, Director of the Office of Arid Lands Studies at the University of Arizona, has used wild seed to produce the equivalent of 10 barrels of bio-crude per hectare. These preliminary results suggest that genetically superior plants could, through extensive research and development, eventually yield 50 barrels per hectare. These output figures need not be so very surprising when we consider that the rubber tree, in its high-yielding plantations, produces the equivalent of 10 metric tons of hydrocarbons per hectare per year, approximating at least 60 barrels of oil.

If these projections, preliminary and approximate as they are, turn out to be realistic, we could envisage a gopher plantation supporting a commercial extractor that converts 1,000 metric tons of biomass a day into 1,500 barrels of bio-crude oil, together with by-products (via pyrolysis of the dried pulp) of 40,000 gallons of ethanol and 25 megawatts of electric power. (In addition, the plantation could yield many valuable materials for chemical industries, including oils, steroids, polyphenols, alkaloids, and other pharmacologically active constituents.) To maintain an operation of this scale would require some 140 km² of gopher plantation, an area about the size of the city of Pittsburgh. This area would prove too small under certain circumstances, e.g., many refineries today work on a production level of 50,000 barrels of oil a day — and to supply a cracking plant of that size, we would need to think in terms of at least 4,600 km² of gopher plantation. Large as this area may sound, there are vast expanses of arid

land in the southwestern United States that remain uncultivated –
128,000 km² in Arizona alone, plus almost as much in New Mexico
and roughly twice as much in Nevada.

We need to be skeptical of projections that may turn out to be less
substantive than has been hoped. According to other researchers in
California (Mendel *et al.*, 1979; Sachs *et al.*, 1981), it would not be
possible to produce 25 barrels of oil per hectare per year with only
5–20 cm of rainfall such as characterizes the drier parts of California
and Arizona – whereas Calvin has postulated that the gopher plant
could probably be cultivated on a large scale with less water than any
established agricultural crop and thereby avoid competition with conventional agriculture. To achieve an output of 25 barrels of oil per hectare per year, a plantation would have to generate over 42 metric tons
of dry biomass, with a rosin (hydrocarbon) content of 10 percent,
some 80 percent of which would have to be extractable. All of this
would require a biomass yield greater than that of virtually all well
known crop plants, with the exception of superswift growers such as
sugarcane. Indeed, recent field trials indicate that the Mojave Desert
of California, viewed by Calvin as a suitable site, would produce a
mere 3 metric tons at most of plant material, yielding only a fraction
of a barrel of oil per hectare per year. In addition, an oil content of 10
percent is probably twice as high as could be practically achieved
through broad-scale cultivation. So, instead of 25 barrels of oil per
hectare per year, we might better think in terms of somewhere between 3 and 7 barrels. Moreover, Calvin's cultivation costs of $375 per
hectare are now being reckoned to be far too optimistic, perhaps only
one-quarter of true costs. The probable upshot is a barrel of oil costing
at least $150 and possibly $250, or between six and ten times as much
as Calvin calculates.

But not all may be lost for the gopher plant. Trial projects at several
localities in California indicate that, with irrigation, the gopher plant
can yield 20–25 barrels of oil per hectare during the February–September growing season. And breeding and selection have not
yet been accounted for, in efforts to improve the yield.

Even if the gopher plant proves to be noneconomic, the prospect of
hydrocarbon crops may be an idea whose time has come. Other plants
of the family Euphorbiaceae offer promise – for example, *Croton
sonderianus*, a plant of northeastern Brazil's drylands, known locally as
black quince or "marmeleiro" (Parente, 1980). Considered a weed
because of its capacity to flourish in unlikely environments, this plant
is estimated to yield at least 15 metric tons of dry material per hectare
per year, sometimes twice and even three times as much. When this
material is treated through steam distillation, it generates a type of oil

suitable for diesel engines without mechanical modifications. Many practical problems remain, however, before the plant can be brought into commercial production. For example, extraction procedures could prove expensive. We are far from having worked out the technology required.

Additional options await the gasoline grower. One lies with a forest tree of Amazonia, that would obviously require plentiful rainfall if it were to be raised as a plantation crop. *Copaiba langsdorfii*, a member of the legume family, grows almost 30 meters high, with a bole 1 meter in diameter. According to preliminary inquiries (Calvin, 1980), the tree's trunk can be tapped for its hydrocarbon fluid, in much the same manner that New Englanders and eastern Canadians tap sugar maples for syrup or Maylasians tap rubber trees for latex. A single-cup bore of tapping can yield between 10 and 20 liters of hydrocarbon fluid within two hours. The sap's makeup turns out to be so close to that of diesel fuel that it can be put straight into the tank of a diesel truck, whereupon the engine fires immediately and the vehicle can be driven away.

Other trees of the *Copaiba* genus are worth evaluation for their hydrocarbon content. They grow throughout Brazil, from Amazonia to Rio de Janeiro, as well as in other parts of northern South America. They are also found in the West Indies and in Central and West Africa. So there is plenty of variety, both among and within species, for geneticists to investigate.

In addition to the Euphorbiaceae and the Leguminosae, several other plant families produce hydrocarbon-bearing latexes, notably the Apocynaceae, Asclepiadaceae, the Compositae, and the Moraceae. Plainly, if a few front-runner candidates fall at the first fences, there are plenty more waiting a chance to show their paces. Even unlikely-looking species could qualify, notably 11 desert plants of Arizona that have been identified as capable of producing bio-crude at prices ranging from $40 to $60 per barrel (McLaughlin and Hoffmann, 1982; McLaughlin *et al.*, 1982). As we have seen already, arid-zone plants tend to be specially suitable sources of hydrocarbons. But many other categories of plants could serve—for instance, the common milkweed (*Asclepias speciosa*), a plant that grows along roadsides in many parts of the world. Test plots in Alabama and Texas, not only under the aegis of universities but of enterprises such as the Simco Corporation, indicate that sizable yields of oil can be derived from milkweed at prices competitive with OPEC oil. The milkweed latex, containing 30 percent hydrocarbons, can be harvested after only two or three months of growth, whereupon its leaves and stems are ground into pulp to release the juices—a process as straightforward as crushing

When a mature milkweed plant is ready for picking, its pods are about to open, releasing a fluffy floss inside. (Credit: U.S. Department of Agriculture)

grapes to make wine. About 75 percent of the latex solids constitute an oil that can be extracted and refined in conventional manner. The remaining 25 percent of the latex proves to be a water-soluble protein, suitable for the food and cosmetic industries.

Finally, let us consider a plant with an established track record. The "petroleum nut tree" of the Philippines (*Pittosporum resiniferum*) was exploited by the Japanese to obtain tank fuel during World War II, by virtue of its highly volatile oil. Its best use today might not be as a fuel for combustion engines, but as a fuel for household uses. A mere half dozen trees planted in a rural backyard can produce 300 liters of oil (roughly 70 gallons) a year, for a variety of fuel purposes (cooking, lighting, etc.). The nuts grow twice yearly, one kilogram of them producing about 70 grams of oil when pressed. The oil contains hydrocarbons of a type rarely found in nature, burning with a smokey flame at a temperature of about 300° C. In fact, the oil is so flammable that when the nuts are freshly picked, they can be lighted with a match.

A crucial characteristic of many of these hydrocarbon trees is that they need relatively little moisture – not all of them, but many of them. This means that they often prosper in drylands, and need not compete with conventional agriculture that demands a fair amount of rainfall.

Vegetable Oils

A final source of plant-derived fuels lies with vegetable oils from soybean, sunflower, peanut, cottonseed, rape, castor, olive, coconut, and several squashes (Bruwer *et al.*, 1980; Hall, 1981; Hoffman *et al.*, 1980). The oil is easy to extract, through mere pressing of the plant seeds, and is suitable for diesel engines. This means that it can be used in most trucks and many automobiles, in tractors and bulldozers, and in irrigation pumps and diesel-powered generators. In fact, as long ago as 1911 the engineer Diesel wrote that he believed vegetable oils would eventually become a prime source of fuel for his engines in agricultural parts of the world. It now seems a practical proposition that a mechanized corn farm in the United States can, by planting 10 percent of its area to sunflowers, achieve self-sufficiency in farming fuels – and this American experience is being replicated in Australia, West Germany, Austria, Brazil, the Philippines, Zimbabwe, and South Africa.

Of all the plants available, the most promising to date seems to be the sunflower. Trials in the U.S. Midwest, as in other parts of the world, show that almost half the weight of the harvested crop is oil. Even with unsophisticated processes for extraction of the oil, one hectare can produce as much as a metric ton of oil, with yields between 2 and 5 metric tons reckoned to be on the cards when geneticists get to work with breeding research. Soviet scientists have drawn on wild varieties to increase oil content from less than 30 percent to around 50 percent; and they have enhanced resistance to several diseases and developed forms that can be mechanically harvested. (Regrettably the genetic variability of wild stocks of sunflower are declining: in the United States, 13 species of sunflower are endangered.)

The sunflower matures in as little as four months. This opens up the prospect in the tropics, with their year-round growth, for a triple-cropping system for the sunflower that could yield as much as 30 barrels of oil per hectare per year, with production costs around $55 per barrel. True, this price is a good way above OPEC prices. But it may prove favorable for tropical developing countries that wish to safeguard their foreign exchange, that seek to exploit their year-round warmth, and that need to free themselves from dependence on foreign sources of fossil fuels. (Brazil calculates that, because of various economic and political factors, each barrel of oil that the nation imports does not cost $35, but eventually costs $100 a barrel when the government takes into account all the associated finance charges, foreign debt problems, and opportunity costs.) A pioneer in the sunflower-fuel field is Zimbabwe, which hopes to obtain between one-tenth and one-fifth of its fuel through the sunflower, together with other plants. Several other African countries plan to follow Zimbabwe's example.

Even without OPEC's emergence, we would swiftly pass through the fossil-fuel era of humankind's energy use. In fact, a mere couple of centures at most would probably have accounted for our swift depletion of Earth's accessible deposits of fossil fuels. The day may come when we shall thank OPEC for giving us the nudge we need to get off our petroleum kick and to devise sustainable ways of producing energy. Our best hope of renewable types of energy appears to lie with the abundant diversity of materials in the 300,000 species of the plant kingdom.

CHAPTER TWELVE

——————————■——————————

Some Esoteric Uses
of Wildlife

Wild creatures increasingly serve esoteric functions in support of humankind. To complete this section on industrial applications of wildlife, let us look at some of these "way out" uses.

Pollution Indicators

In their reactions to pollution and related forms of environmental degradation, wildlife species can serve as indicators of what is happening to our life-support systems (National Academy of Sciences, 1979; Newman, 1980). Pigeons, for example, sometimes suffer sharp decline in their population ostensibly because of atmospheric pollution—and they thereby offer a sensitive register of our fouling of the earth's air mantle (Tansey and Roth, 1970). Wild hares, sparrows, and ducks similarly alert us to rising levels of sulfur dioxide and particulates (McArn et al., 1974; Novakova and Roubal, 1971). Both pigeons and rats serve as biological monitors of lead and asbestos residues.

As for water pollution, wading birds often prove helpful, notably several species of heron, egret, ibis, spoonbill, and stork (Coster and Osborn, 1977). One quarter of a million of these birds breed along the Atlantic shoreline of the United States, a zone where many industrial plants discharge pollutant emissions into estuaries. Since they frequently constitute a terminal link in aquatic food chains, wading birds can reflect changes originating in several different components of their ecosystems. They are sensitive not only to gross habitat disruption, but to covert pollution poisoning, as instanced by the brown pelican of Louisiana and California (Anderson et al., 1975). These birds offer further monitoring advantages in that they tend to have dense population concentrations distributed over wide geographic areas, a pattern that facilitates systematic sampling.

Further first-rate monitors of aquatic ecosystems are mollusks such as oysters, mussels, and clams (Lockwood, 1976). These creatures live in muddy or sandy beds of coastal-zone ecosystems, where sedimentary deposits can accumulate as much as 90 percent of the chemicals carried from terrestrial environments into estuaries and other shoreline habitats. Bivalves pump vast quantities of water each day through their tissues. According to Dr. Mark D. Sobsey, of the University of North Carolina at Chapel Hill, clams and oysters pump almost 400 gallons every day, and certain clams can accommodate 1,000 times more water than a human being drinks in a day. By virtue of these filtering processes, mollusks quickly build up residues of chemical contaminants. Being widely harvested, they can supply systematic streams of data for public health records. Several governments are now collaborating in an international Mussel-Watch Program along their countries' coastlines. Ironically, these sensitive services of mollusks are being discovered precisely at a time when American scientists are finding that as many as half of U.S. mollusks are either extinct or endangered (Davies, 1977).

Among other aquatic creatures that help us with water-body monitoring are certain insects that, being sensitive to slight changes in their habitats, can keep us informed of what we are doing to our water supplies, principally in freshwater ecosystems but also in coastal marine ecosystems. Similarly, goldfish can be put to work to monitor waterborne pollutants. The West German city of Goppingen utilizes goldfish that normally emit several electrical impulses per minute as they swim. If the level of zinc, cadmium, mercury, and other pollutants in the water grows too high, the fish do not generate as much electricity as usual, and the "power shortage" triggers a danger signal at a public-utility headquarters.

Even terrestrial animals can serve as indicators of the health of aquatic ecosystems. In Minamata Bay of Japan, mercury pollution first came to light in the form of aberrant behavior on the part of local cats and birds. This behavior would have been a forewarning, if anybody had cared to take notice, of neurological disorders that eventually overtook local fishermen and their families. Similar indicator services can be supplied by many mammals and birds. Examples include deer, rabbits, pheasants, quail, wild turkeys, cottontail rabbits, muskrats, ground squirrels, woodchucks, voles, foxes, barn owls, house martins, and house sparrows (Balazova and Hluchan, 1969; Dewey, 1973; Gordon, 1969; Heagle, 1973; Karstad, 1970; Kay et al., 1975; Newman and Yu, 1976; Nishino et al., 1973; Trainer, 1973). Also useful are such exotic creatures as spruce gall lice, bark beetles, mites, bees, and even tubifex worms (Wentzel, 1965; Wood, 1973), sawlice, and aphids (Darley, 1966).

Among the best indicators of all are plants (Mansfield, 1976; Schairer et al., 1978). Certain wild plants can even register radiation. An example is the spiderwort, a common wild flower that looks like a normal houseplant with long grassy leaves, a waxy stem, and tiny lavender-hued flowers. The plant has long been known as an indicator of pollution from pesticides, auto exhausts, and sulfur dioxides. Now the tiny plant is revealing itself as an ultrasensitive monitor of ionizing radiation (Ichikawa, 1979). Upon exposure to as little as 150 millirems of radiation, the hair cells of the plant's stamens mutate from a normal blue to pink (we all receive around 100 millirems per year from our natural surroundings). The reason for the change in color is that radiation rapidly destroys the genetic material that gives rise to the usually dominant blue pigmentation of the flower; thus, pink cells serve as a measure of the amount of radiation injury.

So sensitive is the spiderwort that it could prove to be a better measure of radiation than mechanical counters such as a dosimeter. The dosimeter commonly utilized for such purposes is limited to detecting external exposure, whereas living organisms absorb radiation internally. Even more to the point, the spiderwort's stamens turn pink within a mere 10–18 days of exposure, whereas human complications may take as much as 15–40 years to develop – sometimes in the form of cancers. According to preliminary tests in several large industrial cities throughout the United States, where higher-than-normal cancer rates have been documented, the spiderwort could serve as a "sentinel" to warn us of certain environmental hazards that may be implicated in up to 80 percent of all cancers. So promising is the plant that a California company, Protech Products, Inc., of Santa Barbara, is now marketing the spiderwort – and not only as a warning device against potential cancer-causing radiation, but as a monitor of pesticides, fungicides, herbicides, and sulfur dioxide.

Along parallel lines, the U.S. Environmental Protection Agency has been looking at several other plant species that may be unusually sensitive to mutagens (substances capable of causing changes in genetic structures or functions of organisms). Among possible candidates are corn, barley, and a member of the mustard family known as Arabidopsis (Nilan, 1978; Schairer et al., 1978).

According to related research at the University of Illinois at Urbana, seeds of certain strains of corn, when exposed to mutagens, reveal mutations in the genes that control the starch composition in the seeds

(Plawa and Wagner, 1981). Insofar as pollen grains are the functional units for expression of the starch-controlling genes, an iodine-stain test reveals that normal pollen grains become black, while mutants reveal a reddish-brown color. Further work at Washington State University indicates that barley, with large chromosomes that are easily visible through a microscope, is useful in warning of chromosomal damage that can be detected by inspection, i.e. without costly biochemical analysis.

Another common plant that reveals a relationship with radiation, albeit a basically different relationship, is the sagebrush of the Western United States. Satellite images taken over a 12,000-km² section of the Powder River Basin in northeastern Wyoming and southeastern Montana suggest that the sagebrush acts as an indicator of uranium deposits (Raines et al., 1978). Unusually dense patches of the plant appear to be roughly coextensive with uranium deposits.

Plants can likewise help with exploration for minerals in other parts of the world. Along the Copperbelt zone of the Zambia/Zaire borderlands, for example, many species of Crotalaria appear to concentrate metal traces in their tissues, thereby serving as "pointers" to deposits of copper and cobalt (Brooks et al., 1977). Similar concentrations of copper have been noted in plant species in Indonesia (Brooks et al., 1978), and of nickel in various parts of Southeast Asia (Wither and Brooks, 1977), in New Caledonia (Lee et al., 1978), and in certain plants in Europe (Brooks and Radford, 1978). Equally revealing is the accumulation of gold in certain plants in New Zealand (Ward and Brooks, 1978).

In like fashion, a few animals can help us to identify deposits of important minerals. Bees are an example (Warren, 1980). When a honeybee enters its hive, it "wipes" its six feet, causing pollen to fall off at the entrance – and the pollen may contain traces of molybdenum, cadmium, copper, zinc, lead, and iron. According to experiments at the University of British Columbia in Canada, certain pollen collections reveal a molybdenum concentration 40 times greater than would be considered "normal."

Trees as Pollution Cleanup Devices

Trees can perform a distinctive cleanup job on pollution, especially urban pollution – and notably that prime contaminant of industrial localities, sulphur dioxide (Bach, 1972; Roberts, 1974, 1976, and 1979; U.S. Forest Service, 1977). Wherever there is much smelting of sulphur-containing ores or burning of fossil fuels such as coal (also those types of oil with heavy sulphur loads), the atmosphere often contains harmful quantities of sulphur dioxide. If you check the air beneath the canopy of a maple birch or a sweet gum, you can generally find the smog level is significantly less than in the open surroundings. In Hyde Park, a well-treed area of only 2.5 km^2 in central London, the smoke concentration in the mid-1960s was found to be 27 percent less than that in nongreen areas surrounding the park (Meethan, 1964). So when city fathers invest in "green belts" around our conurbations, we can thank them for establishing these "sinks" for the pollutants that would otherwise harm our bodies, let alone our city buildings.

A good number of tree species are fitted for cleanup functions. A beech or an elm, for example, can remove particulate matter from the atmosphere. A 100-year old beech or elm possesses hundreds of thousands of leaves, sometimes as many as half a million or even more. Moreover, these leaves possess millions of stomata, or holes through which carbon dioxide in the atmosphere penetrates into the leaf interior; and because of these openings, the operational "surface" area of the leaf is increased many times over. Hence the leaves of an outsize tree feature a "surface" area of at least one hectare, sometimes a good deal more. The foliage intercepts dust in the air, hundreds of kilograms of it. A one-hectare clump of beech or elm trees can retain at least 40 metric tons of dirt, sometimes much more. Along comes a shower of rain and washes the dust from the leaves into the soil, back where it came from.

Not so effective, but still reasonably efficient, are sycamore trees, able to take 25–30 metric tons of dirt per hectare from the air. Less effective still, because their needlelike leaves offer a smaller surface, are pine trees—yet they can handle at least 15 metric tons of dirt per hectare.

Of course, too much gunk from the atmosphere reduces a tree's health. The dust particles begin to clog its pores. If a beech tree is subject to an undue load of atmospheric pollution, it will eventually die. The same for an elm tree—and it is air pollution that may have caused many elms to start to suffer from "environmental fatigue," making them increasingly subject to attack by the pandemic disease that is causing havoc in parts of North America and Europe. More resistant, hence more capable cleaners in badly polluted localities, are elder, willow, and oak trees. Probably the best of the lot in terms of its readiness to thrive in dirty atmospheres is the plane tree that offers its amenities, both functional and aesthetic, in many urban areas.

These comments apply of course to temperate zones. Tropical trees seem to be still more capable of filtering dust, smoke, soot, and other fine particles from the atmosphere. A tamarind can collect at least

The water hyacinth has proved an expensive weed in those many areas, such as the southern United States, where it chokes irrigation channels. Fortunately, we may soon be able to control the hyacinth through natural controls in the form of plant-eating insects. As an alternative, we may shortly be able to exploit the hyacinth for its capacities as a depolluting agent in sewage lagoons. The plant could even prove to be a fine source of fiber. (Credit: U.S. Department of Agriculture)

twice as much dust per square meter of leaf surface as a maple, a cassia two and a quarter times as much, several flame trees and other flamboyants almost three times as much, a fig tree four times, and a teak five times (Das, 1981).

As for a cleanup agent for bodies of water we can turn to a candidate we have met before (chapter 11), the water hyacinth (*Eichhornia crassipes*) (Tourbier and Pierson, 1976; Wolverton and McDonald, 1979). An infamous aquatic weed in many parts of the world, the water hyacinth multiplies at prodigious rates, covering lakes and blocking canals. A mere 10 plants can multiply to 600,000 in just eight months, forming a carpet a quarter of a hectare in size – and a carpet thick enough for a person to walk across. Fortunately the water hyacinth features an unusual capacity to extract pollutants from sewage. Experiments at the National Space Technology Laboratory in Hancock County, Mississippi, demonstrate the remarkable recycling capacities of the plant. Suspended solids can be reduced by 90 percent, to a mere 10 milligrams per liter – meaning that the hungry plants extract most of the organic material dissolved in the sewage. In addition, the hyacinth reduces ammonia and organically-bound nitrogen by 73 percent, and phosphorus by 57 percent. All in all, one hectare of water hyacinths can eliminate the daily nitrogen and phosphorus wastes of around 850 people. Moreover, the plant can filter out toxic heavy metals such as cadmium, mercury, lead, and nickel. It can also absorb or metabolize trace-organic compounds such as phenols that are suspected of being carcinogenic (Tourbier and Pierson, 1976; Wolverton and McDonald, 1979). The hyacinth's roots concentrate the substances to a level thousands of times higher than in surrounding water. A similar service is supplied by a number of other aquatic plants that are otherwise regarded as weedy pests (Hillman and Culley, 1978; Wolverton and McDonald, 1981). To the extent that these various plant species can efficiently purify contaminated water, they constitute a natural boon for factories that spew out pollutant materials.

Animals and Earthquakes

Certain animals appear to react to seismic disturbances preceding earthquakes. In this sense, they can possibly help us to anticipate the robust earth tremors that shake up our life-styles. True, the animals appear to react similarly in certain other situations (albeit not many), and it is far from clear whether they can really help alert us to impending catastrophes. (We can't have an earthquake alarm every time the animals go into a huddle.) The animals presumably perform their pre-earthquake function by picking up seismic vibrations that lie beyond human sensitivity – and beyond even the sensitivity of our finest technological devices (Anderson, 1973; Kerr, 1980; Kraemer *et al.*, 1978; Simon, 1975).

In June 1976, chimpanzees at the Outdoor Primate Facility at Stanford, California, showed signs of becoming upset. They crowded together, presumably for joint security. This type of behavior in the wild, for example in African parks, often indicates that animals feel bothered about something, whereupon they huddle together for common protection. The day after the aberrant behavior at Stanford, a minor earthquake struck California, without any warning registered on seismic instruments. Again in 1977, animals at the Little Lake Valley area northwest of San Francisco started to act out of character. Dogs and cats set up a shindig, horses kicked their stalls, and other animals refused to leave their shelters to feed outside. Next day the locality was shaken by an earthquake. More recently, in August 1979, a number of animals at Marine World in California started to behave oddly. A group of zebras, ostriches, deer, and antelope that were sharing a common enclosure and were generally ready enough to mingle with each other began to separate out into small groups of individual species. Again, an earthquake struck shortly thereafter.

Scientists can offer little explanation to account for this curious behavior. Indeed many experts think that the out-of-character antics of the animals are coincidental. But there is enough interest for the Stanford Research Institute and other scientific centers in California to start a systematic study. They have sent out questionnaires to qualified observers in many parts of the earthquake-prone state. They are also comparing notes with colleagues in Japan and China, who already utilize animals as early-warning systems.

It is possible that an impending earthquake triggers electric discharges in the earth's atmosphere. Particles known as positive ions released in the air by these electric impulses frequently precede thunderstorms and other electric disturbances in the atmosphere. Such occasions are noted for the irritability and nervousness of certain creatures, also for headaches and nausea in some humans. So could the animals of California be reacting to charged particles in the air? An equally plausible explanation could lie with high- or low-frequency sounds released by anticipatory rumblings of an earthquake – vibrations that arise beyond the range of noises detectable by the human ear but perhaps available to dogs, horses, and other animals with their different hearing ranges.

Research Models for Industry and Manufacturing

As we have seen in the chapters dealing with medicine, wild species can often help us in a role as research models. They can help in the same role in industry.

The woodpecker, for example, may soon help us to design better crash helmets. High-speed films reveal that when the bird is searching for insects or drilling a nesting place in a tree trunk, its beak can hammer away with a speed on impact of around 75 meters per second, or over 300 km per hour. One complete "peck cycle" takes only a 1,000th of a second or less. This means that the deceleration force at the end of each stroke is around 1,000G, where one G is the acceleration needed to counteract earth's gravity. (An astronaut in a Saturn V rocket experiences only 3.5–4G during blast-off.) Yet despite repeated shocks of so great an order, the 28-gram brain of the woodpecker remains uninjured. The bird does not even appear to sustain a headache.

What is the woodpecker's secret? According to Dr. Philip May of the

Neuropsychiatric Institute at the University of California at Los Angeles, and his colleagues at the Brentwood Veterans Administration Hospital in California, the woodpecker's head features a brain case of tough spongy bone, together with sets of opposed muscles that presumably serve as shock absorbers. Equally important, the bird's neck muscles are so finely coordinated that when the woodpecker is hammering away at its target, its head moves forward and backwards in a single plane, allowing no sideways movement at all. If the bird were to strike its tree at even a slight angle, the deviation could cause trouble through internal shearing of the brain within the skull. But because there is no "whiplash" rotation during each stroke, the bird escapes injury to its brain, also to its neck vertebrae and spinal cord.

All this suggests at least two clues to improved crash helmets. First of all, the helmets should be made not only thicker but lighter, with a firm shock-absorbing foam held within a thin surface layer of tougher material to diffuse impact. Second, they should be so designed as to restrict sideways movement, possibly by incorporating some kind of neck brace to reduce whiplash.

The mechanics of movement in other creatures can help us with research models for improved design of industrial equipment. For example, a species of chalcid wasp may help us to build better helicopters (Furber and Ffowes-Williams, 1979). Of the millions of species of flying insects on Earth, the wasp is unique in that its wings interact with one another in a manner that allows each to provide a starting vortex for the other. This mechanism contrasts with the process utilized by other flying animals, known as "vortex shedding." By virtue of its specialized technique, the chalcid wasp achieves a lift coefficient that is double that of vortex shedding, enabling the creature to hover with an aerodynamic performance superior in many respects to anything else known. The interactive movement of the wasp's wings, being radically different in principle from other types of aerodynamic functioning, can supply "design inspiration" for engineers to fashion a more efficient type of helicopter. To the extent that the wasp's mode of aerodynamic lift can be adapted to turbomachinery, it will provide a technological breakthrough for vertical-lift aircraft.

Now for a form of life that may help us to detect further forms of life, in both positive and negative senses. The firefly, whose luminescent antics we often observe at dusk, produces a flash from its tail through the reaction of two chemicals, known as luciferin and luciferase. These two chemicals react with a substance present in all living things, adenosine triphosphate, or ATP for short. When the firefly's chemicals are brought into contact with oxygen, they react to release energy in the form of light. The more ATP, the greater the biological activity, and the more intense the flash of the firefly's tail. Pollution researchers are learning to exploit the firefly's chemicals in order to measure cell growth in eutrophic waters with its high oxygen demand; and equally important, cancer researchers are using the same firefly chemicals to monitor growth rates of cancer cells. In either case, the merest flash response will alert scientists to what they are seeking. As an ultimate "way out" application of the chemicals, space-research engineers place samples in rockets as a device to detect life in outer space. The presence of even one quadrillionth of a gram of ATP would cause a minute glimmer that can be registered by the rocket's instruments.

As an alternative application, chemiluminescent light sources, producing light with little heat and no sparks, can help in circumstances where conventional lighting is extremely dangerous, for example in mines and in industries where flammable or explosive fumes or dust are generated. And the American Cyanamid Company now produces some chemicals for risk-free lighting.

Similar sources of harmless lighting may become available from creatures that live in the oceans at depths where sunlight does not penetrate, ranging from the surface to depths of four or five kilometers (Hastings, 1976). In these zones, animals of numerous species, from shrimplike crustaceans to large fishes, give off light, presumably through biochemical reactions akin to those of the firefly.

Seaweeds

Finally, let us consider an unlikely-looking source of a multitude of products for our material welfare. Seaweeds are algae of types that occur in many shapes and sizes. The Sargasso weed of the Caribbean can be 50 meters or more in length, whereas the tiniest seaweeds measure about 3 micrometers in length (three times one-millionth of a meter). More than almost all other categories of organisms in the oceans, seaweeds offer vast numbers of applications (Chapman, 1976 and 1980; Guiry, 1979; Madlener, 1977; Michanek, 1975, 1978, and 1981; Naylor, 1976). Although most species of seaweeds have yet to be analyzed as food sources, the seaweed-food industry is now worth over $1 billion per year. Large as this sum is, it is surely matched by seaweed products for medicine and industry.

Start-point materials from seaweeds are used for drugs and pharmaceuticals in the form of anticoagulants, antibiotics, and medicinals to treat stomach ulcers, bronchitis, emphysema, epilepsy, blood pressure, cholesterol problems, atherosclerosis, and hypertension. Yet biomedical researchers have only started on their investigations of seaweeds' contributions to modern medicine (Chapman, 1977; Kaul and Sindermann, 1978).

As for industry, seaweeds supply alginate compounds that contribute to literally hundreds of end-products such as plastics, waxes, polishes, transistors, deodorants, soaps, detergents, pharmaceuticals, shampoos, cosmetics, paints, dyes, paper products, photographic films, fire-extinguishing foams, building materials (notably insulation products, sealing compounds, and artificial wood), and lubricants and coolants used in drilling for oil. Seaweeds prove a notable source of vitamin C. They serve as a source or ingredient of poultry meal, food stabilizers, emulsifiers, eggnog mixes, cake batters, pie fillings, pudding thickeners, bakery jellies, doughnut glazes, and meat and fish preservatives. They are further used to make ice cream smooth, to keep the chocolate evenly distributed in chocolate milk, to manufacture sherbets, to grow bacteria, to make candy bars last longer, to keep canned hams from bruising, and to keep toothpaste in the tube.

Among raw materials from seaweeds, a leading item is agar-agar. As a measure of agar-agar's contributions to the U.S. economy, it is utilized to an extent of 450 metric tons per year by the microbiology industry, to suspend, thicken, stabilize, and gell aqueous preparations. Extraction of agar-agar from the seas is primarily conducted by Japan, Spain, and Portugal. But the industry holds great potential for dozens of coastal sectors of Africa and Southern and Southeast Asia. The present global harvest of some 6,000 metric tons of agar-agar could be increased at least 25 times over.

Most of the agar-agar and of a related product, carrageen, utilized in the United States is imported from the three developed nations named, but an increasing amount is imported from the Philippines and Chile, both of which have established mariculture industries. The Philippines has expanded its output of seaweed from some 10,500 metric tons wet weight in the mid-1960s to 70,000 in the late 1970s. Chile's exports have increased from 1,500 metric tons in 1969 to 10,000 metric tons one decade later. Many other developing countries, especially those of the tropics, could follow the example of the Philippines and Chile. Already Brazil is boosting its harvest toward 100,000 metric tons a year.

Even with this expansion of the seaweed industry, total harvest worldwide does not surpass 3 million metric tons of seaweeds a year, of which China accounts for 1,650,000 metric tons. In the early 1950s, China was reaping only a few dozen metric tons of seaweed, all from wild plants in the sea. Then the Chinese started intensive management of a Japanese kelp, *Laminaria japonica*, using a "floating raft" method that keeps plants near the surface at both high and low tides. At the same time, Chinese geneticists bred three superior strains of the kelp, rich in iodine, eventually leading to establishment of nurseries that produce 3,800 million young plants per year for transplanting into the open sea. By 1970 China was harvesting over half a million metric tons of seaweeds. The amount has increased threefold during the 1970s.

These experiences demonstrate how wild plants of the oceans can be domesticated as marine crops. Many other options lie ahead in developing seaweeds, among other plants, as sources of drugs and industrial materials – and more food – supposing the various species retain adequate genetic variability in their populations. Seaweeds can also be exploited as a source of energy in the forms of ethanol and methane gas (Michanek, 1978 and 1981; Wilcox, 1976). If giant kelp is used as a source of bio-energy feedstocks, it converts to 29 kilowatts, or 100 megajoules, per square meter. According to field trials, an ocean farm of 4 km^2 could yield enough energy to support almost 500 persons at today's U.S. per-capita consumption level – plus supply foodstuffs for several times as many people.

PART FOUR

Genetic Engineering

CHAPTER THIRTEEN

■

The Ultimate
Genetic Contribution

As recently as 1980, we heard little about genetic engineering and its associated biotechnologies. A few papers in scientific journals and occasional articles in magazines—that was about it. Today we come across several such reports every week. Genetic engineering has arrived.

Not only has it arrived, it has arrived with a bang. Very soon, within a year or two, it will start to affect our daily lives in myriad ways (the booming literature on this topic is too extensive to review here; the reader is recommended to consult an excellent compendium of latest findings, Office of Technology Assessment, 1981). Each time we reach into the medicince cabinet, sit down at the table, visit a local shopping precinct, use a plastic product, or drive a car, we shall reap the benefits of a revolution whose impact will surely be as widespread as any of the great technical revolutions of history—including the original domestication of crops, discovery of microbial sources of illness, harnessing of electricity, splitting of the atom, and our venturing into space. Among the marvels of genetic engineering that we can confidently anticipate within the present decade should be, for instance, a crop plant that supplies us with edible leaves, high-protein beanlike seeds, large nutritious tubers, and useful fiber from the stalk. Genetic engineering will help us to grow a super-tree that matures in just a few years instead of several decades, incorporating a whole bunch of desirable timber traits in its wood. Genetic engineering will enable us to devise bugs that degrade environmental pollutants, and even help us to extract more minerals from the ground. Genetic engineering will create new life forms (there is no better phrase for the process) that will, with their tailormade attributes, serve our needs in scores of ways.

In short, biotechnology offers us the possibility of building a sustainable future based on renewable resources. Its potential could well bring us closer to material well-being for all citizens on Earth than has been achieved through human ingenuity during the whole of human history. Hence the justification of level-headed observations that biotechnology will be to the 1980s and 1990s what transistors and computers have been to the 1960s and 1970s. Put another way, the biotechnology revolution is already comparable to the microprocessor revolution that started to dominate electronics ten years ago.

In the view of many experts, there are only two limitations to the scope of genetic engineering. The first lies with the imagination and vision of bio-crats. As they learn to flex their scientific muscles, geneticists are comprehending that they hold immense wealth and power in the genes at their fingertips. By figuring out the secrets of these genes, i.e., the strands of DNA that carry the coding for heredity, scientists are manipulating the chemical alphabet of life, with the result that they can now write an entire new lexicon of life forms. It will not take them long to discover whether they possess the creative impulse to put their technical skills to work.

The second limitation could prove just as readily surmountable. But our recent track records suggest that we may allow it to get on top of us. This limitation lies with the Earth's genetic stocks and the rate at which they are being depleted. As this book has made clear time and again, our planet harbors immense stocks of genetic resources, in extraordinarily diversified forms. Yet at the precise stage in human history when we are developing unprecedented capacity to exploit Earth's biotic diversity in order to breed still further diversity on virtually a limitless scale, we are busily destroying the genetic stocks that nature has supplied to us. This aspect of the situation is dealt with in further detail in the final chapter of this book. Suffice it here to note that the extinction spasm that we are imposing on our fellow species could well serve to impoverish humankind, with its scientific talents and its technological inventiveness, as much in the field of genetic engineering as in agriculture, medicine, and other fields. To reiterate the central point, we are now destroying genetic diversity not only among species, but within them as well. Each species has many discrete populations, each possessing its own genetic makeup. With every tick of the clock, we disrupt natural environments and their wildlife communities—and each tick brings an irreversible end to unique genetic material.

In this regard, a species is no longer to be viewed as just a distinctive conglomerate of genes. Thanks to the skills of genetic engineers, a species can now be viewed as a depository of genes that are potentially transferable. This reevaluation confers a new meaning on the phenomenon of extinction. To cite Professor Thomas Eisner of Cornell University, "Extinction does not simply mean the loss of one volume from the library of nature. It means the loss of a loose-leaf book whose individual pages, were the species to survive, would remain available in perpetuity for selective transfer and improvement of other species."

Nature and Scope of Genetic Engineering

Broadly speaking, genetic engineering is an emergent technology that manipulates the molecular structure of cells in order to alter the genetic constitution of life forms. The process can be accomplished in two basic ways. The first is known as tissue culture, coupled with protoplast fusion. The second is recombination of DNA material. More detail on these two strategies will follow, but let us note here that in either case, geneticists achieve a fundamental rejiggering of the genetic makeup of an organism; and in turn this modifies the organism's structure and functions, its growth and adaptability, etc. By transforming the basic alchemy of organisms, scientists can fairly claim to be "inventing" new forms of life. True, they have not proceeded very far down this pioneering track. But they can readily transfer genes between microorganisms, they are well into transferring genes between animals, and they are starting to transfer genes between plants.

Of the two techniques, let us leave tissue culture and protoplast fusion for the moment, returning to it when we look at genetic engineering applications for agriculture, this being the field where the technique is most used. Meanwhile we shall take a quick look at the technique of recombinant DNA.

In order to recombine DNA – the molecule of genetic control – scientists first establish the exact sequence of DNA that they wish to transplant into another organism. At the same time, they identify the appropriate "switch" for that organism, i.e., the correct sequence of DNA that enables the host's cell machinery to exploit the new genetic material. When they are ready to carry out the transfer, they devise their "vector," or a transport system that will carry the foreign genetic information into the new organism without being destroyed by that organism's immune system. Having assembled all the requisite information and spare parts, the scientists can go ahead – and bingo, the genetic material is spliced into a fresh host, whereupon it becomes integrated with a fresh assembly of life processes.

In the case of microorganisms and animals, scientists have now devised several sets of both switches and vectors. In the case of plants, however, they are still trying to develop workable systems. It is one thing to insert a single "foreign" gene into a plant and make it function, but another to insert a whole collection of genes that will work in concert to give the plant an interrelated complex of entirely new and beneficial characteristics. Hence the delay in persuading cereal plants, as notable instances, to fix their own nitrogen; hence also the delay in improving the photosynthetic functions of several valuable but "energy-inefficient" crops. To date, these challenges are regarded as "blue skies" projects that may become possible one day, but that will not be part of the real world until scientists unravel several key problems of plant cell biology. Still, it was only a few years ago that the prospect of gene transfers of any kind were regarded as pie-in-the-sky notions, whereas today they are becoming as much a part of the molecular geneticist's daily routine as brushing his teeth.

What happens in the key process when the fragments of genetic information are spliced together, and implanted into, say, a bacterium? Each time the bacterium divides, the genetic fragments likewise divide – and herein lies the potential of the entire recombinant DNA technique. Implant a human gene that produces, say, insulin into a microorganism that replicates quickly. Within half an hour, the microorganism duplicates itself, and both new individuals contain the insulin-making gene. After another half hour, this population of two divides again. There are four, soon eight, then sixteen. Within 48 hours the single microorganism will reproduce billions of copies of itself, with billions of miniature cellular chemical factories busily manufacturing insulin. Result, an abundance of a high-quality material at little cost.

The technique can be applied with respect to many other genetic combinations. A range of microorganisms can inexpensively produce hormones, enzymes, industrial chemicals, energy materials, plastics, whatever – you name it. The principal applications suggested by these examples of recombinant DNA technology lie with medicine and chemical industry.

Applications in Medicine

Microorganisms, principally bacteria, are now regularly used in the manufacture of an array of medicinal products. These include vitamins, steroids, enzymes, organic acids, vaccines, antibiotics, and antibodies. A specially important category comprises hormones, for example a hormone that prevents certain types of dwarfism. There are specialized chemicals of various sorts, such as endorphins and enkephalins – painkilling materials found in the brains of many animals and hitherto defying the efforts of scientists to manufacture them synthetically and cheaply. In addition, there are large numbers of esoteric-sounding items such as urokinase for treatment of blood clots, somatostatin for brain disorders, and thymosin for controlling the immune response.

We can expect that all these categories of medical products will show great advances in terms of both quantity and quality. Vaccines may soon become available for intractable parasitic and viral diseases such as amoebic dysentery and trachoma, which will lead to a marked decline in morbidity and mortality in developing countries. The burgeoning technology will also help developed-world citizens, through, for example, a vaccine against viral hepatitis. This disease affects 300,000 Americans and threatens another 16 million each year, ranking it among the leading infectious diseases as a cause of death. Hitherto scientists have found it extremely difficult to cultivate the causative agents of the disease, but a breakthrough may be achieved by molecular cloning of a vaccine.

The same molecular cloning technique can help with three other sorts of antigens. It will offer vaccines against parasites such as malaria and hookworm, immunization with respect to cancer treatment, and counteracting agents for auto-immune disease such as multiple sclerosis.

True, some observers remain skeptical about these euphoric predictions from the genetic engineering fraternity. But we can recall the exceptional and unexpected success in development of an organism that produces human insulin to treat diabetes. In the United States, diabetes ranks as the fifth most common cause of death, and the second most common cause of blindness. Two million Americans who daily require injections of insulin will soon receive a more effective, as well as a cheaper, form of insulin.

Similar hopeful prospects await us with respect to interferon. This protein is created by the human body in small amounts to fight viral infections. All types of interferon can induce an antiviral state in susceptible cells, which means that it can be used against influenza, polio, shingles, rabies, various herpes infections, and the common cold. Still greater promise may lie ahead in terms of its use against Hodgkin's disease, leukemia, and breast cancer, among other forms of cancer.

Moreover, genetic engineering will generate sizable economic savings. Genetic improvement of penicillin, for example, has led to 55-fold increases in production processes. Chemically induced mutations yield over 100 times more L-asparaginase (used against leukemia) than the original strain, meaning that a course of therapy now costs only about $300, or one-fiftieth as much as before. Genetic engineering also assists with biosynthetic production of materials that suppress appetite, presumably by way of a satiety signal from the stomach to the brain – and this will make a solid contribution to the anti-obesity market, worth more than $200 million a year in the United States alone.

Biotechnology may even help with a cheaper production process for vincristine, the drug that has led to remission for many sufferers from several forms of cancer. Hitherto the production of vincristine has been a lengthy and costly process. Derived from the rosy periwinkle, the drug has required more than 2,000 kg of plant leaves before pharmacologists could come up with one gram of vinca alkaloid, at a cost of about $250 per gram. As a result of biotechnology techniques, however, scientists can isolate plant cells from the periwinkle, and then culture them. The cultured cells not only continue to synthesize alkaloids at a high rate, they even secrete the material directly into the culture medium instead of accumulating it within the cell, thus eliminating the need for extensive extraction procedures.

In similar fashion, Japanese geneticists are culturing cells from the velvet bean in order to derive L-dopa, a drug used in treatment of Parkinson's disease. Another major pharmaceutical, diosgenin, is the prime raw material for production of corticosteroids and sex steroids, such as the estrogens and progestins used in birth-control pills. The large tuberous roots of diosgenin's plant source, *Dioscorea*, have hitherto been collected from forest habitats in Mexico and parts of Central America. But the plant's cells are now being cultured in the laboratory, making the process much speedier and less costly. Through a parallel technique, the opium poppy's well known alkaloids can be synthesized in a culture medium, together with some further alkaloids that have yet to turn up in extracts from the whole plant.

As for veterinary medicine, scientists are on the point of manufacturing a better and cheaper vaccine for hoof-and-mouth disease. So widespread is the disease virus that around 800 million doses of the present vaccine are required worldwide each year, making it the largest-volume vaccine ever produced. It must be administered frequently to livestock in areas where disease is endemic, including most of the world outside North America. The present methods of producing the vaccine require enormous quantitites of hazardous virus to be kept in stock. Many outbreaks of the disease are attributed to poorly inactivated vaccine, or to the escape of the virus from vaccine-manufacturing factories. Scientists now hope to synthesize portions of the protein produced by the disease virus, and thereby to achieve molecular cloning of the antigen. When once they have identified the segment that turns on antibody production in diseased animals, scientists expect to produce a stable and risk-free vaccine in large quantities, at relatively small expense.

Applications for Industry

Genetic engineering can assist in three main areas of industry, these being mineral leaching and recovery, enhanced oil recovery, and pollution control (Office of Technology Assessment, 1980 and 1981; Sebek and Laskin, 1979; Sharpley and Kaplan, 1976). Each of these three areas is characterized by use of large volumes of microorganisms.

Certain bacteria have the ability to leach minerals from the ground. Although scientists know next to nothing about the precise mechanisms involved, they believe that suitably engineered organisms could be used to help extract minerals from the ground. For example, appropriate types of bacteria could be blown into low-grade copper ores, whereupon the bacteria would produce an enzyme to eat away salts in the ore, leaving behind an almost pure form of copper. This means that low-grade ores that cannot be mined economically through conventional technology, or that lie in rough terrain where conventional mining technologies do not apply, could soon be exploited. This strategy will, in certain circumstances, refine the ores to such an extent that there will be no need to smelt them. Notable elements that often are found in low-grade ores are copper and uranium.

In addition to their use in the mining process, microorganisms can be used to recover valuable metals from industrial effluents. The microorganisms bind metals to their surfaces, and then concentrate them internally.

The second area of application is enhanced oil recovery. Many an oil deposit retains a good half of its material after conventional drilling is completed, because present technology cannot extract more from the oil-bearing strata at economic cost. In some circumstances, however, chemicals can change the oil's flow characteristics, thus enhancing recovery. The present front-runner chemical, xanthan, does not work well, and scientists hope that microorganisms can be engineered to generate more effective chemicals.

Third is pollution control. Many microorganisms already play a role in pollution control by virtue of their natural activities. Many polluted sites of industry reveal unique strains of microorganisms that consume the pollutants, converting them into relatively harmless materials. Scientists now aim to design bacteria with better appetites for waste materials, especially toxins – an exceptionally useful breakthrough for pollution problems like that of the Love Canal crisis. Using the plasmid portions of DNA isolated from naturally occurring bacteria that break down hydrocarbons, bio-engineers plan to modify other microorganisms to digest and degrade a variety of toxins. Already a strain of bacterium has been created that destroys the herbicide 2,4,5-T. At relatively high concentrations of 1,000 parts per million of the toxic chemical in the soil, the new organism goes to work and consumes more than 98 percent. But it takes two weeks to consume one milligram of the chemical, so scientists hope to create an improved bacterium that will do the job in a day or two.

Even the military are finding constructive applications for microorganisms. An enzyme has been discovered that detoxifies nerve gases. So potent are these poisonous gases that a pinhead-sized speck on human skin kills in a few minutes. When the enzyme acts on the nerve gases, it breaks them down into relatively harmless byproducts. The enzyme could be developed as a quick antidote for injection into humans suffering from nerve-gas attack.

Finally, an energy application. As we have seen in Chapter 11, many plants of the family Euphorbiaceae produce hydrocarbons in their tissues. Often enough, the hydrocarbons feature low molecular weights between 10,000 and 20,000 — just the range of molecular weights favored by oil engineers. Because the molecular weights are genetically controlled by the plant, there now appears to be a possibility that scientists can manipulate the plant's genetic constitution to construct materials of the precise molecular weights desired. True, this challenge is a big one, in that the plant, as a highly complex organism, cannot readily be converted into a collecting and constructing vehicle. But the eventual payoff could make the research well worthwhile.

Applications for Agriculture: Tissue Culture and Protoplast Fusion

When working with microorganisms, the bio-engineer's ultimate goal is to accomplish changes at the cellular level. But in crop plants, by contrast, changes at the cellular level accomplish nothing unless they are reproduced in the million of cells of mature plants. So when the first difficult step of growing individual cells in a culture medium has been accomplished, the genetic engineer must then tackle a second and still more difficult step of persuading the culture to reproduce into entire plants with the desired characteristics incorporated into their genetic structures. In order to persuade bacteria to produce human insulin, geneticists have had to transfer only a single gene, but in order to persuade crop plants to make a protein called zein, scientists must manipulate 56 separate genes. All in all, some plants contain more than 100,000 genes.

So the agricultural geneticist has a far greater challenge on his hands than his colleagues in medicine who have accomplished the insulin feat. But a technical strategy has now been established, known as tissue culture, often used in conjunction with protoplast fusion (Barz *et al.*, 1977; Bollinger, 1980; Brill, 1979; Feinert and Bajaj, 1977; Hughes *et al.*, 1978; Office of Technology Assessment, 1981; Shepard, 1982; Struhl *et al.*, 1979). Sometimes known as micropropagation or as cloning of plants, tissue culture really is a more generalized term that is applied to the isolation of embryonic organs, tissues, and cells from plants so that they can be grown through sterile culture on a nutrient medium. The starting point in the process is to take tiny fragments of a plant: a leaf, for example, which can be chopped up into pinhead-sized particles. The material is placed into a nutrient broth or gel with growth hormones to make individual cells develop rapidly. The key is to find the correct combination of growth regulators for the broth; if a single ingredient is off by even one-tenth of a milligram, the cells will not grow. But if the concoction is "on target," the individual cells will form themselves into an amorphous clump known as a "callus," or a glob of cellular material. If the culture conditions are then readjusted, the callus's cells undergo further proliferation – and as they differentiate and become specialized, they start to grow into the well-organized tissues and organs of a whole plant.

It is at the callus stage that the geneticist makes his key contribution. He can disintegrate the callus into a solution of tens of millions of individual cells, all identical. He can then subject these clones to some kind of stress, e.g., by adding salt to the solution medium, or by creating nutrient imbalances, or by inducing high or low temperatures, or by drastically reducing the water content. He thereby causes the great bulk of the cells to die, leaving perhaps only 2 percent to survive by virtue of their special genetic characteristics. These specialist survivors can then be stimulated by hormones to grow and divide until they reconstitute the entire culture. The result is that the progeny of the selected cells develop into finely-tuned organisms adapted to a specific set of environmental conditions. By continually repeating the process, the geneticist develops a plant culture that may be tolerant to the adverse conditions that have meant certain death to the great majority of earlier clones. Finally he exposes the plant culture to more hormones that cause shoots and roots to develop – provided of course (a big proviso, this one) that he has managed to manipulate the chemicals of the medium in such skillful fashion that he has convinced the cells that they are really embryos, capable of growing into complete plants.

The eventual result is a batch of tiny plantlets. When they are sufficiently large, they can be transplanted into open fields, ready to develop into fully functional plants. A single gram of cells at the start can produce as many as 1,000 plantlets, sturdy enough for normal growth in the big wide world. The eventual upshot is a complete crop or plantation of plants, thousands upon thousands of them, all genetically identical to a parent plant from which the original cells were taken.

The advantages of tissue culture are three-fold. It allows mass production of large numbers of exact copies of a "founder plant" to be grown in a limited space and in very little time. Second, the technique enables us to isolate desirable qualities in plant varieties. If we take large populations of individual cells from a particular crop plant, and we then impose a certain type of environmental stress, we swiftly discover which genotypes are most able to cope with the stress. This means that we can selectively culture genetic strains with particular attributes, such as resistance to heat or cold, tolerance for drought, unusual efficiency of photosynthesis, high content of protein, and so forth. Third, tissue culture allows us to develop superior strains of plant species at low cost compared with the traditional techniques of plant breeding. When once the scientist has achieved the key step of embryogenesis, he can turn out immense numbers of the "founder plant," all in identical form, at trifling cost per unit.

The big advantage is that the process allows us to track down answers to difficult questions within a short period, by contrast with other approaches that have demanded large-scale plant-screening programs involving many hectares of plants in poorly controlled selection systems. A research effort that, through conventional plant breeding, would require at least one growing year and generally ten growing years (sometimes as many as 40 years) can be accomplished in the laboratory within just a couple of months. Thanks to the "compressed evolution" that the geneticist can impose upon his cell populations, the breeding breakthroughs that took Dr. Norman Borlaug, "father" of the Green Revolution, a full two decades, can now be accomplished virtually overnight.

To be specific, a single laboratory vial containing half a liter of, say, wheat cell suspension may contain 40 million potential plants, or the equivalent of more than three hectares of field-grown wheat. A small laboratory room can easily contain 35,000 such vials, meaning that the researcher has at his fingertips the genetic equivalent of 112,000 hectares of wheat with 1.4 billion actual plants. Put another way, a single laboratory bench can offer as much experimental scope as a field-breeding program that extends as far as the eye can see. In short, this represents a technique for genetic improvement that will not only duplicate nature's own processes, but improve on them dramatically – and it will not take 500 million years for the job, but only a matter of weeks.

So much for tissue culture. It is one of the most powerful tools that scientists have ever devised to support our effort to grow more food. Yet the technical clout of tissue culture can be greatly reinforced through a related process, known as "protoplast fusion." During the experimental stage when the minute particles of plant tissue are growing away in their nutrient broth, they can be treated with enzymes to dissolve their tough cell walls. The cells are then left "naked," in the form of balls of genetic and physiological material that are protected only by a relatively easy-to-penetrate membrane. These clusters of membrane-bound cells, known as protoplasts, can be very numerous, as many as 10,000 or more to 1 millimeter. If they are then subjected to fusion (by, e.g., a centrifuge), they are forced together until their membranes merge and their genes coalesce. Some of the cells will feature a genetic makeup with desired characteristics, such as disease resistance, or salinity tolerance, etc. These desirable traits can now be incorporated into the fused protoplasts, and the new genetic constitution will be "expressed" in the handful of cells that the scientist persuades to regrow into useful and fertile plants.

True, this last stage can prove tricky, to say the least. While it turns out to be fairly straightforward with some plants, such as carrots and tobacco, and is even becoming routine – in advanced laboratories – with corn, scientists find that most cereals feature very hard cell walls that resist the solution and fusion process. But given the research progress of the last few years, we may not have long to wait before we can hail protoplast fusion of many cereals – a feat that was believed, as recently as the late 1970s, to lie way beyond the realm of possibility, but now is regarded as a highly probable accomplishment before 1985.

All in all, the technological breakthroughs of protoplast fusion represent, for the hidden world of the plant cell's nucleus, as great an advance as the piecing together of a Skylab for space technology.

The combined strategies of tissue culture and protoplast fusion are likely to become a major avenue for broad crosses between existing plants. Hitherto these broad crosses have proved almost impossible, because of sterility barriers between fairly closely related species, let alone between distinct genera. But this daunting problem should soon recede into agricultural history.

Still more important, the cellular approach to plant breeding could lead to formation of entirely new varieties, and even new species, of crop plants with a host of much-sought-after qualities. Already genetic engineers have come up with a type of asparagus that matures more quickly, produces better-quality "spears," and offers a threefold increase in yield. With citrus fruits, geneticists are eliminating a number of viruses. With coffee, they have induced resistance to many diseases. With pineapples, they have incorporated improved taste, together with higher productivity. With strawberries, they have achieved ultrarapid introduction of new strains. With potatoes, sweet potatoes, rhubarb, gooseberries, hops, and many ornamental flowers, they have devised virus-free varieties. A number of geneticists are even working on putting back the flavor into tomatoes.

What further successes can we anticipate in the near future? One lies with the prospect of dryland rice that is not overwhelmed with disease. Dryland areas of the tropics tend to suffer from rice blast, a fungus that presents the major barrier to rice growing on drylands. It turns out, however, that certain wild strains of rice possess several genes that protect them from the blast (Nelson and MacKenzie, 1980). Scientists hope that they will soon isolate these genes and breed them into cultivated rice in order to produce varieties that can survive the rice blast. This research breakthrough will enable dryland rice growers to produce as much as 5 metric tons of rice a hectare, across many millions of hectares of potential rice-growing drylands that have remained "off limits" because of the blast.

A second big breakthrough could lie with the nitrogen-fixing capabilities of the soybean. As a legume, the soybean lives in mutualism with a bacterium that fixes nitrogen from the atmosphere. But this plant-bacterium partnership is not very efficient, losing a good deal of fixable nitrogen in the process. Fortunately, about 20 percent of soybeans grown in the United States contain the gene for an enzyme that prevents nitrogen from "leaking out" of the plant. Genetic engineers hope to transfer this "anti-leak" gene into other strains of soybeans. This change, if it becomes possible, could increase the protein yield of soybeans by some 15–20 percent.

Of course most plants have no evolutionary "arrangement" with microorganisms that might share the plants' root tissues and fix nitrogen. What if we could take the genetic system that enables legumes to insure their nitrogen independence via a partnership with rhizobia and transfer it into nonlegumes? It appears that about 15 genes are involved, and geneticists have identified the functions of about half these genes. Each of the 15 will have to be manipulated independently until the entire system has been decoded, if scientists are to devise a way to insert the functioning gene arrangement into plants such as cereals. This is a massive challenge by any standards – and one that, having been dismissed in the late 1970s as indefinitely impossible, may well be accomplished within just the next few years.

Some scientists are skeptical, however, of the benefit of a nitrogen-fixing system in nonleguminous plants. The process saps a great deal of the plant's energy, resulting in lower food yields per hectare. So how about approaching the nitrogen-fixation issue in other ways? One option lies with the so-called "hydrogen afterburner" genes found naturally in some of the bacteria that live in root nodules of legumes. The scientific goal here is to improve the symbiotic relationship between the nodule bacteria and the host plants. The natural nitrogen-fixing process yields hydrogen as a by-product; certain bacteria in the root nodules secrete a catalyst called nitrogenase, which recycles the hydrogen and makes the process more efficient. Bio-engineers are trying to clone the hydrogen-afterburner genes so that all root nodule bacteria can incorporate them and secrete nitrogenase.

A still further strategy could lie with genetic improvement of plants in order to reduce the natural attrition of nitrogen nutrients through processes known as nitrification and denitrification (see Chapter 3). If "custom-designed" plants could be devised to counter these losses, the savings could total as much as $6 billion per year.

A still further major advance is expected with wheat. A strain that possesses some resistance to cold weather and to drought could extend the growing period of wheat by 15–20 days at either end of the season, thus enabling farmers in northern latitudes to grow two wheat crops a year instead of the traditional one. Other wheat genes are being manipulated to produce a variety with twice as much protein as conventional wheat.

Not only can established crop plants be genetically improved, but new ones can be created. Scientists believe there is much scope for genetic engineering of entirely new crop species. As we have already noted in Chapter 4, scientists have devised an entirely new crop species, triticale, a cross between wheat and rye. More recently, geneticists have come up with a cross between the potato and tomato, known as the "pomato." Latest news flashes from the research laboratories indicate that genetic engineers have devised a sunflower that contains protein-synthesizing genes from the French bean, leading to a plant with the inviting name of "sunbean."

Despite these early accomplishments, however, the technology is complex in the extreme. The genetic makeup of plants is thousands of times more complex than that of bacteria with which genetic engineers have scored one success after another. Plant researchers still cannot find a transmitting material, i.e., a plasmid, that can reliably introduce genes into plant cells. Moreover, present knowledge of plant genes is patchy at best, and most genes have not yet been matched up with the traits they produce, which means that nobody has yet been able to culture a callus leading to an improved form of corn, or an improved legume such as a pea or a bean, or indeed any of most other major crops. In any case, certain plant characteristics turn out to reflect not a single gene, but several genes. For example, the salt tolerance of certain plants involves at least 6 or 8 and possibly more genes – though if scientists can work out the mechanism involved, they will be well on the way to improving species that are very sensitive to salt, notably corn.

As with agriculture, so with forestry. Geneticists consider that they may soon be able to propagate pine trees by methods that bypass sexual reproduction, and enable a single tree to produce huge numbers of descendants that are genetically identical to it. Bio-engineers have just achieved as much with specimens of the American chestnut tree and the coast redwood.

To date, the selective breeding of tree species has been a very drawn-out process. Trees that reach sexual maturity within five years still require as much as another five decades, spanning numerous generations, to produce the useful homozygous strains that have been a prerequisite for further breeding. Species such as the sequoia, which do not flower until they are 15–20 years old, require between one and two centuries for their genetic traits to become stabilized so that preliminary field trials can be evaluated. But now forestry geneticists have achieved tissue culture of 2,500 redwood trees, grown under field conditions for comparison with regular sexually produced seedlings. Still more significant, those prime species of the American timber industry, loblolly pine and Douglas fir, are being cultured, and the number of trees that can be grown from cells in 100 liters of media in three months is enough to reforest roughly 50,000 hectares of land at a 4 × 4-meter spacing.

These advances in tree breeding are only a start. Geneticists realize that they can now accelerate the detection of desirable and heritable traits in individual trees, making possible the replication of such trees in large numbers. Before long, they hope to improve even the fastest-growing trees we know from nature, such as the giant ipilipil, which grows to a person's height within just a few months. The time may come when we shall produce superstrains of trees that grow faster than mushrooms sprout – one will just have to plant a seedling, then jump aside.

Epilogue

Dollars and Sense

To conclude this book, let us quickly remind ourselves of the scale of wildlife's contributions to our daily welfare, by reviewing some notable instances.

In agriculture, the genetic share in the increased productivity of United States agriculture can be put at 1 percent of the annual farmgate value of crops, or some $1 billion a year. In the Third World, genetically improved types of a single crop, wheat, have boosted output by an amount estimated at $2 billion a year by the mid-1970s, and genetically superior strains of rice in Asia have helped expand output by $1.5 billion a year. Not all the credit can go, of course, to genetic infusions. One must consider extra fertilizer, improved machinery, and better farm practices all around. But extra fertilizer and the rest accomplish nothing without genetically adapted varieties of crops to take advantage of them.

The genetic enhancement applies not only to food crops. In England, barley has been complemented by wild hops that bring "better bitterness" of taste, rejoicing English beer drinkers and the brewing industry to an extent of $15 million in 1981.

Agriculture can be further helped through cutting down on damage caused by insect pests. Just in the United States, food losses to insects amount to $5 billion a year. Many insect pests can be controlled by other insects, notably by predators and parasites (such as wasps) that attack crop plant eaters. In California alone, during the period 1928–1979, seven leading biological-control projects have reduced crop losses to insects, and have likewise reduced the need for pesticidal chemicals, to an extent of savings worth $987 million, showing an average return on investment of 30:1. In Australia, four biological-control programs are producing benefits that, projected to the year 2000, are expected to exceed the cost of research to develop them by $286 million.

As for medicine, the value of drugs and pharmaceuticals that are derived in some form or other from plants has now reached $20 billion a year in the United States. When we take the rest of the developed world into account, the total can fairly be supposed to double. The rosy periwinkle, to cite a notable instance, supplies alkaloidal materials for two potent anticancer drugs that now generate worldwide sales of more than $100 million a year.

Industry too benefits from plants of diverse sorts. American chemical enterprises import plant materials such as oils, fats, and waxes worth many millions of dollars a year, using them to manufacture a vast array of end-products whose ultimate economic value is many times greater than the cost of the raw materials. During the 1970s, the cost of newsprint in the United States rose from $170 to over $500 a metric ton due to shortages of wood pulp. Some of the pulp deficits may soon be met by a wild annual plant known as kenaf, related to okra, hollyhock, and marijuana. And if the threefold increase in the price of newsprint has hit our pockets hard, that is a trifling price hike as compared with that of petroleum. But thanks to a number of hydrocarbon-bearing plants, both woody and herbaceous species, we may soon be able to establish "petroleum plantations" and grow our own gasoline.

Finally, the emergent technology of bio-engineering may shortly enable us to derive unprecedented support from Earth's stocks of genetic materials. Take penicillin, for instance: genetic improvements have led to a 55-fold increase in production processes. Similarly, chemically induced mutations of L-asparaginase now yield over 100 times more of the key antileukemia drug than the original strain, meaning that a course of therapy for a leukemia sufferer now costs only about $300, or one-fiftieth as much as before. Genetic engineering is also assisting with biosynthetic production of materials that suppress human appetite, presumably through a satiety signal from the stomach to the brain; this research breakthrough will make a solid contribution to the anti-obesity market, now worth more than $200 million a year in the United States.

A major problem for livestock, hoof-and-mouth disease, is currently resisted through 800 million doses worldwide per year of a vaccine that is the largest-volume vaccine ever produced. Molecular cloning of an antigen may shortly lead to a bettter and cheaper vaccine for livestock in many parts of the world. Agricultural experts hope they are within a few years of introducing a nitrogen-fixing capacity into several major crop plants, thus reducing the need for chemical nitrogen fertilizer that now costs the world's farmers a whopping $15 billion a year.

So much for some figures on wildlife's benefits to us. They are impressive figures as measured by everyday criteria of economics. Yet they are still more impressive when we compare them with what we – great beneficiaries that we are – do for wildlife in return. By proportion, we spend scarcely a cent on safeguarding our fellow species, precisely at a time when the earth's wildlife is declining with every tick of the clock. The rest of this Epilogue will take a look at this problem – and at some opportunities for turning an appalling problem into a creative challenge.

It is ironic that at a time when we are learning to bring species into our service on a scale hardly dreamed of before, we are also busily pushing them over the edge into oblivion with far greater energy than humankind has ever been able to muster before. Right now we are almost certainly eliminating one species per day, out of Earth's 5–10 million species. By the end of the century we could well account for at least 1 million – and possibly several more million within the next few decades, or until such time as humankind establishes ecologically acceptable life-styles. It is far from fanciful to suppose that by the time today's children grow old, we could well have lost one-quarter, possibly one-third, and conceivably one-half of all species that now share the One Earth home.

True, extinction has been a fact of life virtually right from the start of life on Earth 3.6 billion years ago. At least 90 percent of all species that have existed have disappeared. But almost all of them have gone under by virtue of natural processes. During the present phase of evolution's course, the "natural rate" of extinction could be about one species per year. But people are able to impose extinction of a less natural kind, and almost always an unnecessary kind. With our growing numbers and our growing expectations, allied with our growing technological muscle, we can now elbow a species off the face of the planet with scarcely a thought – or, much more often, with no thought at all. Between the years 1600 and 1900, our predecessors are known to have eliminated some 75 species at least, almost all of them mammals and birds. But virtually nothing has been established about how many reptiles, amphibians, fishes, invertebrates, and plants disappeared during the same period of time; it is very likely that their total greatly exceeds the 75 known species mentioned above. During the course of the present century, we have stepped up the pace and eliminated a further 75 known species. Again, they are all mammals and birds – and again, we know hardly anything about how many other creatures we have taken from the scene.

The rate of human-caused extinctions from the year 1600 to the year 1900 works out at roughly one known species every four years. The rate during most of the present century works out at about one known species each year. These rates are to be compared with a rate that averaged possibly one species every 1,000 years during the "great dying" of the dinosaurs and their kin.

Since the end of the Second World War, when growth in human numbers and human aspirations began to exert greater impact on natural environments, vast territories in several major regions of the world have become so modified as to be cleared of much of their wildlife. The result is that the extinction rate has certainly soared, though the details remain mostly undocumented. A single ecological zone, the tropical moist forests, is believed to contain between 2 and 5 million species. If present patterns of exploitation persist (commercial lumbering, and the like), much undisturbed forest of the present time is likely to be grossly disrupted, if not destroyed outright, by the end of the century. This degradative process will cause huge numbers of species to disappear.

Similar depletive processes are at work in other major environments, notably grasslands and wetlands. While not so ecologically diverse as tropical moist forests, these biomes feature their own rich arrays of species. They are likewise undergoing fundamental modification at the hands of humans. The United States once featured around 1 million km² of pristine prairie, but now it has disappeared under the plow or has been otherwise transformed, except for about 16,000 km² in Kansas. Grasslands in many other parts of the world are similarly giving way to cultivated crops in order to feed hungry human populations. In advanced and developing regions alike, wetlands are being drained, dug up, or filled in and paved over, so that they can be converted from their present "useless" state into something profitable for the human economy. The overall result has been the elimination of whole plant-animal communities virtually overnight.

Let us suppose that, as a consequence of this manhandling of natural environments, the final quarter of this century witnesses the elimination of 1 million species. This would work out, during the course of 25 years, at an average extinction rate of 40,000 species per year, or more than 100 species per day. The greatest exploitation pressures will not be directed at tropical forests and other species-rich biomes until toward the end of the period. That is to say, the 1990s could see many more species accounted for than the previous several decades. But already the disruptive processes are well underway: hence it is not unrealistic to suppose that, right now, at least one species is disappearing per day. By the late 1980s, we could be facing a situation where one species becomes extinct each hour. By the late 1990s, we could conceivably be losing several hundred species every day. In terms of numbers of species involved, and the compressed time scale of the extinction spasm, this will amount to a biological debacle greater than all mass extinctions of the biological past.

Where are the greatest losses likely to occur? Very roughly speaking, we can assume that the tropical moist forests of Latin America harbor 1 million species, the forests of Asia about three-quarters of a million, and those of Africa about one-third of a million. This makes a total of rather over 2 million. Of course these figures are no better than informed estimates; if they are off target, they are almost certainly on the low side, in that they are calculated with a deliberately cautious bias – and many scientists believe the forests could contain twice as many species. All other environments on Earth possibly contain as many as 3 million species, if not twice as many, making an overall total of some 5–10 million species. If we now look at deforestation projections as postulated by some recent studies (Myers, 1980), we find that by the year 2000 Latin America's tropical forests could lose about one-third of their species complement, Asia's forests at least two-fifths, and Africa's over one-eighth (Asia's forest expanse is likely to be worst hit in proportion to its relatively small area on the grounds that this is where the great bulk of tropical forestland farmers live). If, however, deforestation rates turn out to be higher than projected (and in several sectors of the biome they are accelerating rapidly right now), each of the three major regions could lose as many as half of its species. Other parts of the earth will probably fare rather better, perhaps losing only one-tenth of their species. Overall, it is plain that we can reasonably expect that we shall bid adieu to a full 1 million species by the end of the century, the greatest fallout occurring in tropical forests.

Moreover, the wholesale elimination of species is not the entire story. As we have seen at various points in this book, certain species feature much genetic variability among their subspecies. True, this does not apply to all species, not by a long way; but it surely applies to enough species to cause us to consider that we should not always confine our wildlife conservation efforts to species alone, but that sometimes we should extend our efforts to subspecies and races, even distinct populations. For example, certain strains of willow tree produce twice as much wood per growing season as do other willows. A few populations of the rosy periwinkle feature ten times as much alkaloidal material, used to prepare anticancer drugs, as do most populations of the plant. By drawing on genetic variability in the wild, rubber tree breeders have been able to increase productivity by 2,000 percent during the past three decades.

We face, then, the imminent elimination of many of the species that have shared the One Earth home with humankind for millennia, but are now to be denied living space during a phase that may last no more than half a century. This extinction spasm will amount to an irreversible loss of unique resources. Earth is currently afflicted with other forms of environmental degradation, but from the standpoint of permanent despoliation of the planet, no other form is anywhere near so significant as the fallout of species. If we choose to foul up our rivers and lakes, and to treat the atmosphere as a garbage can, we can always change our minds, and set about cleaning up the mess. But species extinction is final – and the impoverishment of life on Earth falls not only on present society but on all generations to come.

Any reduction in the natural resource stocks represented by species will reduce our ability to respond to new problems and opportunities. To the extent that we cannot be certain what needs may arise in the future, it makes sense to keep our options open, provided of course that a strategy of that sort does not unduly conflict with other major purposes of society. This rationale for conservation applies to the planet's stock of species more than to virtually any other category of natural resources. We cannot point to any other stock of resources that offers such immense potential for us as we confront the unknown challenges of the future.

The position has been well stated by Professor Thomas Eisner of Cornell University, when he views the loss of a single species not merely as "the loss of one volume from the library of nature, but the loss of a loose-leaf book whose individual pages, were the species to survive, would remain available in perpetuity for selective transfer to other species." And when considering the biological secrets locked up in a species, let us reflect that a butterfly is far more complicated than any machine ever devised by man, including the most advanced computer. Moreover, when one such species is gone, it is gone forever. To cite the words of a great American naturalist, William Beebe, "The beauty and genius of a work of art may be reconceived, though its first material expression be destroyed; a vanished harmony may yet again inspire the composer; but when the last individual of a race of living things breathes no more, another heaven and another earth must pass away before such a one can be again."

To view the situation in alternative terms, we can heed the view of Professor Edward O. Wilson of Harvard University, when he asserts that "there is far more biological complexity in a handful of soil in Virginia than on the entire surface of Jupiter." Because of the microorganisms living in it, the Virginia soil provides far greater opportunity for scientific advance. Yet we invest more money in exploration of the planets than in finding out how humankind's life-support systems work here on Earth. Indeed we now know more about several sectors of the moon's surface than we know about the depths of tropical rainforests – and the moon is probably going to stay around, undisturbed, far longer than tropical rainforests.

A switch of a mere 10 percent of funding from space exploration into ecological understanding of our Earth home would increase our biological research budgets many times over, and would greatly enhance our skills in planetary management. At present, total funding worldwide for research into tropical forests amounts to only some $30 million (Raven, 1981); the National Science Foundation of the United States, which accounts for about two-thirds of all America's support for tropical biology, is actually cutting back its funding. The figure of $30 million is to be compared with total global expenditures on research and development amounting to $150 billion a year, much of which is spent on activities such as space exploration and military buildup.

For sure, at a time of economic recession there is need to reduce our public outlays of money for scientific research. But let us likewise recall that when we look at lists of leading plant-derived medicines, we find that 90 percent of the 63 main genera in question occur in the tropics (Staritsky, 1980). Among drugs derived from the tropical moist forest zone, we can include not only the anticancer drug vincristine, but also reserpine, emetine, cocaine, codeine, quinine, and morphine – all of them major items in a modern pharmacopoeia.

We discern a similar tale of neglect for species conservation when we look at the activities of agencies that depend on genetic resources. In the agricultural field, two main international bodies are charged with responsibility for protection of crop germ plasm. The International Board for Plant Genetic Resources, administered by the Food and Agriculture Organization, devotes a mere $3 million a year to genetic resources, reflecting the low priority accorded to crop germ plasm by the Board's member governments. The Consultative Group for International Agricultural Research, housed within the World Bank, coordinates the programs of rather over one dozen research centers, such as the International Rice Research Institute in the Philippines and the International Center for Improvement of Maize and Wheat in Mexico. The combined budget of these centers now amounts to almost $150 million per year. Only a small part of this funding is devoted to efforts to track down gene reservoirs in the wild, let alone to efforts to safeguard them. Yet as we have seen, the collection of wild rice germ plasm held by IRRI, critically valuable as this genetic material is, is deficient in virtually every main aspect – even though it was a single strain of wild rice from India that supplied the answer to the brown hopper insect crisis.

In terms of agriculture overall, with its promise of a Gene Revolution to far surpass the feats of the Green Revolution, we find that research funding is grotesquely meager. Worldwide it amounts to less than $5 billion, or a mere 3 percent of all research support. In the United States, it now amounts to only 2 percent, a decline from 39 percent in 1940, and a proportion greatly exceeded by the Soviet Union's allocation to agriculture and especially to genetic adaptations of leading food crops. Plant science generally in the United States is in a parlous state, with federal funding only a little over $200 million a year. The Department of Agriculture allocates no more than $25 million to genetic avenues for crop improvement, including such prime areas as nitrogen fixation and photosynthesis. For all that the agricultural geneticist is no better than the gene stocks he has to work with, the sum allocated by the Department of Agriculture to gene conservation is a mere $12 million in 1982, or less in real terms than in 1979 – even though genetic experts believe that the field could absorb five times as much funding forthwith if it is to respond to the most urgent priorities (General Accounting Office of the United States, 1981).

Perhaps less surprising, though no more rational, is the trifling contribution of private enterprise to conservation of crop genetic resources. As Chapter 13 has made plain, the scope for genetic engineering of agricultural breakthroughs is estimated to be on a scale of $50–100 billion a year by the end of the 1980s, through contributions to new vaccines, growth hormones, bacterial feeds, anabolic steroids, pesticides, nitro-fixed osmoregulation, nitro-fixed cereal enzymes, and dozens of other strategies to achieve a quantum advance in our capacity to feed a hungry world (Murray et al., 1981). Yet at a time when hundreds of private corporations are investing at least $100 million a year in laboratory research (some observers believe the sum could be many times more), we are almost certainly losing one plant species every week, and scores of populations every day. Why, one wonders, do not private enterprises, with their innovative genius, join hands with governments and conservationists to safeguard the resource base on which the future of genetic engineering will depend? To cite a leading exponent of the biotechnology wonders that lie ahead of us, Professor William Brill (1979), "We are entering an age in which genetic wealth, especially in tropical areas such as rainforests, until now a relatively inaccessible trust fund, is becoming a currency with high immediate value. Estimates place the annual extinction rate as high as 1,000 species per year, and there is still little organized effort for maintaining genetic reserves."

A similar discrepancy between benefits and costs arises with regard to biological-control agents of agricultural pests. In California during the period 1928–1979, seven control projects, utilizing wild species, have generated savings worth $987 million. Yet the main research centers that identify biological agents, such as wild beetles and wasps – the Divisions of Biological Control at the Berkeley and Riverside campuses of the University of California – receive only about $1 million for their research efforts each year.

Although American farmers now use twice as much pesticide on their crops as in 1950, and now lose twice as much food to pests (which breed resistance to toxic chemicals), the chemical industry goes on its merry way in developing more pesticides, at an average cost of $18 million for each new product. During the 1970s, the American chemical industry was spending an average of well over $100 million a year on research and development of synthetic pesticides. All in all, retail sales of pesticides in the United States are now worth more than $3 billion a year. These figures are to be contrasted with U.S. government outlays on research and development of natural enemies of crop pests – from the period of the program's start-up in the late 1880s to the early 1970s, a paltry $20 million. Would it not be economcally rational to allocate further funds to research on the hundreds of insect control species that are believed available in the wild, with huge potential advantages for American agriculture? To date, we do not know which of the many thousands of insect predators and parasites, such as wasps and other Hymenoptera, can best assist the agricultural cause. But we can be pretty sure that very large numbers of such species could do the trick for us. We can be equally certain that these species are disappearing with every day that goes by.

As large as the pesticide industry is in the United States, it is only about one-third as large as the chemical fertilizer industry. As has been recounted in Chapters 3 and 13, scientists are working to transfer the nitrogen-fixing capacities characteristic of legume species into crops that need lots of fertilizer, such as corn, wheat, and rice. These research scientists receive sizable research budgets to support their work. Wildlife botanists would need only a fraction as much funding to document the genetic makeup of the many members of the legume family that have scarcely been investigated by scientists – and that, in certain instances, face threat of extinction before we can form the faintest idea of their possible utility to us.

One way to raise the research and conservation funding required would be to levy a trifling tax on the fertilizer and pesticide industries.

Just 1 percent would increase present research and conservation budgets several times over. The commercial interests in the fertilizer and pesticide sectors need not complain. Chemical fertilizer cannot be produced indefinitely from fossil fuels; we will simply run out of a supply of these fuels. Chemical pesticides are becoming less and less effective, while causing more and more harm to the general environment. Thus both economic sectors will have to make basic shifts within the foreseeable future anyway. Why not help to investigate one of the most promising alternatives available to us – and also help to safeguard that option before it becomes foreclosed to us through mass extinction of species?

A parallel money-raising approach can be adopted with respect to crop genetic resources. Among leading beneficiaries are commercial seed companies, with global sales now well above $10 billion a year. A 1 percent tax could produce the $100 million that many agricultural experts believe is required for a crash budget to finance the conservation of key gene reservoirs before it is too late.

Most of these fund-raising considerations apply primarily to developed nations. How about developing nations – what is in genetic conservation for them? In fact, the same agricultural factors apply, only more so. It is Third World citizens who are growing more numerous and more hungry. Ironically it is also Third World nations of the tropics that possess the most abundant and diverse stocks of genetic resources, with extinction of species occurring fastest. If ever these nations are to feed their peoples, they will need to draw on the many resource materials available to them in the form of species stocks and genetic reservoirs. In fact, the Third World could eventually enjoy a Gene Revolution on a scale even greater than that in prospect for the advanced nations.

Equally to the point, Third World nations could look to their energy problems and investigate the opportunity to mobilize bio-energy as a way to get themselves off the "fossil fuel hook." Between 1970 and 1990, developing nations are projected to increase their imports of petroleum four times over, and in terms of cost as measured by constant 1980 dollars, their bill is projected to expand 20 times over. So how about looking at the prospects for developing "green gasoline"? Developing nations of the tropics possess almost three-quarters of all plant species, with their potential to yield "bio-crude" and fuels in a dozen other forms. In the tropical forests of South America, there are believed to be more than 1,000 possible plant candidates, of which 95 percent occur in Amazonia, 10 percent in the coastal forest of eastern Brazil, and 10 percent in the Pacific Choco region of Colombia (Plotkin, 1982). Brazil alone possesses at least 700 of these plant species: what an opportunity for a single nation to grow its own energy in infinitely renewable form!

Still further advantages could accrue to Brazil from its botanical endowment. The nation now imports large amounts of olive oil, a commodity which is in such tight supply that its price has increased eight times during the 1970s. Brazil's import bill for olive oil has now topped $20 million a year. Yet two genera of Amazonian palm trees, *Oenocarpus* and *Jessenia*, produce a high-quality edible oil that is almost indistinguishable from olive oil (Plotkin, 1982). Moreover, world demand for edible oils is already great and growing, which means that the price will soar. Brazil could embark on an edible-oil bonanza, both for its own needs and for the export trade. Brazil could likewise look to its long-term future as an emergent industrial power, and to its growing need for raw materials of ever-greater diversity – materials for which there is no more abundant and varied stock available than in Brazil itself. Fortunately, Brazil is now starting to learn the immense benefits of wildlife conservation, and it has recently become a pioneer among large tropical forest nations in establishing new parks and reserves.

Let us now move on to the field of medicine. In Chapters 6, 7, 8, and 9 we reviewed the many plants and animals that already serve our health needs. Yet scientists have so far conducted detailed examination of only about 5,000 of Earth's estimated 250,000 species of flowering plants. Of these 5,000 species analyzed, 41 have come up with the goods, i.e., one species out of every 122 (Farnsworth, 1982). These 41 species now generate commercial sales each year in the developed world worth around $40 billion, or an average of almost $1 billion each. If the 245,000 species still to be subjected to systematic analysis were to come up with "winners" at a rate of one for every 122, this would mean another 2,008 prime candidates – with a putative worth of over $2,000 billion per year.

While this arithmetic is rudimentary to a degree, it surely indicates that we would find it a suitable investment to allocate far greater funds than at present to safeguarding the spectrum of plant species on Earth. So far as we can estimate, at least one plant species in ten is now threatened and could well be eliminated by the year 2000. If these 25,000 species offer medical potential at a rate of one in every 122 species, this means that we shall lose 205 species with material for drugs. In terms of the "back of an envelope" arithmetic presented here, this spasm of plant extinctions could cost us a solid $205 billion each year in medicinal terms.

So how about a tax on commercial drug sales in order to stimulate pharmaceutical research? A 1 percent tax on plant-derived drugs and pharmaceuticals, both prescription and nonprescription items, in the United States alone would generate about $200 million a year. This sizable sum would enable government agencies and foundations, presumably in conjunction with private enterprises, to embark on a comprehensive survey of the plant kingdom. When we think what the $3 million a year for anticancer screening of plants (see Chapter 7) has achieved, we could probably work wonders with $200 million a year. The one factor that does not tell in our favor is time. The clock already tells a quarter to midnight.

Of course the tax would be passed on, in the form of slightly increased prices, to the consumer. This is where it surely belongs. The consumer can hardly protest. After all, Americans spend far greater amounts on their health each year, at least $50 million for diet books, $200 million for diet pills, $6 billion for diet drinks, $3 billion for health foods, and $3 billion for health clubs. Clearly consumers are prepared to dig deep into their pockets in order to safeguard their physical welfare.

These proposals of conservation and research tied to taxes raise two basic questions about conservation of species. How much in fact is already being spent on conservation? How much do we need to do a proper job?

To answer the first of these questions, let us take a quick look at some of the main agencies involved in the United States. The Endangered Species Office under the Department of the Interior receives about $20 million a year. This amount does not even enable the Office to describe and document the full scale of the problem it confronts! If the agency cannot even get a clear idea of the problem, how can it hope to come up with responses? By comparison, the U.S. government spends at least 10,000 times as much on military activities each year. Put another way, annual spending on endangered species matches only the amount by which military spending increases from one day to the next.

As for private organizations, the U.S. National Appeal of the World Wildlife Fund now enjoys a budget of about $3 million a year, which, thanks to the growing awareness of American citizens, is a great deal more than it was a few years back. However, because of the spreading degradation of wildlife habitats around the earth, the growing World Wildlife Fund budget in the United States is becoming less and less capable of matching conservation needs. (As for the World Wildlife Fund worldwide, with its 26 National Appeals, the organization now raises about $6 million each year.)

So much for some current sources of conservation funds. How far do they fall short of meeting their targets? A minimum guideline has been established by UNESCO, which proposes that each of the planet's biotic provinces, around 200 of them, should feature at least one Biosphere Reserve. To date, less than one-quarter of these provinces feature such a Reserve. To establish a typical Reserve now costs around $200,000, and to maintain it another $100,000 a year. So a program to set up a further 150 Reserves, and to run them until the end of the century, would cost $300 million, or an average of a little over $15 million a year. This network of Reserves would serve to safeguard representative examples of wildlife communities and would thereby help protect an "average array" of species. Of course a representative system of Reserves would tend to omit a key component of a comprehensive strategy for conservation – the unique (as opposed to representative) wildlife communities, notably those with high concentrations of species and exceptional levels of endemism. To establish further Reserves for these unique areas, and to run them until the end of the century, could bring the total cost to at least $20 million a year.

Yet even an approach along these lines would respond only to the known needs of conservation. Most sectors of tropical forests still remain to be investigated. We also know all too little about tropical coral reef ecosystems, wetland communities such as swamps and salt marshes, and other ecological zones that are unusually rich in species. So far as we can estimate, we have identified between one in three and one in six of all species on the face of the planet. In order to mount a comprehensive research program to tackle these many lacunae in our knowledge with due dispatch, we would need to think of a budget of some $50 million a year. When we have identified these major gaps left in our conservation strategy (after we have taken the preliminary step as proposed under the UNESCO plan for Biosphere Reserves), we would probably have to expend a further $30 million a year to set up and to run the additional Reserves required. So the total sum in question could well amount to a full $100 million a year.

One hundred million dollars a year is not peanuts. Indeed it is a substantial sum as compared with the money that is being spent right now on conservation of threatened species. Yet as compared with other outlays that supposedly support our welfare, the sum *is* peanuts, because it is only what the global community will spend on armaments in the next 90 minutes. It is a good deal less than the cost of a single AWACS reconnaissance plane; it is about one-third the cost of a Trident I missile; and it is only one-fifth as expensive as a B-1 bomber. Are we so sure that each additional reconnaissance plane or Trident missile or strategic bomber adds so much to our long-term security that we prefer to allocate the funds in that way? Might not a similar sum achieve greater long-run security by safeguarding the planetary heritage of species, thereby preserving an unusually valuable stock of natural resources and raw materials with which we can hope to boost our agriculture, improve our medicine, and expand our industry into the indefinite future? Many military conflagrations erupt over natural resources. Would we not reduce the prospect of further conflicts in the future if we move to safeguard some of the most diversified and potentially valuable resources of all?

Of course an annual save-species bill of $100 million would fall on those members of the global community who can best afford to pay it – meaning the citizens of the affluent world, around 1 billion of them. A matter of one dime per head per year. No great outlay, when we remember that the folks who possess the technological skill to exploit genetic resources are those same citizens of advanced nations.

A save-species effort would probably have to be broached as part of a comprehensive strategy to protect the entire global environment. Whatever the merits of a strategy geared to helping threatened wildlife alone, we would find that we could not practically pursue it in isolation from an across-the-board campaign to cover conservation needs for the entire human environment, including, for example, safeguarding measures to halt the spread of deserts. It is not realistic at this stage to try to put a figure on the costs of an all-embracing campaign. Let us simply note that an antidesertification program has been estimated by the United Nations at some $600 million a year – and let us also note that such a program would not only relieve destructive pressures on several ecological zones that border existing deserts, but it would assist several Mediterranean-type areas with their extraordinary assemblies of endemic species.

A broad-front campaign to halt desertification, deforestation, pollution, and other degradation of the planetary ecosystem could well cost many billions of dollars a year. No small sum. Yet the bill is surely not beyond our means. The United States now devotes around $1,000 per citizen each year to military expenditures. If the nation were to allocate $100 per citizen, or a total of $230 billion, to safeguard the One Earth habitat, in which Americans tend to enjoy a privileged place, would the outlay not prove ultimately worthwhile? And if all nations were to similarly divert one-tenth of what they now spend on armaments to environmental safeguards, would not this move be a sound investment to secure a planetary home with living space and material welfare for all?

As with so many aspects of environmental conservation, the issue hangs on perceptions of priorities. In the United States, parents now spend a full $100,000 to bring up a child until the end of the college years – a sizable financial investment in the future, as well as a tremendous gesture of faith. A small fraction of that amount spent on global conservation would help to ensure for each child a worthwhile patch of the One Earth home to spend the rest of his or her life in.

In short, the question is not whether we can afford to support conservation of our joint natural heritage. The real question is, can we afford *not* to support it? The time is arriving when we shall find that there is little difference between being idealistic and being realistic.

I would like to end this book on a personal note. To write the final chapter, I have come to Island Camp at Lake Baringo in Kenya's Rift Valley. I am sitting on a bluff on the island, looking out over the lake. From the verandah of my tent, I can see a grove of thorntrees along the island shoreline. Once again I ask myself, as I have done on thousands of occasions during my quarter century in East Africa: Are the crowns of the trees flat because all branches reach up equally to the sun's light, or because the canopy has been beaten down by the sun's glare? Whatever the reason, the trees are filled with weaver birds, flycatchers, and a dozen other species. Down by the waterside a single bush features a cormorant, a darter, two sorts of kingfisher, and three sorts of bee-eater. Wheeling overhead is a fish eagle, calling with plaintive cry, one of the wildest sounds that I ever hear in Africa. Across the placid surface of the lake, three or four miles distant, is the wall of the Rift Valley, backed by hills and mountains, row upon blue row of them.

Within those distant landscapes, stretching to the furthest horizons, I know there must be creatures still waiting to be discovered. Most of them will be insects – beetles and ants and butterflies. But in some of the valleys and ravines, and atop an isolated peak that is barely discernible 100 kilometers away in Kenya's northern region, there must surely be a few plants that remain unknown to science, and probably a snake or a frog, plus a bat or two. So much new life, not yet documented in shape and color, let alone investigated for possible benefit to us. Perhaps there is an obscure bush, akin to the one discovered across the border in Ethiopia, with capacity to kill bilharzia snails and thus bring relief to the hundreds of millions of snail-fever sufferers in developing countries. Or perhaps there is a shrub to match the one found near Mombasa on Kenya's coast, with compounds in its tissues that resist several types of cancer.

A little way along the edge of the island, where I am on safari, I have seen a crocodile basking, lying in-shore from the lagoon where fellow visitors and I go water skiing. (I know the crocodile is not supposed to bother us because of all the fish in the lake that it can consume at leisure. But does the crocodile know?) I speculate about whether medical physiology might not have something to learn from an air-breathing creature that can stay submerged for a whole hour if necessary–that must possess secret ways to depress its metabolism and generally put its life processes "on hold," thus offering all manner of insights for modern surgery, which depends on suspending key functions in human patients while they undergo hours-long operations.

In the string of lakes along the Rift Valley–Lake Baringo is a prominent member–there are reputed to be several hundred fish species waiting to be tracked down, notably the tilapia forms that are specially succulent on the supper table, and that offer untold potential for fish farming in many parts of the world.

All these wild species, and many more that lie beyond my imagination, have followed their slow evolutionary way until they now present refinements of form and function that we cannot start to visualize until we take a long, close look at them. We shall not get around to that task tomorrow, or next week, or next year. And yet we must surely reckon, I surmise as I sit on Island Camp's hilltop, that during my three-day safari Africa will probably lose at least one species, its habitat eliminated by hundreds of digging hoes or by a squad of bulldozers. Whether spider or flower or lizard, it will be gone for good–and that will be for bad, for us as well as for the creature.

There is no point, I reflect, in protesting that humankind must be stupid or selfish or worse, to deny wild creatures their living space with such casual disregard. People are not so uncaring. It is not that they lack compunction. Rather they lack the imagination that would allow them to see beyond the bounds of their daily lives. Perched on my island bluff and gazing out over Lake Baringo, I feel stirred by the vistas of savanna Africa that are opened up before me. I am rarely stirred that way while sitting in Nairobi–there my imagination lacks the "stretch" that it could have if I gave it proper exercise. Those people with their digging hoes, they are not callous toward wildlife, they just do not think about it. The drivers of the bulldozers harbor no malice toward antelopes and zebras, they merely clear bush to convert savannas into pasturelands on which commercial stockmen, as some of the more enterprising of Kenya's yeoman farmers, can raise extra beef for export markets in Europe. European citizens like to enjoy a regular diet of red meat at "reasonable," i.e., noninflationary, prices–and they can derive cheap meat from the spreading cattle ranches of Kenya and Botswana and other countries of savanna Africa. With their knives and forks, these millions of Europeans are speeding the demise of giraffes and gazelles just as effectively as the spears and arrows of Africa's few thousand poachers are doing.

I am lucky to have lived in a land of wide horizons, horizons of the spirit as well as of the landscape. Within one month of leaving Island Camp, I shall depart from Kenya with my family, to set up home in Oxford, England. As I sit here in camp clad in my bush shirt and safari shorts, I speculate whether I shall retain the sense of spacious vision that I enjoy while looking out over Lake Baringo to the far escarpments of the Rift Valley, and to the mountains beyond that make me ache just to gaze at their distant outline and wonder at all that lies between them and me. Can I grow fast enough to accommodate all that the vista offers me? And when I shall become preoccupied with the nuts and bolts of daily life in Britain, will I still think spaciously enough about Africa's wildlife, about lizards as well as lions, caterpillars as well as flamingoes, prickly plants as well as stately giraffes? And if I do think on a broad enough scale, what shall I then do about it?

Well, I shall send off a subscription to yet another conservation group. I shall send off further pieces of paper that cost little and mean much, being letters to political leaders that tell them about the concerns of this version of John Citizen. I shall write more articles for newspapers to tell the tale of threatened species, and I shall spread the message by radio and television.

Equally important, I shall support my wife in her view that red meat for the family should not be a daily expectation, it should be a weekly treat. And while I do my marathon training along the banks of the River Thames, I shall wonder about my overall life-style, and how it impinges on the survival prospects of wild creatures in far-off Africa — and in Amazonia and Borneo and in whatever lands lie many horizons away from Oxford. Or will these remote places remain hidden beyond the horizons of my mind?

My wife and I are leaving Kenya primarily for our children's sake. What point, I wonder, in dragging up our roots from dear old Kenya in order to safeguard our children's future, while allowing them to grow up in a world that could become impoverished through a virtually instantaneous loss of life forms that have endured on Earth for many millennia but are to be snuffed out in a twinkling of a geologic eye? When my children are grown up and they may wish to take a safari to Kenya, shall we still enjoy the plains herds, the birdlife throngs, and the safari territories that are the glory of Kenya? This question belongs, in the first place, with Kenyans themselves. But in the last place, and in all places in between, it is a responsibility for all members of the global village.

References

Ackefors, H. and C. G. Rosen. 1979. Farming Aquatic Animals. *Ambio* 8(4).

Altschul, S. von R. 1977. Exploring the Herbarium. *Scientific American* 236(5): 96-104.

Anderson, C. J. 1973. Animals, Earthquakes and Eruptions. *Field Museum of Natural History Bulletin* 44:5, 9-11.

Anderson, D. W. and five others. 1975. Brown Pelicans: Improved Reproduction on the Southern California Coast. *Science* 190:806-808.

Anderson, G.R.V. and five others. 1981. The Community Structure of Coral Reef Fishes. *American Naturalist* 117(4):476-495.

Andrews, N. J. and D. C. Pratt. 1978. The Potential of Cattails (*Typha* spp.) as an Energy Source: Productivity in Managed Stands. *Journal of Minnesota Academy of Sciences* 44:5-8.

Applezweig, N. 1977. *Dioscorea*–the Pill Crop. Pp. 149-164 in D. S. Seigler (ed.), *Crop Resources*. Academic Press, New York.

Asahinat Y. and S. Shibata. 1971. *Chemistry of Lichen Substances*. A. Asher & Co. Ltd., Amsterdam.

Austin, R. B. 1978. Actual and Potential Yields of Wheat and Barley in the United Kingdom. *ADAS Quarterly Review* 2:76-87.

Ayensu, E. S. 1978. *Medicinal Plants of West Africa*. Reference Publications Inc., Algonac, Michigan.

Bach, W. 1972. *Atmospheric Pollution*. McGraw-Hill, New York.

Bagby, M. O. 1977. Kenaf: A Practical Fiber Resource. *TAPPI/Press Reports: Non-Wood Plant Fiber Pulping Progress Report No. 8*:75-80. TAPPI, Atlanta, Georgia.

Bakus, G. J. and G. Green. 1974. Toxicity in Sponges and Holothurians. *Science* 185:951-953.

Balazova, G. and E. Hluchan. 1969. The Influence of Fluoride Emissions on the Animals in the Vicinity of An Aluminum Factory. Pp.275-279 in *Proceedings of European Congress on Influence of Air Pollution*.

Balick, M. J. 1979. Amazonian Oil Palms of Promise: A Survey. *Economic Botany* 33(1)1:11-28.

Barclay, A. S. 1978. Personal Communication. National Cancer Institute, Bethesda, Maryland.

Barclay, A. S. and R. E. Perdue. 1976. Distribution of Anti-Cancer Activity in Higher Plants. *Cancer Treatment Reports* 60(8):1081-1113.

Barz, W., E. Reinhard, and M. H. Zenk (eds.). 1977. *Plant Tissue Culture and Its Bio-technological Application*. Springer-Verlag, Berlin and New York.

Bassham, J. A. 1977. Increasing Crop Production Through More Controlled Photosynthesis. *Science* 197:630-638.

Batra, S.W.T. 1982. Biological Control in Agroecosystems. *Science* 215:135-139.

Beadle, G. W. 1980. The Ancestry of Corn. *Scientific American* 242(1):112-119.

Bemis, W. P. and four others. 1975. *The Buffalo Gourd: A Potential Crop for the Production of Protein, Oil and Starch on Aridlands*. Office of Agriculture, Agency for International Development, Washington, D.C.

Bendz, G. and J. Santesson (eds.). 1974. *Chemistry in Botanical Classification*. Nobel Foundation, Stockholm, Sweden.

Benedict, H. M. *et al.* 1979. *A Review of Current Research on Hydrocarbon Production by Plants*. Solar Energy Research Institute, Golden, Colorado.

Benemann, J. R. 1979. *Energy from Aquaculture Biomass Systems: Fresh and Brackish Water Aquatic Plants*. Office of Technology Assessment, U.S. Congress, Washington, D.C.

Bente, P. F. (ed.). 1981. *Proceedings of Bio-Energy Conference*. Bio-Energy Council, Washington, D.C.

Bertrand, A. R. 1980. Personal Communication, in his capacity as Director of Science and Education, U.S. Department of Agriculture, Washington, D.C.

Bingel, A. S. and N. R. Farnsworth. 1980. Botanical Sources of Fertility Regulating Agents: Chemistry and Pharmacology. In *Advances in Hormone Biochemistry and Pharmacology*. Eden Press, New York.

Bodenheimer, F. S. 1951. *Insects as Human Food*. W. Junk, The Hague, Netherlands.

Bollinger, W. H. 1980. Sustaining Renewable Resources: Techniques from Applied Botany. Pp. 379-390 in *Renewable Resources: A Systematic Approach*, Academic Press, New York.

Borgese, E. M. 1980. *Seafarm: The Story of Aquaculture*. Abrams Publishers, New York.

Braekman, J. C. (ed.). 1981. *Proceedings of Third International Symposium on Marine Natural Products*, September 16-19, 1980. International Institute of Pure and Applied Chemistry, Brussels, Belgium.

Braun, A. 1968. Cultivated Palms of Venezuela. *Principes* 12:111-113.

Brewbaker, J. L. 1979. Diseases of Maize in the Wet Lowland Tropics and the Collapse of the Classic Maya Civilization. *Economic Botany* 33(2):101-118.

Brewbaker, J. L. and Ta Wei Hu. 1981. *Nitrogen Fixing Trees of Importance in the Tropics*. Nitrogen Fixing Tree Association, University of Hawaii, Honolulu, Hawaii.

Brill, W. J. 1979. Nitrogen Fixation: Basic to Applied. *American Scientist* 67:458-465.

Brisky, E. J. (ed.). 1981. *Advances in Food Producing Systems for Arid and Semi-Arid Lands*. Whitlock Press, Middletown, Connecticut.

Bristowe, W. S. 1932. Insects and Other Invertebrates for Human Consumption in Siam. *Transactions of the Entomological Society of London* 80:387-404.

Brooke, P. 1978. *Cancer: Drug Utilization and Drug Prospects*. Drug and Medical Follow-up No. 78-29. Cyrus J. Laurence, Inc., New York.

Brooks, R. R. and C. C. Radford. 1978. Nickel Accumulation by European

Species of the Genus *Alyssum. Proceedings of Royal Society of London* 200:217–224.

Brooks, R. R., J. A. McCleave, and F. Malaisse. 1977. Copper and Cobalt in African Species of *Crotalaria. Proceedings of Royal Society of London* 197:231–236.

Brooks, R. R., E. D. Wither, and L. Y. Th.Westra. 1978. Biochemical Copper Anomalies on Salajar Island in Indonesia. *Journal of Geochemical Exploration* 10:181–188.

Brown, C. R., W. Hauptli, and S. K. Jain. 1979. Variation in *Limnanthes alba:* A Biosystematic Survey of Germ Plasm Resources. *Economic Botany* 33(3):267–274.

Bruwer, J. J. *et al.* 1980. *The Use of Sunflower Seed Oil In Diesel-Engined Machinery.* Division of Agricultural Engineering, Department of Agriculture, Silverton, South Africa.

Bryson, R. A. and T. J. Murray. 1977. *Climates of Hunger.* University of Wisconsin Press, Madison, Wisconsin.

Buchanan, R. A., I. M. Cull, F. H. Otey, and C. R. Russell. 1978. Hydrocarbon and Rubber-Producing Crops. *Economic Botany* 32:131–153.

Buchanan, R. A. and F. H. Otey. 1979. Multi-Use Oil- and Hydrocarbon-Producing Crops in Adaptive Systems for Food, Material and Energy Production. *Biosources Digest* 6:176–202.

Buvet, R. *et al.* (eds.). 1977. *Living Systems as Energy Converters.* Elsevier, Amsterdam, Netherlands.

Calvin, M. 1977. Green Factories. *Chemical and Engineering News* 56:30–36.

———— . 1980. Hydrocarbons From Plants: Analytical Methods and Observations. *Naturwissenschaften* 67:525–533.

Case, T. J. and R. K. Washino. 1979. Flatworm Control of Mosquito Larvae in Rice Fields. *Science* 206:1412–1414.

Cassady, J. M. and J. D. Douros (eds.). 1980. *Design and Synthesis of Potential Anti-Cancer Agents Based on Natural Product Models.* Academic Press, New York.

Chapman, V. J. 1976. *Seaweeds and Their Uses.* Second edition. Methuen, London, U.K.

———— (ed.). 1977. *Ecosystems of the World.* Volume 1: *Wet Coastal Systems.* Elsevier, Amsterdam, Netherlands.

———— . 1980. Organic Chemicals From the Sea. Pp. 551–564 in L. E. St. Pierre and G. R. Brown (eds.), *Future Sources of Organic Raw Materials.* Pergamon Press, New York.

Chatterjee, S. K. 1980. Cultivation of Medicinal Plants in India, with Special Reference to the Eastern Himalayan Regions. Paper presented at Fourth Asian Symposium on Medicinal Plants and Spices, UNESCO and Faculty of Science, Mahidol University, Bangkok, Thailand. In UNESCO, 1981:100.

Chikov, P. 1973. Herbal Medicines in the Soviet Union. *World Health*, September 1973:18–23.

Child, J. J. 1977. New Developments in Nitrogen Fixation Research. *BioScience* 26(10):614–617.

Chin, K. K. and T. N. Gohj. 1978. *Bioconversion of Solar Energy and Methane*

Production From Water Hyacinth. Institute of Gas Technology, Chicago, Illinois.

Christiansen, M. N. and C. F. Lewis (eds.). 1982. *Breeding Plants For Less Favorable Environments.* Wiley-Interscience, New York.

CIMMYT. 1974. *Annual Review.* International Centre for Improvement of Maize and Wheat, Mexico.

_____. 1976. *CIMMYT Review, 1976* (Tenth Anniversary 1966–1976). International Centre for Improvement of Maize and Wheat, Mexico.

_____. 1978. Evaluating the Impact of Research on Wheat for 1976/77. *CIMMYT Review, 1978:*129–136. International Centre for Improvement of Maize and Wheat, Mexico.

Cmelik, S.H.W. and C. C. Douglas. 1970. Chemical Composition of "Fungus Gardens" from Two Species of Termites. *Comparative Biochemistry and Physiology* 36:493–502.

Cohen, E. (ed.). 1979. *Biomedical Applications of the Horseshoe Crab (Limulidae).* Alan R. Liss, New York.

Connell, J. H. 1978. Diversity in Tropical Rainforests and Coral Reefs. *Science* 199:1302–1310.

Convit, J. and M. E. Pinardi. 1974. Leprosy: Confirmation in the Armadillo. *Science* 184:1191–1192.

Cordell, G. A. 1978. Alkaloids. Pp. 883–943 in *Encyclopedia of Chemical Technology.* Vol. I, third edition. John Wiley & Sons, New York.

Coster, T. W. and R. G. Osborn. 1977. *Wading Birds as Biological Indicators: 1975 Colony Survey.* Special Scientific Report on Wildlife No. 206, Fish and Wildlife Service of U.S. Department of the Interior, Washington, D.C.

Council on Environmental Quality. 1980. *Global 2000 Report.* Council on Environmental Quality, Washington, D.C.

Cowell, R. (ed.). 1979. *Proceedings of First International Symposium on Tropical Tomato.* Asian Vegetable Research and Development Center, Publication 78–59, Taiwan.

Crabbe, P. 1979. Mexican Plants and Human Fertility. *Courier* (UNESCO monthly), May 1979: 33–34.

Culbertson, C. F. 1969. *Chemical and Botanical Guide to Lichen Products.* University of North Carolina Press, Chapel Hill, North Carolina.

Cushing, D. H. and J. J. Walsh (eds.). 1976. *The Ecology of the Seas.* Blackwell Scientific Publications, Oxford, U.K.

Dalrymple, D. G. 1979. The Adoption of High-Yielding Grain Varieties in Developing Nations. *Agricultural History* 53(4):704–726.

_____. 1980. *Development and Spread of Semi-Dwarf Varieties of Wheat and Rice in the United States: An International Perspective.* Agriculture Economic Report No. 455. Office of International Cooperation and Development, U.S. Department of Agriculture, Washington, D.C.

Darley, E. F. 1966. Studies on the Effects of Cement-Kiln Dust on Vegetation. *Journal of Air Pollution Control Association* 16:145–151.

Das, T. M. 1981. Plants and Pollution. *Proceedings of 68th Session of the Indian Science Congress, Section of Agricultural Sciences,* Part II: 1–17. Indian Science Congress Association, Calcutta, India.

Davies, G. M. 1977. Rare and Endangered Species: A Dilemma. *Frontiers* (publication of the Academy of Natural Sciences of Philadelphia) 41(4): 12-14.

Day, P. R. 1977. Plant Genetics: Increase in Crop Yield. *Science* 197: 1334-1339.

de Padua, L. S., G. C. Logot, and J. V. Pancha. 1977. *Handbook on Philippines Medicinal Plants*. Two volumes. UPLB Technical Bulletin 3(3). University of the Philippines at Los Baños, Philippines.

DeBach, P. 1974. *Biological Control by Natural Enemies*. Cambridge University Press, New York.

Delucchi, V. L. (ed.). 1976. *Studies in Biological Control*. Cambridge University Press, Cambridge, U.K.

DeWet, J.M.J. 1979. *Tripsacum* Introgression and Agronomic Fitness in Maize (*Zea Mays* L.). Pp. 203-210 in *Proceedings of the Conference on Broadening the Genetic Base of Crops*. A. C. Zeven and A. M. van Harten (eds.), Pudoc, Wageningen, Netherlands.

Dewey, J. E. 1973. Accumulation of Fluoride by Insects near an Emission Source in Western Montana. *Environmental Entomology* 2(2):179-182.

Dixon, B. 1976. Smallpox – An Unresolved Dilemma. *New Scientist* 69(989): 430-432.

Dobereiner, J., J. M. Day, and P. J. Dart. 1972. Nitrogenase Activity in Rhizospheres of Sugar Cane and Some Other Tropical Grasses. *Plant Soil* 27:191-196.

Dobereiner, J., D. Burrio, and A. Hollaender (eds.). 1978. *Limitations and Potentials for Biological Nitrogen Fixation in the Tropics*. Plenum Press, New York.

Douros, J. D. 1976. Lower Plants as a Source of Anticancer Drugs. *Cancer Treatment Reports* 60(8):1069-1080.

Douros, J. D. and M. Suffness. 1978. New Natural Products of Interest Under Development at the National Cancer Institute. *Cancer Chemotherapy Pharmacology* 1:91-100.

_____ . 1980. The National Cancer Institute's Natural Products Antineoplastic Development Program. In S. K. Carter and Y. Sakurai (eds.), *Recent Results in Cancer Research* 70:21-44.

_____ . 1981. New Antitumor Substances of Natural Origin. *Cancer Treatment Reviews* 8:63-87.

Downton, W.J.S. 1973. *Amaranthus edulis*: A High Lysine Grain Amaranth. *World Crops* 25(1):20.

Duckham, A. M., J.G.W. Joans, and E. H. Roberts (eds.). 1976. *Food Production and Consumption*. North Holland Publishing Co., Amsterdam, Netherlands.

Duke, J. A. 1978. The Quest for Tolerant Germplasm. In *Crop Tolerance to Suboptimal Land Conditions*: 1-61. American Society of Agronomy, Madison, Wisconsin.

_____ . 1979. Ecosystematic Data on Economic Plants. *Quarterly Journal of Crude Drug Research* 17:91-110.

_____ . 1980. *Neotropical Anti-Cancer Plants*. Economic Botany Laboratory, Agricultural Research Service, Beltsville, Maryland.

_____ . 1981. *The Gene Revolution*. Office of Technology Assessment, U.S. Congress, Washington, D.C.

Duke, J. A., S. J. Hurst, and E. E. Terrell. 1975. *Ecological Distribution of 1000 Economic Plants.* Agronomia No. 1, IICA-TROPICOS, Turrialba, Costa Rica.

Duvick, D. N. 1977. Genetic Rates of Gain in Hybrid Maize Yields During the Past 40 Years. *Maydica* 22:187–196.

———. 1981. Genetic Diversity in Major Farm Crops on the Farm and in Reserve. In *Proceedings of 13th International Botanical Congress,* Sydney, Australia, August 12–28.

Dynatech Research and Development Corporation. 1978. *Cost Analysis of Aquatic Biomass Systems.* U.S. Department of Energy, Washington, D.C.

Edwards, D. 1976. Floral Resources of Southern Africa. Pp. 154–160 in G. Baker (ed.), *Resources of Southern Africa Today and Tomorrow.* Associated Technical and Scientific Societies of Southern Africa, Johannesburg, South Africa.

Ehrlich, P. R. 1975. The Population Biology of Coral Reef Fishes. *Annual Review of Ecology and Systematics* 6(1975).

Ehrlich, P. R., A. H. Ehrlich, and J. P. Holdren. 1977. *Ecoscience: Population, Resources, Environment.* W. H. Freeman, San Francisco, California.

Ekong, D.E.U. 1979. African Medicinal Plants Under the Microscope. *Courier* (UNESCO monthly), May 1979: 17–18.

Emlen, J. M. 1973. *Ecology: An Evolutionary Approach.* Addison-Wesley, Reading, Massachusetts.

Epstein, E. and J. D. Norlyn. 1976. Seawater-Based Crop Production: A Feasibility Study. *Science* 197:249–251.

Epstein, E. and six others. 1980. Saline Culture of Crops: A Genetic Approach. *Science* 210:399–404.

Farnsworth, N. R. 1969. Drugs From The Sea. *Tile and Till* 55.

———. 1978. Indigenous Plants for Fertility Regulation. *Proceedings of IUPAC Eleventh International Symposium on Chemistry of Natural Products* 4(2):475–489. International Union for Pure and Applied Chemistry, Brussels, Belgium.

———. 1979. The Present and Future of Pharmacognosy. *American Journal of Pharmaceutical Education* 43:239–243.

———. 1982. The Consequences of Plant Extinction on the Current and Future Availability of Drugs. Paper Presented at AAAS Annual Meeting, Washington, D.C., January 3–8. University of Illinois Medical Center, Chicago, Illinois. 19 pp. mimeo.

Farnsworth, N. R. and G. A. Cordell. 1976. A Review of Some Biologically Active Compounds Isolated from Plants as Reported in the 1974–1975 Literature. *Lloydia* 39(6):420–455.

Farnsworth, N. R. and J. M. Farley. 1980. *Traditional Medicine Programs of the World Health Organization.* Department of Pharmacognosy and Pharmacology, College of Pharmacy, University of Illinois at the Medical Center, Chicago, Illinois.

Farnsworth, N. R. and C. J. Kaas. 1978. An Approach Utilizing Information From Traditional Medicine to Identify Tumor Inhibitory Plants. In *Proceedings of Consultations Meeting on the Potentials for Use of Plants Indicated* by *Traditional Medicine in Cancer Therapy*. World Health Organization, Geneva, Switzerland.

Farnsworth, N. R. and R. W. Morris. 1976. Higher Plants – the Sleeping Giant of Drug Development. *American Journal of Pharmacy* 148(2):46-52.

Feinert, J. and Y.P.S. Bajaj (eds.). 1977. *Plant Cell, Tissue, and Organ Culture*. Springer-Verlag, New York.

Feldman, M. and E. R. Sears. 1981. The Wild Gene Resources of Wheat. *Scientific American* 244(1):98-109.

Felger, R. S. and M. B. Moser. 1973. Eelgrass (*Zostera marina* L.) in the Gulf of California: Discovery of its Nutritional Value by the Seri Indians. *Science* 181:355-356.

Felker, P. and R. S. Bandurski. 1979. Uses and Potential Uses of Leguminous Trees for Minimal Energy Input Agriculture. *Economic Botany* 33(2): 172-184.

Ferwerda, F. P. 1976. Coffees. Pp. 252-260 in N. W. Simmons (ed.), *Evolution of Crop Plants*. Longman, New York.

Fisher, A. C. 1982. Economic Analysis and the Extinction of Species. Department of Agriculture and Resource Economics, University of California at Berkeley. 6 pp. mimeo.

Flores-Moya, P., R. E. Evenson, and Y. Hayami. 1978. *Social Returns of Rice Research in the Philippines: Domestic Benefits and Foreign Spillover*. Economic Growth Center No. 270. Yale University, New Haven, Connecticut.

Food and Agriculture Organization. 1978. *1977 Yearbook of Forest Products*. Food and Agriculture Organization, Rome, Italy.

Franda, M. 1980. New Roads to Nitrogen Fixation. *Kettering's Nitrogen Fixers Part III:* 5-9. General Report No. 15, American University Field Staff, Hanover, New Hampshire.

Frankel, O. H. and J. G. Hawkes (eds.). 1974. *Plant Genetic Resources for Today and Tomorrow*. Cambridge University Press, London, U.K.

Franz, C. (ed.). 1978. *Proceedings of First International Symposium on Spices and Medicinal Plants*, July 31-August 4, 1977. Freising-Weihenstephan, West Germany.

Fryer, G. 1980. *Conserving and Exploiting the Biota of Africa's Great Lakes*. Freshwater Biological Association, The Ferry House, Ambleside, Cumbria, U.K., 34 pp. mimeo.

Fulder, S. 1980. *The Root of Being*. Hutchinson, London, U.K.

Furber, S. B. and J. E. Ffowes-Williams. 1979. Is the Weis-Fogh Principle Exploitable in Turbomachinery? *Journal of Fluid Mechanics* 94(3):519-540.

Gabel, M. 1979. *Ho-Ping: Food for Everyone*. Anchor Press/Doubleday, New York.

Gasser, W. R. 1981. *Survey of Irrigation in 8 Asian Nations*. Foreign Agricultural Economic Report No. 165. Economics and Statistics Service, U.S. Department of Agriculture, Washington, D.C.

General Accounting Office of the United States. 1981. The Department of Agriculture Can Minimize the Risk of Potential of Crop Failures. General Accounting Office of United States, Washington, D.C.

Ghosh, K. and T. Ghosh. 1971. Ramie Cultivation in India. *Jute Bulletin* April–May:15–18.

Gibbs, R. D. 1974. *Chemotaxonomy of Flowering Plants.* McGill-Queens University Press, Montreal, Canada.

Glendinning, D. R. 1979. The Potato Gene-Pool, and Benefits Deriving From Its Supplementation. Pp. 187-194 in A. C. Zeven and A. M. van Harten (eds.), *Proceedings of the Conference on Broadening the Genetic Base of Crops.* Pudoc, Wageningen, Netherlands.

Gold, J. and W. Cates. 1980. Herbal Abortifacients. *Journal of the American Medical Association* 243:1365–1366.

Goldman, J. C. *et al.* 1977. *Report on Sources and Systems for Aquatic Plant Biomass as an Energy Source.* Dynatech Research and Development Corporation, Cambridge, Massachusetts.

Gordon, C. C. 1969. *East Helena Report.* Department of Environmental Studies, University of Montana, Missoula, Montana.

Gottlieb, O. R. and W. R. Mors. 1980. Potential Utilization of Brazilian Wood Extractives. *Journal of Agricultural and Food Chemistry* 28:196–215.

Grojean, R. E., J. A. Sousa, and M. C. Henry. 1980. Utilization of Solar Radiation by Polar Animals: An Optical Model for Pelts. *Applied Optics* 19(3):339–346.

Guiry, M. D. 1979. Commercial Exploitation of Marine Red Algal Polysaccharides – Progress and Prospects. *Tropical Science* 21(3):183–196.

Gupta, R. 1981. Genetic Resources of Medicinal Plants in a World Perspective. Paper presented at FAO/UNEP/IBPGR Technical Conference on Crops Genetic Resources, April 6–10. Food and Agriculture Organization, Rome, Italy.

Hall, D. O. 1981. Put a Sunflower in your Tank. *New Scientist* 89(1242): 524–526.

Hall, D. O. and K. K. Rao. 1980. *Photosynthesis.* Edward Arnold, London, U.K.

Hall, D. O., G. W. Barnard, and P. A. Moss. 1982. *Biomass for Energy in the Developing Countries.* Pergamon Press, Oxford, U.K.

Hanlon, J. 1979. When the Scientist Meets the Medicine Man. *Nature* 279:284–285.

Hardy, M. R. 1980. *Report of International Paper Sales Kenaf Newsprint Project.* International Paper Sales Co., Inc., Atlanta, Georgia.

Harlan, J. R. 1969. Ethiopia: A Center of Diversity. *Economic Botany* 23(4):309–314.

_____ . 1975. *Crops and Man.* American Society of Agronomy, Madison, Wisconsin.

_____ . 1976. Genetic Resources in Wild Relatives of Crops. *Crop Science* 16:329–333.

_____ . 1981. Evaluation of Wild Relatives of Crop Plants. Paper presented at FAO/UNEP/IBPGR Technical Conference on Crop Genetic Resources, April 6–10. Food and Agriculture Organization, Rome, Italy.

Hartwell, J. L. 1976. Types of Anticancer Agents Isolated From Plants. *Cancer Treatment Reports* 60(8):1031–1068.

Hastings, J. W. 1976. Bioluminescence. *Oceanus* 19(2):17-27.

Heagle, A. S. 1973. Interactions Between Air Pollutants and Plant Parasites. *Annual Review of Phytopathology*, 11:365-388.

Herklots, G.A.C. 1972. *Vegetables in Southeast Asia.* George Allen and Unwin, London, U.K.

Hester, F. J. 1976. *Economic Aspects of the Effects of Pollution on the Marine and Anadromous Fisheries of the Western United States of America.* FAO Fisheries Technical Paper 162. United Nations Food and Agriculture Organization, Rome, Italy.

Higginbotham, J. D. 1979. Protein Sweeteners. In C.A.M. Hough, K. J. Parker, and A. J. Vletof, *Developments in Sweeteners*, Applied Science Publishers, London, U.K.

Hillman, W. S. and D. D. Culley. 1978. The Uses of Duckweed. *American Scientist* 66(4)442-451.

Hodge, W. H. 1975. Oil-Producing Palms of the World – A Review. *Principes* 19:119-136.

Hodge, W. H. and H. H. Sineheh. 1956. The Mexican Candelilla Plant and its Wax. *Economic Botany* 10(2):134-154.

Hoffman, J. *et al.* 1980. *Sunflower Oil as a Fuel Alternative.* Cooperative Extension Service Bulletin, North Dakota State University, Fargo, North Dakota.

Hollaender, A., J. C. Aller, E. Epstein, A. S. Pietro, and O. R. Zaborsky (eds.). 1979. *The Biosaline Concept.* Environmental Science Research Vol. 14. Plenum Publishing, New York.

Horrobin, D. F. 1980. A Biochemical Basis for Alcoholism and Alcohol-Induced Damage Including the Fetal Alcohol Syndrome and Cirrhosis: Interference with Essential Fatty Acid and Prostaglandin Metabolism. *Medical Hypotheses* 6:929-942.

Hudson, M. S. 1979. *Anticancer Agents From Tree Sap.* M. S. Hudson Inc., Charlottesville, Virginia.

Huffaker, C. B. 1980. Use of Predators and Parasitoids in Biological Control. Pp. 173-198, in R. C. Staples and R. J. Kuhr (eds.), *Linking Research to Crop Production*, Plenum Publishing, New York.

Huffaker, C. B. and P. S. Messenger (eds.). 1976. *Theory and Practice of Biological Control.* Academic Press, New York.

Hughes, K. W., R. Henke, and M. Constantin (eds.). 1978. *Propagation of Higher Plants through Tissue Culture.* National Technical Information Service, Springfield, Virginia.

Ichikawa, S. 1979. Personal Communication. Environmental Protection Agency, Washington, D. C.

Iltis, H. H., J. F. Doebley, R. M. Guzmán, and B. Pazy. 1979. *Zea diploperennis* (Gramineae), a New Teosinte From Mexico. *Science* 203:186-188.

Imle, E. P. 1978. *Hevea* Rubber: Past and Future. *Economic Botany* 32:264-277.

Indian Council of Medical Research. 1976. *Medicinal Plants of India.* Vol. 1. Indian Council of Medical Research, New Delhi, India.

Inglett, G. E. 1981. Sweeteners – A Review. *Food Technology*, March 1981: 37-41.

Inman, R. 1977. *Silvicultural Biomass Farms.* Six volumes. MITRE Corporation, McLean, Virginia.

International Marketing Statistics. 1981. *National Prescriptions Audit.* I.M.S. Limited, Ambler, Pennsylvania.

International Paper Sales. 1980. Joint Kenaf Project: Technical Report Summary. International Paper Sales Co., Inc., Atlanta, Georgia.

International Rice Research Institute. 1977. *Utilization of the Azolla-Anabaena Complex as a Nitrogen Fertilizer for Rice.* Research Series No. 2, International Rice Research Institute, Los Baños, Philippines.

Jackson, J.B.C. and L. Buss. 1975. Allelopathy and Spatial Competition Among Coral Reef Vertebrates. *Proceedings of the National Academy of Sciences* 72(12):5160-5163.

Jalliff, G. D., I. J. Tinsley, W. Calhoun, and J. M. Crane. 1981. *Meadowfoam (Limnanthes alba): Its Research and Development as a Potential New Oil Seed Crop for the Willamette Valley of Oregon.* State Bulletin No. 648. Agricultural Experiment Station, Oregon State University, Corvallis, Oregon.

Jennings, D. L. 1976. Cassava. Pp. 81–84 in N. W. Simmonds (ed.), *Evolution of Crop Plants.* Longman, London, U.K.

Jensen, N. F. 1978. Limits of Growth in World Food Production. *Science* 201:317-320.

Johnson, J. D. and T. W. Hinman. 1980. Oils and Rubber from Arid Land Plants. *Science* 208:460-464.

Jones, J. L. et al. 1979. *Extraction of Hydrocarbon Liquids from Euphorbia Type Plants.* Stanford Research Institute International, Menlo Park, California.

Jung, G. A. (ed.). 1978. *Crop Tolerance to Suboptimal Land Conditions.* Special Publication No. 32, American Society of Agronomy, Madison, Wisconsin.

Jury, W. A., H. Frankel, H. Fluhlel, D. Devitt, and L. H. Stoley. 1978. Use of Saline Irrigation Waters and Minimal Leeching for Crop Production. *Hilgardia* 46:169-192.

Justice, O. L. and L. N. Bass. 1978. *Principles and Practices of Seed Storage.* Agriculture Handbook No. 506. Science and Education Administration, U.S. Department of Agriculture, Washington, D.C.

Kandel, E. R. 1979. Behavioral Biology of *Aplysia.* W. H. Freeman, San Francisco, California.

Kanjanopothi, D. and four others. 1980. Antifertility Activity of *Mentha Arvensis* in Rats: Postcoital Contraception. Paper presented at Fourth Asian Symposium on Medicinal Plants and Spices, UNESCO and Faculty of Science, Mahidol University, Bangkok, Thailand. In UNESCO, 1981:62.

Karstad, L. 1970. Wildlife in a Changing Environment. Pp. 73–80 in D. F. Elrich (ed.), *Environmental Change.* Simon and Schuster, New York.

Kaul, P. N. 1979. The Sea's Biomedical Potential. *Impact of Science on Society* 29(2):123-134.

Kaul, P. N. and C. J. Sindermann (eds.). 1978. *Drugs and Food From the Sea.* University of Oklahoma Press, Norman, Oklahoma.

Kay, C. E., P. C. Tourangeau, and C. C. Gordon. 1975. Industrial Fluorosis in Wild Mule and Whitetail Deer from Western Montana. *Fluoride* 8(4):182-191.

Kempanna, C. 1974. Prospects for Medicinal Plants in Indian Agriculture. *World Crops* 26:166-168.

Kerr, R. A. 1980. Quake Prediction by Animals Gaining Respect. *Science* 208:695-696.

King, E. W. 1976. *Insects as Food.* Department of Entomology, Clemson University, Clemson, South Carolina.

Kingsolver, B. E. 1982. *Euphorbia lathyris* Reconsidered: Its Potential as an Energy Crop for Arid Lands. *Biomass* 2:281-298.

Kitzke, E. D. and D. Johnson, 1975. Commercial Palm Products other than Oils. *Principes* 19:3-26.

Kong, Y. C., S. Y. Hu, and P. But. 1980. A Critical Review of the Medicinal Plant Resources in Chinese Flora. Paper presented at Fourth Asian Symposium on Medicinal Plants and Spices, UNESCO and Faculty of Science, Mahidol University, Bangkok, Thailand. In UNESCO 1981:39.

Kovaly, K. A. 1979. Better Ways to Fix Nitrogen. *Technology Tomorrow* 2(5):6-7.

Kraemer, H. C., B. E. Smith, and S. Levine. 1978. *An Animal Behavior Model for Short-Term Earthquake Prediction.* National Center for Earthquake Research, U. S. Geological Survey, Menlo Park, California, and Department of Psychiatry and Behavioral Sciences, Stanford University, Stanford, California.

Kumpf, H. E. 1977. *Economic Impact of the Effects of Pollution on the Coastal Fisheries of the Atlantic and Gulf of Mexico Regions of the United States of America.* FAO Fisheries Technical Paper 172. United Nations Food and Agriculture Organization, Rome, Italy.

Kupchan, S. M. 1976. Novel Plant-Derived Tumor Inhibitors and Their Mechanisms of Action. *Cancer Treatment Reports* 60(8):1115-1127.

Kuru, A. 1978. The Environmental Impact of Agriculture in Ethiopia. *Environmental Conservation* 5(3):213-221.

Laufs, R. and H. Steinke. 1975. Vaccination of Non-Primates Against Malignant Lymphoma. *Nature* 253:71-72.

Lee, D. 1980. *The Sinking Ark.* Heinemann Educational Books (Asia) Ltd., Kuala Lumpur, Malaysia.

Lee, J., R. D. Reeves, R. R. Brooks, and T. Jaffrey. 1978. The Relation Between Nickel and Citric Acid in Some Nickel-Accumulating Plants. *Phytochemistry* 17:1033-1035.

Legner, E. F. 1978. Mass Culture of *Tilapia zillii* (Cichlidae) in Pond Ecosystems. *Entomophaga* 23(1):51-55.

Legner, E. F. and T. W. Fisher. 1980. Impact of *Tilapia zillii* on *Potamogeton pectinatus, Myriophyllum spicatum* var. *exalbescens,* and Mosquito Reproduction in Lower Colorado Desert (USA) Irrigation Canals. *Acta Oecologia Appl.* 1(1):3-14.

Legner, E. F. and F. W. Pelsue. 1980. Bioconversion: Tilapia Fish Turn Insects and Weeds into Edible Protein. *California Agriculture* 34(11 & 12):13-14.

Lemma, A., D. Heyneman, and H. Kloos (eds.). 1979. Studies on Molluscicidal and Other Properties of the Endod Plant, *Phytolacca Dodecandra.* Department of Epidemiology and International Health, University of California, San Francisco, California.

Lemma, A. and P. Yau. 1974. Studies on the Molluscicidal Properties of Endod. *Ethiopian Medical Journal* 13:115–124.

Levin, D. A. 1976. The Chemical Defenses of Plants to Pathogens and Herbivores. *Annual Review of Ecology and Systematics* 7:121–159.

Lewis, G. 1979. Natural Vegetable Fibres as Reinforcement in Cement Sheets. *Magazine of Concrete Research* 31(107):104–108.

Lewis, W. H. and M.P.F. Elvin-Lewis. 1977. *Medical Botany*. John Wiley & Sons, New York.

Lipinsky E. S., S. Kresovich, and A. Scantland. 1980. Fuels from New Crops. Pp. 307–328 in *Renewable Resources: A Systematic Approach*. Academic Press, New York.

Lockwood, A.P.M. (ed.). 1976. *Effects of Pollutants on Aquatic Organisms*. Cambridge University Press, Cambridge, U.K.

Lovejoy, T. E. 1978. Royal Water Lilies: Truly Amazonian. *Smithsonian* (1):78–83.

Lovell, R. T. 1979. Fish Culture in the United States. *Science* 206:1368–1372.

Lowe-McConnell, R. H. 1977. *Ecology of Fishes in Tropical Waters*. Studies in Biology No. 76, Edward Arnold Ltd., London, U.K.

Lumpkin, T. A. and D. L. Plucknett. 1982. *Azolla as a Green Manure: Use and Management in Crop Production*. Westview Press, Boulder, Colorado.

MacArthur, R. H. 1972. *Geographical Ecology: Patterns in the Distribution of Species*. Harper and Row, New York.

Madlener, J. C. 1977. *The Seavegetable Book: Foraging and Cooking Sea Weeds*. Clarkson N. Potter, New York.

Man, A. B. and D. Blandford. 1980. *The Outlook for Natural Rubber*. Cornell International Agriculture Mimeograph No. 78. Cornell University, Ithaca, New York.

Mann, J. D. 1978. Production of Solasodine for the Pharmaceutical Industry. *Advances in Agronomy* 30:207–245.

Mansfield, T. A. (ed.). 1976. *Effects of Air Pollutants on Plants*. Cambridge University Press, Cambridge, U.K.

Marsden, J. S., G. E. Martin, D. J. Parham, T. J. Ridsdill-Smith, and B. G. Johnston. 1980. *Returns on Australian Agricultural Research*. Division of Entomology, Commonwealth Scientific and Industrial Research Organization, Canberra, Australia.

Marzola, D. L. and D. P. Bartholomew. 1979. Photosynthetic Pathway and Biomass Energy Production. *Science* 205:555–559.

Mason, I. L. 1975. Beefalo: Much Ado About Nothing? *World Review of Animal Production* 11(4):19–23.

Mass, E. V. and R. H. Nieman. 1978. Physiology of Plant Tolerance to Salinity. Pp. 277–299 in G. A. Jung (ed.), *Crop Tolerance to Suboptimal Land Conditions*. Special Publication No. 32, American Society of Agronomy, Madison, Wisconsin.

Maugh, T. H. 1982. Leprosy Vaccine Trials to Begin Soon. *Science* 215:1083–1086.

May, R. M. 1973. *Stability and Complexity in Model Ecosystems*. Princeton University Press, Princeton, New Jersey.

McArn, G. E., M. L. Boardman, R. Munn, and S. R. Wellings. 1974. Relationship of Pulmonary Particulates in English Sparrows to Gross Air Pollution. *Journal of Wildlife Diseases* 10:335-340.

McClure, R. 1980. Personal Communication. Department of Cellular Biology, University of California, Los Angeles, California.

McGinnies, W. G. and E. F. Haase (eds.). 1975. *Proceedings of International Conference on the Utilization of Guayule*. Office of Arid Lands Studies, University of Arizona, Tucson, Arizona.

McLaughlin, S. P. and J. J. Hoffmann. 1982. A Survey of Biocrude-Producing Plants from the Southwest. *Economic Botany* 36:323-339.

McLaughlin, S. P., B. E. Kingsolver, and J. J. Hoffmann. 1982. Bioenergy Production in Arid Lands. *Economic Botany* (in press).

Meethan, A. R. 1964. *Atmospheric Pollution: Its Origins and Prevention*. Third edition, revised. Pergamon Press, Oxford and New York.

Mendel, D. A., F. A. Schooley, and R. L. Dickenson. 1979. *A Production Cost Analysis of* Euphorbia lathyris. Stanford Research Institute, Menlo Park, California, and U.S. Department of Energy, Washington, D.C.

Meyers, W. M. and six others. 1981. Naturally Acquired Leprosy in a Mangabey Monkey. *Laboratory Investigation* (Annual Meeting Abstracts) 44:A44.

Michanek, G. 1975. *Seaweed Resources of the Ocean*. United Nations Food and Agriculture Organization, Rome, Italy.

―――――. 1978. Trends in Applied Physiology with a Literature Review: Seaweed Farming on an Industrial Scale. *Botanica Marina* 21:469-475.

―――――. 1981. Getting Seaweed to Where It's Needed. *Ceres* 14(1):41-44.

Miller, L. P. (ed.). 1973. *Phytochemistry*, Vol. 3. Van Nostrand-Reinhold, New York.

Miller, K. R. 1980. Threatened Species and Protected Zones. Paper presented at Third International Conference on the Environment, December 9-11, Paris, France. School of Natural Resources, University of Michigan, Ann Arbor, Michigan.

Mitsui, A. and C. C. Black (eds.). 1982. *Biosolar Resources*. CRC Press Inc., Palm Beach, Florida.

Moore, H. E. 1978. Endangerment at the Specific and Generic Levels in Palms. Pp. 267-282 in G. T. Prance and T. S. Elias (eds.), *Extinction is Forever*. New York Botanical Garden, Bronx, New York.

Mors, W. B. and C. T. Rizzini. 1966. *Useful Plants of Brazil*. Holden-Day, San Francisco, California.

Morton, J. F. 1971. The Wax Gourd―A Year-Round Florida Vegetable With Unusual Keeping Quality. *Proceedings of Florida State Horticulture Society* 84:104-109.

―――――. 1977. *Major Medicinal Plants*. Charles C. Thomas, Springfield, Illinois.

Mudie, J. P. 1974. The Potential Economic Uses of Halophytes. In R. J. Reinold and W. H. Queen (eds.), *Ecology of Halophytes*. Academic Press, New York.

Murata, M., E. E. Roos, and T. Tsuchiya. 1981. Chromosome Damage Induced by Artificial Seed Ageing in Barley. *Canadian Journal of Genetic Cytology* 23:267–280.

Murray, J. R., L. Teichner, A. Hiam, and R. Rosenberg. 1981. *An Assessment of the Global Potential of Genetic Engineering in the Agribusiness Sector.* Policy Research Corporation and The Chicago Group, Inc., Chicago, Illinois.

Mussell, H. W. and R. C. Staples (eds.). 1979. *Stress Physiology in Crop Plants.* Wiley-Interscience, New York.

Myers, N. 1972. *The Long African Day.* Macmillan, New York.

_____. 1979. *The Sinking Ark.* Pergamon Press, Elmsford, New York, and Oxford, U.K.

_____. 1980. *Conversion of Tropical Moist Forests.* National Research Council, Washington, D.C.

_____. 1981. Corn Genes and Big Dollars. *Technology Review* 84(2):8–9, 64.

_____. 1982. *The Use of Wild Plants for Traditional Medicine in Africa.* Report to World Health Organization, Geneva, Switzerland. Norman Myers Consultancy, Ltd., Nairobi, Kenya.

Nabham, G. P. 1979. Cultivation and Culture. *The Ecologist* 9(8 & 9) 259–263.

National Academy of Sciences. 1972. *Genetic Vulnerability of Crops.* National Academy of Sciences/American Association for the Advancement of Science, AAAS 126–72, Washington, D.C.

_____. 1975. *Underexploited Tropical Plants with Promising Economic Value.* National Academy of Sciences, Washington, D.C.

_____. 1976. *Making Aquatic Weeds Useful.* National Academy of Sciences, Washington, D.C.

_____. 1979. *Tropical Legumes: Resources for the Future.* National Academy of Sciences, Washington, D.C.

National Research Council. 1977. *Appropriate Technologies for Developing Countries.* National Research Council, Washington, D.C.

National Science Foundation. 1977. The Desert Pupfish and Human Kidney Research. *Mosaic*, January/February 1977.

Nault, L. R. and W. R. Findley. 1981. Primitive Relative Offers New Traits for Corn Improvement. *Ohio Report* 66(6):90–92.

Naylor, J. 1976. *Production, Trade and Utilization of Seaweeds and Seaweed Products.* FAO Fisheries Technical Paper 159. United Nations Food and Agriculture Organization, Rome, Italy.

Neill, W. T. 1974. *Reptiles and Amphibians in the Service of Man.* Pegasus Press, London, U.K.

Nelson, R. A. 1977. *Urea Metabolism in the Hibernating Black Bear.* Mayo Clinic, Rochester, Minnesota.

Nelson, R. R. and D. R. MacKenzie. 1980. Personal Communication. Department of Plant Pathology, Pennsylvania State University, University Park, Pennsylvania.

Nemethy, E. K., J. W. Otvos, and M. Calvin. 1979. Analysis of Extractables from one *Euphorbia. Journal of American Oil Chemists Society* 56:957–960.

Newman, J. R. 1980. *Effects of Air Emissions on Wildlife Resources.* Report FWS/OBS-80/40.1 of National Power Plant Team, Biological Services Program, U.S. Fish and Wildlife Service, Department of the Interior, Washington, D.C.

Newman J. R. and M. Yu. 1976. Fluorosis in Black-tailed Deer. *Journal of Wildlife Diseases* 12:39–41.

Newton, W. E. and D. J. Nyman (eds.). 1976. *Proceedings of First International Symposium on Nitrogen Fixation* (two volumes). Washington State University Press, Pullman, Washington.

Nickell, L. G. 1977. Plant Growth Regulators. *Advances in Chemistry* 159:6–22.

Nilan, R. A. 1978. Potential of Plant Genetic Systems for Monitoring and Screening Mutagens. *Environmental Health Perspective* 27:181.

Nishino, O., M. Arari, I. Senda, and K. Kuboto. 1973. Influence of Environmental Pollution on the Sparrow. *Japanese Journal of Public Health* 20(10):1.

North, W. J. 1979. Marine Macroscopic Plants as Biomass Sources. W.M. Keck Engineering Laboratories, California Institute of Technology, California.

Novakova, E. and Z. Roubal. 1971. Calcium and Phosphorus Ratios in the Blood Serum of Hares Subject to Air Pollution. Pp. 529–536 in *Proceedings of Tenth Congress of Union of International Game Biologists*.

Office of Technology Assessment. 1980. *Energy From Biological Processes*. Westview, Press, Boulder Colorado.

_____ . 1981. *Impacts of Applied Genetics: Micro-Organisms, Plants and Animals*. Office of Technology Assessment, U.S. Congress, Washington, D.C.

Oldfield, M. 1979. *The Use and Conservation of Biotic Genetic Resources*. Report to National Parks Service, U.S. Department of Interior, Washington, D.C. Texas System of Natural Laboratories, Inc., Austin, Texas.

_____ . 1981. *The Value of the Conservation of Genetic Resources*. Department of Agriculture, University of Texas, Austin, Texas.

Oomen, H.A.P.C. and G.J.H. Grubben. 1977. Tropical Leaf Vegetables in Human Nutrition. In *Communication* 69:24–41 and 51–55. Department of Agricultural Research, Koninklijk Instituut voor de Tropen, Amsterdam, Netherlands.

Papavizas, R. (ed.). 1982. *Proceedings of the Beltsville Symposium on Agricultural Research: Biological Control in Crop Production*. Allenheld Osmun, Montclair, New Jersey.

Parente, E.J.S. 1980. Internal Report. Energy Nucleus, Federal University of Ceará, Fortaleza, Brazil.

Peoples, T. R. and ten others. 1981. *Euphorbia lathyris* L.: A Future Source of Extractable Liquid Fuels. *Biosources Digest* 3:117–123.

Pearson, F. C. 1978. A Living Fossil Rediscovered and Put to Use. *Maritimes* 22(2):4–6.

Pearson, F. C. and M. Weary. 1980. The *Limulus* Amebocyte Lysate Test for Endotoxin. *BioScience* 30:461–464.

Pelletier, S. W. (ed.). 1970. *Chemistry of the Alkaloids*. Van Nostrand-Reinhold, New York.

Perdue, R. E. 1976. Procurement of Plant Materials for Anti-Tumor Screening. *Cancer Treatment Reports* 60(8):987–1030.

Peyster, A. and Y. Y. Wang. 1979. Gossypol – Proposed Contraceptive for Man

Passes the Ames Test. *New England Journal of Medicine* 301(5):275-276.

Phillips, D. A. 1980. Efficiency of Symbiotic Nitrogen Fixation in Legumes. *Annual Review of Plant Physiology* 31:29-49.

Piatelli, M. 1979. Neptune's Pharmacopoeia. *Courier* (UNESCO monthly), May 1979: 29-32.

Pimentel, D. and 12 others. 1980. Environmental and Social Costs of Pesticides: A Preliminary Assessment. *OIKOS* 34:126-140.

Plawa, M. J. and E. D. Wagner. 1981. Germinal Cell Mutagenesis in Specially Designed Maize Genotypes. *Environmental Health Perspective* 37:61-73.

Plotkin, M. J. 1982. *Conservation and Ethnobotany in Tropical South America.* Progress Report to World Wildlife Fund – U.S. Harvard Botanical Museum, Cambridge, Massachusetts.

Prance, G. T. and M. F. da Silva. 1973. Caryocaraceae. *Flora Neotropica* 12:1-75.

Pratt, D. C. and N. J. Andrews. 1980. Cattails as an Energy Source. Paper presented at the Institute of Gas Technology Symposium, Orlando, Florida, January 1980. Department of Botany, University of Minnesota, St. Paul, Minnesota, 22 pp. mimeo.

Prescott-Allen, R. and C. Prescott-Allen. 1981. *Wild Plants and Crop Improvement.* World Conservation Strategy Occasional Paper No. 1, World Wildlife Fund, Godalming, Surrey, U.K.

Princen, L. H. 1977. Need for Renewable Coatings Raw Materials and What Could Be Available Today. *Journal of Coatings Technology* 49(635):88-93.

_____ . 1979. New Crop Development for Industrial Oils. *Journal of the American Oil Chemists' Society* 56(9):845-848.

_____ . 1982. Personal Communication. Northern Regional Research Center, Agricultural Research Service, U.S. Department of Agriculture, Peoria, Illinois.

Pritchard, G. I. 1980. *Fisheries and Aquaculture in the People's Republic of China.* International Development Research Center, Ottawa, Canada.

Protein Advisory Group of the United Nations. 1973. Proteins From Microalgae and Microfungi. *Tropical Science* 15:77-81.

Pryde, E. H. 1977. Non-Food Uses for Commercial Vegetable Oil Crops. Pp. 25-46 in D. S. Seigler (ed.), *Crop Resources.* Academic Press, New York.

_____ (ed.). 1979. *Fatty Acids.* American Oil Chemists' Society, Champaign, Illinois.

Pryde, E. H., L. H. Princen, and K. D. Mukherjee (eds.). 1981. *New Sources of Fats and Oils.* Monograph No. 9, American Oil Chemists' Society, Champaign, Illinois.

Quin, P. J. 1959. *Foods and Feeding Habits of the Pedi.* Witwatersrand University Press, Johannesburg, South Africa.

Raffauf, R. F. 1970. *Handbook of Alkaloids and Alkaloid-Containing Plants.* John Wiley & Sons, New York.

Raines, G. L., T. W. Offield, and E. S. Santos. 1978. Remote-Sensing and Subsurface Definition of Facies and Structure Related to Uranium Deposits, Powder River Basin, Wyoming. *Economic Geology* 73:1706-1723.

Raven, P. H. 1981. *Research Priorities in Tropical Biology*. National Research Council, Washington, D.C.

Ray, J. P. 1981. *The Effects of Petroleum Hydrocarbons on Corals*. National Academy of Sciences, Washington, D.C.

Reitz, L. P. and J. C. Craddock. 1969. Diversity of Germ Plasm in Small Grain Cereals. *Economic Botany* 23:315-323.

Rick, C. M. 1977. Conservation of Tomato Species Germplasm. *California Agriculture* 31:32-33.

_____ . 1979. Potential Improvement of Tomatoes by Controlled Introgression of Genes from Wild Species. Pp. 167-173 in A. C. Zeven and A. M. van Harten (eds.), *Proceedings of the Conference on Broadening the Genetic Base of Crops*. Pudoc, Wageningen, Netherlands.

_____ . 1982. Personal Communication. College of Agriculture, University of California, Davis, California.

Riggs, T. J. and five others. 1981. Comparison of Spring Barley Varieties Grown in England and Wales between 1880 and 1980. *Journal of Agricultural Science, Cambridge* 97:599-610.

Rinehart, K. L. and 25 others. 1981a. Marine Natural Products as Sources of Antiviral, Antimicrobial and Antineoplastic Agents. *Pure and Applied Chemistry*, April 1981.

Rinehart, K. L. and 8 others. 1981b. Didemnins: Antiviral and Antitumor Depsipeptides From a Caribbean Tunicate. *Science* 212:933-935.

Ritchie, G. A. (ed.). 1979. *New Agricultural Crops*. Westview Press, Boulder, Colorado.

Roberts, B. R. 1974. Foliar Sorption of Atmospheric Sulphur Dioxide by Woody Plants. *Environmental Pollution* 7:133-140.

_____ . 1976. *Air Pollution—How Do Plants Cope?* Nursery Crops Research Laboratory of U.S. Department of Agriculture, Delaware, Ohio.

_____ . 1979. *Trees as Biological Filters*. Nursery Crops Research Laboratory of U.S. Department of Agriculture, Delaware, Ohio.

Robinson, M. H. and B. Robinson. 1976. The Ecology and Behavior of *Nephila maculaga*: A Supplement. *Smithsonian Contributions to Zoology* 218:1-22.

Robinson, T. 1975. *The Organic Constituents of Higher Plants*. Third edition. Cordus Press, North Amherst, Massachusetts.

Rodriguez, E. 1981. *Chemical Patterns of Some Dominant Desert Shrubs of the Chihuahuan and Baja Californian Deserts*. Department of Biology, University of California, Riverside, California. 38 pp. mimeo.

Ronsivalli, L. J. 1978. Sharks and Their Utilization. *Marine Fisheries Review* 40(2):1-13.

Roos, E. E. 1977. Genetic Shifts in Bean Populations During Germplasm Preservation. *Annual Report of the Bean Improvement Cooperative* 20:47-49.

Ross, H. 1979. Wild Species and Primitive Cultivars as Ancestors of Potato Varieties. Pp. 237-245 in A. C. Zeven and A. M. van Harten (eds.), *Proceedings of the Conference on Broadening the Genetic Base of Crops*, Pudoc, Wageningen, Netherlands.

Ruddle, K. 1973. The Human Use of Insects: Examples from the Yukpa. *Biotropica* 5(2):94-101.

Ruggieri, G. D. 1975. Aquatic Animals and Biomedical Research. *Annals of New York Academy of Science* 245:39–56.

————. 1976. Drugs from the Sea. *Science* 194:491–497.

Ruggieri, G. D. and N. D. Rosenberg. 1978. *The Healing Sea.* Dodd Mead and Co., New York.

Runeckles, V. C. (ed.). 1975. *Recent Advances in Phytochemistry*, Vol. 9. Plenum Publishing, New York.

Rush, D. W. and E. Epstein. 1976. Genotypic Responses to Salinity: Differences Between Salt-Sensitive and Salt-Tolerant Genotypes of the Tomato. *Plant Physiology* 57:162–166.

Russell, W. A. 1974. Comparative Performance for Maize Hybrids Representing Different Eras of Maize Breeding. Pp. 81–101 in *Proceedings of 29th Annual Corn and Sorghum Research Conference.* American Seed Trade Association, Washington, D.C.

Ryther, J. H. 1979. Aquaculture in China. *Oceanus* 22(1):21–28.

Ryther, J. H. *et al.* 1979. *Biomass Production by Some Marine and Freshwater Plants.* Woods Hole Oceanographic Contribution No. 4163. Marine Biological Laboratory, Woods Hole, Massachusetts.

Sachs, R. M., C. B. Low, J. D. MacDonald, A.R. Awad, and M. J. Sully. 1981. *Euphorbia lathyris*: A Potential Source of Petroleum-Like Products. *California Agriculture* 35(7–8):21–32.

Saterson, K. A. *et al.* 1979. *Herbaceous Species Screening Program.* Arthur D. Little, Inc., Cambridge, Massachusetts.

Sailer, R. I. 1979. Use of Biological Control Agents. Pp. 139–151 in W. B. Ennis (ed.), *Introductions to Crop Protection.* American Society of Agronomy and the Crop Science Society of America, Madison, Wisconsin.

————. 1981. Progress Report on Importation of Natural Enemies of Insect Pests in the USA. Pp. 20–26 in J. R. Coulson (ed.), *Use of Beneficial Organisms in the Control of Crop Pests.* Entomological Society of America, College Park, Maryland.

Schairer, L. A., J. V. Hof, C. G. Hayes, R. M. Burton, and F. J. de Serres. 1978. Exploratory Monitoring of Air Pollutants for Mutagenicity Activity with the *Tradescantia* Stamen Hair System. *Environmental Health Perspective* 27:51–60.

Schaller, C. W. 1977. Utilizing Genetic Diversity in the Improvement of Barley Cultivars. *California Agriculture* 31(9):18–19.

Scheuer, P. J. 1973. *Industry of Marine Natural Products.* Academic Press, New York.

————. 1979. Living Marine Resources for Industry and Medicine. Report to United Nations Industrial and Development Organization, Vienna, Austria.

Schmitz, F. J. and eight others. 1981. Recent Developments in Research on Metabolites from Caribbean Marine Invertebrates. *Pure and Applied Chemistry* 53(4):853–866.

Schopf, T.J.M. (ed.). 1972. *Models in Paleobiology.* Freeman Cooper and Co., San Francisco, California.

Schultes, R. E. 1976. *Hallucinogenic Plants.* Golden Press, Racine, Wisconsin.

_____. 1980. The Amazonia as a Source of New Economic Plants. *Economic Botany* 33(3):259-266.

Schultes, R. E. and A. Hofmann. 1979. *Plants of the Gods.* McGraw-Hill, New York.

Schultes, R. E. and T. Swain. 1976. The Plant Kingdom: A Virgin Field for New Biodynamic Constituents. Pp. 133-171 in N. J. Finer (ed.), *The Recent Chemistry of Natural Products, Including Tobacco: Proceedings of the Second Philip Morris Science Symposium.* Philip Morris, Inc., New York.

Scobie, G. M. and R. T. Posada. 1977. *The Impact of High-Yielding Rice Varieties in America, with Special Reference to Colombia.* International Center for Tropical Agriculture (CIAT), Cali, Colombia.

Sebek, O. K. and A. I. Laskin (eds.). 1979. *Genetics of Industrial Microorganisms.* American Society for Microbiology, Washington, D.C.

Sen, D. N. 1982. *Environment and Plant Life in Indian Desert.* Geobios International, Jodhpur, India.

Shapley, D. 1973. Sorghum: "Miracle" Grain for the World Protein Shortage? *Science* 182:147-148.

Sharpley, J. M. and A. M. Kaplan (eds.). 1976. *Proceedings of the Third International Bio-Degradation Symposium.* Applied Science Publishers, New York.

Shepard, J. F. 1982. The Regeneration of Potato Plants From Leaf-Cell Protoplasts. *Scientific American* 246(5):154-166.

Short, R. V. 1976. The Introduction of New Species of Animals for the Purpose of Domestication. *Symposium of Zoological Society of London* 40:1-13.

Siegel, M. M. *et al.* 1970. Anticellular and Antitumor Activity of Extracts from Tropical Marine Invertebrates. In *Proceedings of Food and Drugs from the Sea.* Marine and Technological Society, Washington, D.C.

Sikes, S. K. 1966. Observations on the Ecology of Arterial Diseases in the African Elephant in Kenya and Uganda. *Symposium of Zoological Society of London* 21:26-42.

Silvey, V. 1981. The Contribution of New Wheat, Barley and Oat Varieties to Increase in Yield in England and Wales 1947-78. *Journal of National Institute of Agricultural Botany* 15:399-412.

Simmonds, N. W. (ed.). 1976. *Evolution of Crop Plants.* Longman, London, U.K.

Simmonds, F. J. and F. D. Bennett. 1976. Biological Control of Agricultural Pests. Pp. 464-472 in *Proceedings of 15th International Congress of Entomology.* Commonwealth Institute of Biological Control, Curepe, Trinidad.

Simon, R. B. 1975. Animal Behavior and Earthquakes. *Earthquake Information Bulletin* 7(6):9-11.

Slayter, L. E. and S. K. Levin (eds.). 1982. *Contending with Climate's Impact on Food.* American Association for Advancement of Science, Washington, D.C.

Slesser, M. and C. Lewis. 1979. *Biological Energy Resources.* Spon Publishers, London, U.K.

Smith, N. 1974. Agouti and Babassu. *Oryx* 12(5):581-582.

Smith, R. L. and seven others. 1976. Nitrogen Fixation in Grasses Inoculated with *Spirillum lipoferum. Science* 192:1003-1005.

Söderman, S. 1980. *Short Rotation Forestry in Sweden.* Department of Forestry, Stockholm, Sweden.

Soedigdo, S. and three others. 1980. Studies on the Chemistry and Pharmacology from Indonesian Medicinal Plants. Paper presented at Fourth Asian Symposium on Medicinal Plants and Spices, UNESCO and Faculty of Science, Mahidol University, Bangkok, Thailand. In UNESCO, 1981:112.

Soejarto, D. D. 1975. *The Plant Kingdom and the Search for Antifertility Agents.* Botanical Museum of Harvard University, Cambridge, Massachusetts.

Soejarto, D. D., A. S. Bingel, M. Slaytor, and N. R. Farnsworth. 1978. Fertility-Regulating Agents from Plants. *Bulletin of World Health Organization* 56:343-352.

Soepadmo, E. 1979. The Role of Tropical Botanic Gardens in the Conservation of Threatened Valuable Plant Genetic Resources in Southeast Asia. Pp. 63-74 in H. Synge and H. Townsend (eds.), *Survival or Extinction.* Royal Botanic Gardens, Kew, Richmond, Surrey, U.K.

Spjut, R. W. and R. E. Perdue. 1976. Plant Folklore: A Tool for Predicting Sources of Anti-Tumor Activity? *Cancer Treatment Reports* 60(8):979-985.

Sprague, G. F. 1979. Personal Communication, letter dated June 4, 1979. Department of Agronomy, College of Agriculture, University of Illinois, Urbana, Illinois.

Sprague, G. F., D. E. Alexander, and J. W. Dudley. 1980. Plant Breeding and Genetic Engineering: A Prospectus. *BioScience* 30(1):17-21.

Staritsky, G. 1980. Is There a Future for Medicinal Crops? *Span* 23(2):8-82.

Starr, T. B. 1977. The Role of Climate in American Agriculture. *The Ecologist* 7(7):262-267.

Stevens, L. M., A. L. Steinhauer, and J. R. Coulson. 1975. Suppression of the Mexican Bean Beetle on Soybeans with Annual Inoculative Releases of *Pediobius foveolatus. Environmental Entomology* 4:947-952.

Struhl, K., D. T. Stinchcomb, S. Scherer, and R. W. Davis. 1979. High-frequency Transformation of Yeast: Autonomous Replication of Hybrid DNA Molecules. *Proceedings of National Academy of Sciences* 76(3):1035-1039.

Suffness, M. 1978. Personal Communication. National Cancer Institute, Bethesda, Maryland.

Suffness, M. and J. Douros. 1979. Drugs of Plant Origin. Pp. 73-126 in V. T. DeVita and H. Busal (eds.), *Methods in Cancer Research,* Vol. XVI, Part A. National Cancer Institute, Bethesda, Maryland.

Swain, T. (ed.). 1972. *Plants in the Development of Modern Medicine.* Harvard University Press, Cambridge, Massachusetts.

Swift, C. C. 1979. *Fishes: A Report Prepared for the IUCN World Conservation Strategy.* International Union for Conservation of Nature and Natural Resources, Gland, Switzerland.

Talbot F. H., B. C. Russell, and G.R.V. Anderson. 1978. Coral Reef Fish Communities: Unstable, High-Diversity Systems. *Ecological Monographs* 48:425-440.

Tansey, M. F. and R. P. Roth. 1970. Pigeons, a New Role in Air Pollution. *Journal of Air Pollution Control Association* 20(5):307-309.

Tatom, J. W. 1981. Pyrolysis Experience in Developing Countries. Pp.

180-183 in P. F. Bente (ed.), *Proceedings of Bio-Energy 1980.* Bio-Energy Council, Washington, D.C.

Tatum, L. A. 1971. The Southern Corn Leaf Blight Epidemic. *Science* 171:1113-1116.

Taylor, R. L. 1975. *Butterflies in My Stomach.* Woodbridge Press, Santa Barbara, California.

Taylor, R. L. and B. J. Carter. 1979. *Entertaining with Insects: The Original Guide to Insect Cookery.* Woodbridge Press, Santa Barbara, California.

Teteny, P. 1979. Medicinal and Aromatic Plants in the Present and Future. *Chronica Horticultura* 19(1):3-5.

Thompson, E. H. 1981. Hop Industry Committee: Analysis of Hops of the 1980 Crop. *Journal of Institute of Brewers* 87:180-184.

Thomson, P. 1975. Value Is Extracted from a Nuisance. *Smithsonian* 6(1):40-47.

Thorhaug, A. 1979. Utilizing Botanical Resources in the People's Republic of China. *Resource Recovery and Conservation* 4:105-110.

Tingey, W. M., S. A. Mehlenbacher, and J. E. Laubengayer. 1981. Occurrence of Glandular Trichomes in Wild *Solanum* Species. *American Potato Journal* 58:81-82.

Tourbier, J. and R. W. Pierson (eds.). 1976. *Biological Control of Water Pollution.* University of Pennsylvania Press, Philadelphia, Pennsylvania.

Trease, G. E. and W. C. Evans. 1972. *Pharmacognosy.* Balliere Tindall, London, U.K.

Trainer, D. O. 1973. Wildlife as Monitors of Disease. *American Journal of Public Health* 63(3):201-203.

Turner, W. B. 1971. *Fungal Metabolites.* Academic Press, London, U.K.

U.S. Forest Service. 1977. *How Trees Help Clean the Air.* Agriculture Information Bulletin No. 412. U.S. Forest Service, U.S. Department of Agriculture, Washington, D.C.

UNESCO. 1977. *Proceedings of Third Asian Symposium on Medicinal Plants and Spices,* Colombo, Sri Lanka, February 1977. UNESCO Special Publication, United Nations Educational, Cultural, and Scientific Organization, Paris, France.

―――― . 1978. *Tropical Forest Ecosystems.* United Nations Educational, Scientific, and Cultural Organization, Paris, France.

―――― . 1981. *Proceedings of Fourth Asian Symposium on Medicinal Plants and Spices,* Bangkok, Thailand, September 1980. UNESCO Special Publication, United Nations Educational, Scientific, and Cultural Organization, Paris, France.

University of Puerto Rico. 1978. *Production of Sugarcane and Tropical Grasses as a Renewable Energy Source.* Agricultural Experiment Station, University of Puerto Rico, Rio Piedras, Puerto Rico.

Uphof, J. C. 1968. *Dictionary of Economic Plants.* S-H Service Agency, Inc., Riverside, New Jersey.

Uvarov, B. P. 1966. *Grasshoppers and Locusts: A Handbook of General Acridology.* Cambridge University Press, Cambridge, U.K.

U.S. Department of Agriculture. 1976. *Introduction, Classification, Mainten-*

ance, Evaluation, and Documentation of Plant Germplasm. National Research Program Report No. 20160. Agricultural Research Service, U.S. Department of Agriculture, Washington, D.C.

Valentine, J. W. 1973. *Evolutionary Paleoecology of the Marine Biosphere.* Prentice-Hall, Englewood Cliffs, New Jersey.

Van Bulow, J.F.W. and J. Dobereiner. 1975. Potential for Nitrogen Fixation in Maize Genotypes in Brazil. *Proceedings of the National Academy of Sciences* 72:2389-2393.

Van den Bosch, R. 1978. *The Pesticide Conspiracy.* Doubleday, Garden City, New York.

Van den Bosch, R., P. S. Messenger, and A. P. Gutierrez. 1982. *An Introduction to Biological Control.* Plenum Publishing, New York.

Vaughan, J. G. 1977. A Multidisciplinary Study of the Taxonomy and Origin of *Brassica* Crops. *BioScience* 27(1):35-38.

Wagner, H. and P. Wolff. 1977. *New Natural Products and Plant Drugs.* Springer-Verlag, New York.

Walsh, J. 1981. Germplasm Resources are Losing Ground. *Science* 214: 421-423.

Ward, R. F. 1981. *Alcohols as Fuels: The Global Picture.* Solar Energy Research Institute, Golden, Colorado.

Ward, N. I. and R. R. Brooks. 1978. Gold in Some New Zealand Plants. *New Zealand Journal of Botany* 16:175-177.

Warren, H. V. 1980. Pollen: A Possible Tool for Exploration Geologists and Environmentalists. *Western Miner*, March 1980:35-36.

Watanabe, I., C. R. Espinas, N. S. Berja, and B. V. Alimagno. 1977. *Utilization of the Azolla-Anabaena Complex as a Nitrogen Fertilizer for Rice.* IRRI Research Paper Series No. 11. International Rice Research Institute, Los Baños, Philippines.

Waterhouse, D. F. 1979. Reduction of Some Biological Constraints on the World's Food Supply. *Proceedings of Ninth International Congress of Plant Protection*: 6-9.

Watson, S. A. 1977. *Corn and Corn Improvement.* Monograph No. 18, American Society of Agronomy, Madison, Wisconsin.

Weatherly, A. H. and B.M.G. Cogger. 1977. Fish Culture: Problems and Prospects. *Science* 197:427-430.

Weinheimer, A. J., J. A. Matson, T.K.B. Karns, M. B. Hossain, and D. Van der Helm. 1978. Some New Marine Anticancer Agents. Pp. 117-121 in P. N. Kaul and C. J. Sindermann (eds.), *Drugs and Food From The Sea.* University of Oklahoma Press, Norman, Oklahoma.

Weisz, P. B. and J. F. Marshall. 1979. High-Grade Fuels from Biomass Farming: Potentials and Constraints. *Science* 206:24-29.

Wentzel, K. F. 1965. Insects as Emission-Related Pests. *Naturwissenschaften* 52(5):113.

Westphal, E. 1974. *Pulses in Ethiopia, their Taxonomy and Agricultural Significance.* Centre for Agricultural Publishing and Documentation, University of Wageningen, Netherlands.

Wetterberg, G. B. *et al.* 1976. *An Analysis of Nature Conservation Priorities in the Amazon.* Technical Series No. 8. Brazilian Institute for Forestry Development, Brasília, Brazil.

Whistler, R. and T. Hymowitz. 1976, *Guar: A Food and Industrial Crop.* American Association of Cereals Chemists, St. Paul, Minnesota.

Wilcox, B. A. 1980. Insular Ecology and Conservation. Pp. 95–118 in M. E. Soule and B. A. Wilcox (eds.), *Conservation Biology.* Sinauer Associates, Sunderland, Massachusetts.

Wilcox, H. A. 1976. *The Ocean Food and Energy Farm Project.* Naval Undersea Center, San Diego, California.

Wilkes, H. G. 1972. Maize and its Wild Relatives. *Science* 177:1071–1077.

_____. 1977. Hybridization of Maize and Teosinte in Mexico and Guatemala and the Improvement of Maize. *Economic Botany* 31:254–293.

_____. 1979. Mexico and Central America as a Center for the Origin of Agriculture and the Evolution of Maize. *Crop Improvement* 6(1):1–18.

Williams, J. T., C. H. Lamoureux, and N. Wulijarni-Soetjipto (eds.). 1975. *Southeast Asian Plant Genetic Resources.* BIOTROP, Bogor, Indonesia.

Wither, E. D. and R. R. Brooks. 1977. Hyperaccumulation of Nickel by Some Plants of Southeast Asia. *Journal of Geochemical Exploration* 8:579–583.

Withner, C. L. (ed.). 1974. *The Orchids.* John Wiley & Sons, New York.

Wittwer, S. H. 1979. The Shape of Things to Come. In P. Carlson (ed.), *Biology of Crop Productivity.* Academic Press, New York.

_____. 1980. Carbon Dioxide and Climatic Change: An Agricultural Perspective. *Journal of Soil and Water Conservation* 35(2):116–120.

_____. 1981. *The Further Frontiers: Research and Technology for Global Food Production in the 21st Century.* Michigan Agricultural Experiment Station, East Lansing, Michigan, 40 pp. mimeo.

_____. 1982. Worldwide Influences on U.S. Farm Production. Paper Presented at Annual Meeting of the American Association for Advancement of Science, January 5. Michigan Agricultural Experiment Station, East Lansing, Michigan.

Wolf, S. G. 1978. Contributions of the Sea to Medicine. Pp. 7–16 in P. N. Kaul and C. J. Sindermann (eds.), *Drugs and Food from the Sea.* University of Oklahoma Press, Norman, Oklahoma.

Wolverton, B. C. and R. C. McDonald. 1979. Water Hyacinth Productivity and Harvesting Studies. *Economic Botany* 33(1):1–10.

_____. 1981. Natural Processes for Treatment of Organic Chemical Waste. *The Environmental Professional* 3:99–104.

Wood, D. L. 1973. The Impact of Photochemical Air Pollution on the Mixed-Conifer Forest Ecosystem – Arthropods. Pp. 1–25 in O. C. Taylor (ed.), *Oxidant Air Pollution Effects on a Western Coniferous Forest Ecosystem* (Task B Report, Part C). Air Pollution Research Center, University of California, Riverside, California.

Woodson, R. E., H. W. Younken, E. Schlitter, and J. A. Schneider. 1957. *Rauwolfia: Botany, Pharmacognosy, Chemistry and Pharmacology.* Little, Brown, Boston, Massachusetts.

World Bank. 1978. *The Consultative Group on International Agricultural Research: An Integrative Report.* World Bank, Washington, D.C.

_____ . 1980. *Energy Needs and Opportunities in Third World Countries.* World Bank, Washington, D.C.

Wright, M. J. (ed.). 1976. *Plant Adaptation to Mineral Stress in Problem Soils.* Agricultural Research Center, U.S. Department of Agriculture, Beltsville, Maryland.

Wyatt, R. G. and eight others. 1980. Human Rotavirus Type 2: Cultivation in Vitro. *Science* 207:189–191.

Yanchinski, S. 1981. Who Will Save the Caribbean? *New Scientist* 92(1278):388–389.

Zaman, M. B. and M. S. Khan. 1970. *One Hundred Drug Plants of Pakistan.* Medicinal Plant Branch of Pakistan Forest Institute. Ferozsens Limited, Peshawar, Pakistan.

Zelitch, I. 1975. Improving the Efficiency of Photosynthesis. *Science* 188:626–633.

Zeven, A. C. 1977. Breeding Green Revolution. *World Crops and Livestock* 29(3):123–124.

Zuber, M. S. and L. L. Darrah. 1979. U.S. Corn Germplasm Base. In *Proceedings of the 35th Annual Corn and Sorghum Industry Research Conference.*

Index

Other Titles of Interest from Westview Press

† *Available in hardcover and paperback.*

About the Book and Author

A Wealth of Wild Species:
Storehouse for Human Welfare
Norman Myers

As environmentalists and wildlife enthusiasts argue for preservation of wild species, they sometimes overlook a most compelling fact – the survival of wild species directly benefits humans. Like the Earth's most precious minerals, the planetary gene pool is a valuable natural resource that is vulnerable to irreversible harm. Yet, if present trends toward extinction persist, possibly one-third and conceivably one-half the entire spectrum of species may be lost to us within another century.

What does this mean?

In 1960, a child suffering from leukemia had only one chance in five of remission. Today, thanks to a drug developed from an obscure tropical forest plant, the rosy periwinkle, the odds are reversed and that child has an 80 percent chance. In fact, each time we take a doctor's prescription to a pharmacy, there is a one-in-two chance that the medication we collect originated in the unique properties of a wild plant or animal.

Wild species of plants also hold the promise of revolutionizing agriculture around the world, and their uses as foods, sources of new chemicals for pest control, and even new kinds of contraceptives are being developed.

Wild animals likewise have made great – and often little known – contributions to mankind. Studies of a woodpecker's vertebrae have led to better design for antiwhiplash equipment in automobiles, and engineering information derived from studies of hummingbirds is contributing to improved helicopters.

Norman Myers, well-known author of *The Sinking Ark,* goes beyond traditional moral, philosophical, and ecological arguments for preservation of wild species to present a synoptic review of the contributions that these resources make, and can make, to our daily lives. While presenting a vast range of examples of how humans have benefited from wild species (emphasizing the dollar value of each), Dr. Myers continually reminds us that for every wild species lost, we also have lost the potential to deal with yet-unknown problems of the future. That we do not wish to live without wild beings is only one side of the coin. That perhaps we *cannot* live without them is a vastly more important reason for preservation.

Dr. Myers, a consultant on environmental issues and resource economics, is best known as author of *The Long African Day* and *The Sinking Ark.* This book is a continuation of the arguments he first presented in *The Sinking Ark.*